The Cooper Files

Dr. Sherry Cooper

The Cooper Files

KEY PORTER BOOKS

Canadian Cataloguing in Publication Data

Cooper, Sherry S.
  The Cooper files

Includes bibliographical references.

ISBN 1-55263-81-1

1. Economic forecasting—Canada.   2. Canada—Economic conditions—
1991–   .

I. Title.

HC115.C6928 1999   330.971'001'12   C99-931227-8

THE CANADA COUNCIL | LE CONSEIL DES ARTS
FOR THE ARTS | DU CANADA
SINCE 1957 | DEPUIS 1957

The publisher gratefully acknowledges the support of the Canada Council for the Arts and the Ontario Arts Council for its publishing program.

Canada

We acknowledge the financial support of the Government of Canada through the Book Publishing Industry Development Program (BPIDP) for our publishing activities.

Key Porter Books Limited
70 The Esplanade
Toronto, Ontario
Canada M5E 1R2

www.keyporter.com

Electronic formatting: Heidy Lawrance Associates
Design: Peter Maher

Printed and bound in Canada

99 00 01 02 03 6 5 4 3 2 1

For Peter and Stefan, you are my life's blessings.
For Mom and Charlotte, my roots, you are
my teachers who guide my path.
For Dad, thanks for reading over my shoulder.

Acknowledgments

Many people have helped to make this book a reality, and to all of them I am grateful. I want to thank Allan Fotheringham for inviting me to Anne's birthday dinner, where I met Anna Porter. Anna, publisher and CEO of Key Porter Books, called me a few days later and suggested that I write a book. I had already begun to do just that, but Anna provided the final impetus. Her suggestions and edits have humanized the subject of economics, giving me the courage to allow myself to show through. Susan Renouf, my editor, provided invaluable critique and, most importantly, unbridled enthusiasm. As a self-proclaimed econo-phobe, her interest and expressed delight gave me the self-confidence to plough ahead under unreasonable time constraints. John Sweet, my copy editor, made a meaningful contribution. By correcting my all too prevalent tendency to rely on economic jargon, he turned it into plain English.

Time, the currency of life, is what I owe to my family. My husband, Peter Cooper, and my son, Stefan Atkinson, patiently and stalwartly supported my long-held dream of writing this book, throughout the nights, weekends and vacations it consumed. My book was conceived and born in the beautiful wine country near Cape Town, South Africa. The ocean air, mountain vistas and profusion of scented flowers provided the perfect backdrop for creativity. I forged and honed my ideas while running on the beach. No one could ever have had a better sounding board, cheering section or editorial team than Peter and Stefan. They are two of the smartest guys I will ever meet. And when I succumbed to the strain of a more-than-full-time job on top of the demands of the book, I could not have had more loving soul mates to keep me going. Peter and Stefan, you're the best; thank you.

I also want to thank my mom and stepdad, Vilma and Bernie Liedman, for your comments on the first draft. I wanted this book to be accessible to people of all ages with little knowledge of economics. You helped me see what I needed to define and explain. But even more, your enthusiasm and support gave me the confidence I needed to keep going. Mom, you are a gracious, charming lady who has mentored me through life.

My second family, the economics department of Nesbitt Burns, has also made an enormous contribution to this book. Nancy Huether provided crucial research assistance and kept my life in order, no easy task. Her diligence and dedication were essential to the successful completion of this book. The economists—David Rosenberg, Douglas Porter, Robert Spector, Jennifer Lee and Scott Kinnear—read the early drafts of this manuscript on their own time, taking precious hours away from their family and friends. Dave taught me Canadian economic history— *à la* Dave—and helped me to stand by the courage of my convictions when the occasional critic questioned my right to "walk the sidewalks of Canada." Doug, the consummate diplomat, smoothed the sharper edges of Dave's rendition of history, adding a decidedly human side to what it means to be Canadian. Robert assisted me in the intricate world of stock market technical analysis. Jennifer has become a global corporate tax-rate guru and Scott is our resident certified financial planner. I have learned much from each of them; their ideas, comments and criticisms were extremely helpful and made for some lively debate.

Conrad DeQuadros offered enormous data and technical support; thanks, Conrad, for returning my frantic weekend phone calls. Also, much appreciation for the contribution of John Szauer and Patrick Grixti, my ever-trusted computer-graphics wizards extraordinaire. Bobby Briones, Daniel Jankowski and Bindia Ravindran contributed meaningfully to this book and to my Web site.

A special thanks goes to Caitlin MacNamara, my colleague, protégée and friend. From the beginning, Caitlin believed I could pull this off, despite my gruelling schedule. Her dauntless enthusiasm and positive attitude kept me going. Her edits and critique were wise and insightful, and gave me invaluable firsthand knowledge of Generation X. I would also like to express appreciation to Caitlin's parents, Mark and Margaret MacNamara, for their expertise in successful retirement planning.

I also want to thank the senior executives of Nesbitt Burns, who never questioned my ability to carry out this project as well as meet the ongoing demands of my job. Special thanks go to Brian Steck, Gilles Ouellette and John MacNaughton for their continuing support. You have made Nesbitt Burns a wonderful place to work.

A special tribute goes to Tony Comper, CEO of the Bank of Montreal, for his confidence and support. Tony, with his remarkable personal touch, truly does make the bank a caring organization.

I would also like to acknowledge the long list of individuals who provided enormously helpful comments and critique: Erich Almasy, Rob Bourgeois, Peter and Jo Flach, Brian Foody, Michael Galper, Rod MacGillivray, the Nesbitt Burns Financial Planning Group, Richard Mills, Lynda Palazzi, Brian Piccioni, John Platt, Jackie Swanson and Kris Vikmanis. My enduring gratitude also goes to my mentor, deputy director at the Federal Reserve Board in Washington, D.C., Edward Ettin, who read every word of the first draft and contributed significantly to its improvement.

To all of these people and the many I may have forgotten, thank you. The errors and omissions remain my own, but the successes I share with them.

And finally, the views expressed in this book are my own and not necessarily shared by Nesbitt Burns or the Bank of Montreal.

Contents

Part 4 A New Economic Paradigm

Part 5 Canada in the Global Economy

Part 6 What All of This Means to You

Introduction

This book is about change—about managing it and profiting from it. Never before in history has change been so rapid or so pervasive. We are in a period of major transformation. Breakthrough technologies are changing the way we communicate, shop, play, read, research, do business and sell our own labour services. Innovations in the life sciences will alter the way we procreate, live our lives, battle handicaps and fight disease; they will revolutionize the way in which the world is fed and all life forms are reproduced.

Technological innovation fosters globalization. Our competitors are no longer the businesses down the street or in the same town; our competition is global. We should see ourselves as self-employed consultants, regardless of where we work. We are each the president of our own personal services company, responsible for the ongoing improvement of the service we offer. Each of us is in competition with everyone everywhere. If we aren't constantly improving, getting smarter, increasing efficiency, adding more value, we are falling behind.

You are responsible for yourself. No one else can take care of you—not government, big business, daddy's money or a rich spouse. Security comes from providing a service the market values, and then salting away at least 10 to 15 percent of your gross income, investing it regularly over a long period of time. Very few people do that; you can be among the minority of those with a secure financial future.

The future, as always, is unpredictable and therefore frightening, particularly with so much in flux. But it is exciting too, and provides opportunities for all of us. This book describes those opportunities and how to benefit from them. I believe we are in the very early days of a long-term upswing in global economic activity, a twenty-plus-year period of non-inflationary growth. It won't be painless. Many of the world's economies experienced a sharp economic downturn in 1997 and 1998; some are still recovering. Enormous volatility will remain. Old businesses will die only to be replaced by new ones. New ones will come and go. The technology life cycle is very short; obsolescence is rapid, and foreign and domestic competitors are quick to copy new products at lower costs. This "creative destruction"—a phrase coined by Harvard economist Joseph Schumpeter in 1942—is a necessary part of economic progress, but it is also very difficult, fraught with human costs.

Innovation often leads to business restructuring. Competitive pressures force companies to cut costs and then to cut them again. Successful new products attract new entrants into the industry, increasing supply. This puts downward pressure on prices and squeezes profits for all but the most fleet of foot. Technology companies, therefore, must be ever innovating, cost cutting and price slashing. This is a tall order. Remember, every successful new technology is eventually mass produced, ultimately becoming a commodity—a product that is undifferentiated by manufacturer, a product for which price is the only distinguishing factor. Telephones, radios, televisions, cash registers, calculators, automobiles and microwave ovens were all high-tech products at one time. Very quickly, they became low-growth, low-margin commodities.

Going forward in the technology revolution, fortunes will be made and lost, jobs created and destroyed. Today's hottest stocks may not exist five years from now, and the biggest companies of tomorrow are still a figment of someone's imagination today. It took one hundred years to industrialize the United States; it took a fraction of that time to do the same in much of Asia. But as we have seen in Asia, with the financial crises and economic slowdowns in Thailand, Malaysia, Japan and elsewhere, fortunes come and fortunes go and nobody knows for sure when and why. This book shows you how to prosper in threatening times, what to look for and do to ensure your own financial security and that of your children.

Demographics—the vital statistics of a country's population—play a key role in the outlook, but demography alone is not enough to predict the future. As Michael Adams suggests in his book *Sex in the Snow*, demography is not destiny. The popularization of the demographic story—Boomers drive all markets and aging Boomers will behave like their parents as they move towards retirement and beyond—is oversimplified. The simplistic prediction that Baby Boomers will behave like the generation before them ignores the changes that have occurred—dramatic lifestyle and work-style changes. It ignores the substantial differences in attitudes and values between the generations.

My parents were nineteen and twenty-two years old when I was born. Today, that seems exceedingly young. They were both Depression babies, conscious of the risk of potential financial crisis all their lives. They understood sacrifice and denial, and knew how to save money. Not only were their attitudes and values quite different from those of today's Boomers, but so were their lifestyles. Mom stayed home with the kids and dad was a lawyer. My dad thought a fax machine was a newfangled annoyance. He hated airplanes, rarely travelled more than 150 miles in any direction and assessed the value of any new place by how closely it resembled home (Baltimore, Maryland). They smoked cigarettes, ate fried and canned foods, and never, ever exercised—certainly in contrast with today's health-conscious Boomers.

When it came time for his eldest daughter (me) to go to university, my dad favoured a small women's college in Baltimore, so that I could live at home. (Little did he know it was a hotbed of late 1960s bra-burning feminism.) His secretary took dictation, typed his legal papers and answered the phone. She even made coffee. He never quite cottoned to women lawyers, never mind women judges. Today, close to 50 percent of the labour force are women, and almost 70 percent of women with children under the age of six are in the workforce. Women represent 51 percent of law-school and medical-school classes, and record numbers are getting advanced degrees.

My dad mistrusted the stock market, invested his money in Treasury and municipal bonds, and benefited meaningfully from the inflation of the 1970s and 1980s, in terms of both high interest rates on his bonds and bank deposits and rising house prices. His home was his best investment, a very unlikely state of affairs today. He died young, much too young, because of heart disease and diabetes. He died before he ever had the opportunity to take life easier.

In true Baby Boomer fashion, my sister and I have very different attitudes and values. We grew up during a period of economic prosperity. Unlike our parents, we were confident that the good times would never end. This created a sense of expectation and entitlement in us that we share with our generation. With the idea that the future was secure, we Boomers, unlike our parents, felt free to focus on ourselves—the "me" generation. We stressed the importance of experimentation and self-fulfillment. We are still doing that. So why would our preferences, our spending and saving patterns, mirror those of our parents as we move into middle age and retirement? They won't.

The demography-tells-all school suggests that Boomers will behave more or less uniformly, and more or less like their parents. They will soon become empty-nesters, sell their houses and cause a crash in residential real estate values. They will retire en masse at age sixty-five or before and sell their stocks, causing a crash there as well. But the truth is, nobody knows for sure what the future will bring. Demography is powerful, but with growing globalization who is to say that it is the demography of the domestic population alone that matters most? Perhaps younger foreign investors will take up the slack. Maybe immigration of highly skilled, high-paid labour will create growing demand for our houses. And Boomers, after all, may not mirror their parents. Many may choose to live in family houses, enjoying the space. Today's lifestyles will cause many to convert their four-bedroom houses to two-bedroom-one-study-and-a-gym houses. The reality of adult children returning home after university, as well as the rapidly increasing numbers of telecommuters and the self-employed, will maintain the demand for larger living spaces among aging Boomers.

Will Boomers retire en masse? Maybe not. In true Boomer fashion, self-denial and saving are very difficult. Savings rates for this generation have fallen to their lowest levels in history. Many cannot afford to retire fully, and many will prefer not to. Boomers have always self-actualized in their work, much more so than the generation that followed them. Many will remain active in the workforce for a lot longer, either by necessity or through choice. And they will not sell their stocks in unison at age sixty-five. With life expectancy rising sharply in the next twenty years, many will continue to invest in stocks well beyond traditional retirement age. Biotechnological and pharmaceutical breakthroughs will extend life and improve its quality, changing markedly what it means to be old. More and more people will work longer, save more and keep it invested in relatively high-risk assets to ensure they don't run out of money before they run out of time. In the United States today, there are just as many people under the age of eighteen as there are Baby Boomers. Maybe these Echo Boomers will jump on the stock market bandwagon before the Boomers sell out.

This book looks at these issues and what they mean for Canada and Canadians. The U.S. has been the global leader in the information economy. This book examines why—the strengths the U.S. possesses, and the opportunities for Canada to share in those strengths and to make the most of our own. Economic well-being has declined in Canada relative to the U.S. since the end of the 1970s. In this book we analyze why and suggest what can be done about it. There are great Canadian success stories, cities and towns that are building and attracting new growth companies and new technologies. But the successes are still too few.

Tax rates are onerous in Canada, for both individuals and businesses, and they are holding us back. Since the tax gap has widened in relation to the U.S., so have the gaps in job creation, unemployment, economic growth and stock market performance. The Canadian dollar has been on a downward trend for the better part of twenty-three years. This, combined with the relative underperformance of our stock market since 1980, has markedly reduced the wealth and economic well-being of Canadians, especially in comparison to our number-one trading partner and ally to the south. Tax rates must come down. When they do, the economy will boom, non-inflationary growth will be staggering and government tax coffers will swell. More money, not less, will be available for health care and education. The Canadian stock market will start to outperform other stock markets around the world once again, and family living standards will rise. This book tells you how you can help as a citizen and prosper as an individual.

You need a financial blueprint to navigate these rocky shoals, to keep what you have and to garner more. You too can be a great success in the information age. You too can work as long as you wish and retire in financial security and comfort. You too can navigate your career through seemingly treacherous waters, set your kids in the right direction, maximize your personal desires given budget and wealth constraints, and ensure that those constraints become ever less binding.

It is an exciting journey into the twenty-first century, fraught with dips and bends. The outlook, although volatile, is spectacular, the opportunities immense. Any barriers to success will be of your own creation, so you and you alone can knock them down. The past has been prelude, the future is now.

Prologue

I came to Canada in January 1983 in the dying days of a troubled marriage. I came to save the marriage, to make a fresh start, to make my husband happy. He had landed a great job in Toronto, a job he wanted very much. We had a two-year-old son, my miracle baby, the baby my doctors said I would never have. I almost didn't. I spent four of my nine pregnant months in bed, but in June 1980 I gave birth to one of the world's most longed-for babies. I had recently lost another one; an ectopic pregnancy had sent me into emergency surgery, my third baby-related operation in two years. I was of a mind to make my marriage work.

When my husband told me he was applying for the job in Toronto, I was only four months into a new job myself. After spending five incredible years as a research economist at the Federal Reserve Board (the Fed) in Washington, DC, the U.S. central bank, I became Director of Financial Economics at the Federal National Mortgage Association (better known as Fannie Mae).

Potomac Fever

My years at the Fed were eye-opening and tremendously exciting, an outstanding entrée to the real world of economic analysis. I joined the Fed staff in 1977, in the final stages of writing my doctoral dissertation. What a thrill it was to be there. Very quickly I had what they call Potomac fever.

One hundred and fifty economists work at the Federal Reserve Board in Washington and that many more at the twelve regional Reserve banks, monitoring and analyzing the U.S. and global economies. These are among the brightest financial economists in the world. Graduate students with an interest in monetary policy and financial markets vie for jobs. Even those who ultimately intend to work on Wall Street recognize the value of the education. It is seen as a critical post-doctoral experience. The Fed recruits from the top U.S. graduate schools each year. Jobs are tough to get, and the application process is competitive, requiring multiple interviews and the oral presentation of a major research paper.

The economists at the Fed have access to the most complete databases in the world, both proprietary and public, as well as leading-edge technology. Yet as I quickly discovered, forecasting the economy and financial markets is just as difficult at the Fed as anywhere else, owing to data inadequacies and random unexpected shocks. When the statistical-model predictions of the economy contradict the judgmental forecasts, they generally go with judgment.

I had been trained in the monetarist tradition, believing that the Fed's role should be to steer the growth of the money supply to some constant optimal pace consistent with price stability. What a naive person I was. Very quickly after joining the capital markets section as thrift-institution economist, responsible for monitoring and assessing the activity of savings and loan associations, I discovered how the real world really worked. Firstly, there is no set optimal money-supply growth pace; it changes all the time because of changing circumstances. Secondly, even measuring the money supply is difficult and uncertain. Finally, the Fed couldn't control money growth with any degree of precision even if it wanted to. What the Fed can control is very short-term interest rates, and then only in the short run. No one, not even the Fed, can control the bond and stock markets.

This doesn't, however, detract from the power and importance of the institution. The world's financial markets are rocked regularly by Fed action or inaction. Wall Street and Bay Street economists, indeed economists all over the world, watch the Fed, attempting to predict its coming moves. Stock markets and interest rates everywhere gyrate on these predictions. Economic activity in every country can be influenced; spending by households and businesses, job creation, and other central bank policies are all affected. For a young economist, the pace and the power are dizzying.

Trial by Fire—Briefing the Board

When I joined the Fed, Arthur Burns was Chairman—a burly old gentleman and a data junky. He knew more about my sector, the savings and loan associations, than I did. He could spot data errors instantly, and ruthlessly questioned the staff on minutia at weekly board briefings.

Oh, those briefings. What a way to ruin a weekend. Every Monday morning at ten a.m., select members of the research staff would brief the Chairman and the six governors on all economic and capital market developments. The massive boardroom, with its huge mahogany table, was awesome. The three briefers sat at the table with the Board and the most senior staff. Behind was a group of economists sent to help answer the questions any briefer missed—a black mark on the briefer's record. The Chairman began the questioning. Arthur Burns was relentless, and went straight for the jugular at the slightest sign of weakness. A misstep in the answer beckoned a staff study—hours of work with rapid turnaround.

By my third year at the Fed, I was in the regular briefing rotation. By then, the chairmanship had shifted to G. William Miller and then to the revered Paul Volcker. Miller, a Carter appointment, had been a business executive at Textron Corporation and had little expertise in economics or financial issues. His stay at the post was very brief. President Carter soon appointed him Treasury Secretary.

Paul Volcker, on the other hand, was a pro. Appointed as Chairman in 1979, he had been the President of the New York Federal Reserve Bank, the home of the Fed's trading desk. He was an expert; there was nothing about the workings of Fed policy that Volcker didn't understand. At six feet seven inches tall, with an ever-present cigar in his mouth, he was an impressive sight. I could see eye to eye with his belt buckle. He scared me to death. He had perfected the art of devil's advocacy, often questioning your every statement only for you to find out later that he had agreed with you all along.

Special Assistant to the Chairman

In 1980, I became special assistant to Paul Volcker. President Jimmy Carter had just introduced the ill-conceived credit controls. Americans misunderstood their meaning and literally stopped spending. The economy went into a tailspin, causing Carter to quickly rescind the controls. Interest rates were sky-high; the housing market had tanked. Builders all over the country were going bankrupt. So were farmers and many others. Paul Volcker was blamed.

He had hiked interest rates sharply beginning in October 1979. Inflation was hitting unprecedented heights. By 1980, protesters were burning his body in effigy outside his office window on Constitution Avenue. I have been told that similar protests were held at the Bank of Canada headquarters. The hate mail came pouring in. Bags and bags of obscenity-laden wood blocks were sent to the Chairman by enraged homebuilders. Ordinary people wrote to the Fed begging for cuts in interest rates; stories of mortgage foreclosures, repossessed furniture and cars, and personal bankruptcies hit my desk. My job was to respond to each of these protests. I was to consult with Volcker about the answers.

Many letters came from members of Congress, demanding explanation for the pain in their districts. Those responses received the scrutiny of the senior staff and the Chairman. Volcker was asked repeatedly to testify before Congress. I often wrote the testimony and suffered through countless rewrites into the early morning hours. Volcker himself was a workaholic. He lived alone in Washington in an apartment near the Fed; his family had remained in New York. My years at the Fed were gruelling and wonderful, the experience invaluable. My move to Fannie Mae was the next step: more money and more autonomy, a chance to apply what I had learned to the real world.

The Move to Toronto

I loved Washington. We had a beautiful new house in McLean, Virginia. We hadn't been there two years. I remember dreaming that our baby, Stefan, would go to Langley High School, only three blocks away.

My family lived reasonably near by. I grew up in Baltimore, Maryland, but my mother's parents lived in Richmond, Virginia. Our house was in between, about an hour's drive from each. My parents and sister from Baltimore and my grandparents from Richmond would descend on us one Sunday a month for lox and bagels and a day of close family connection. My grandmother was dying of cancer and my father wasn't well. I didn't want to move to Toronto. Not that I had anything against Toronto; I had never been there.

It is frightening to move so far away from home—to a new country, a new culture. I had been away before, but I didn't like it. I had gone to graduate school in Pittsburgh, and in the first year of my marriage I had lived in Oxford, Ohio, where I wrote most of my doctoral dissertation. I had missed my family and friends.

Washington was perfect—just far enough away from family to be independent, but close enough to see them and spend holidays and celebrations together. We had made many friends there. Washington is like that. Almost everyone is a transplant; no one was born there, so people are very friendly, forming families with each other. Many of my Fed colleagues have become lifelong friends. One was my mentor, Ed Ettin, who was also often my slave driver. I have never learned so much from anyone before or since. Ed is Deputy Director, Division of Research and Statistics, a trusted adviser to Chairman Alan Greenspan and many Federal Reserve Chairmen before him. He attends all policy-making meetings of the Federal Open Market Committee, the famous FOMC (composed of the Chairman, the Board of Governors and a rotating subgroup of the Federal Reserve Bank Presidents).

We visited Toronto and I liked it. It was much more cosmopolitan than McLean, Virginia, and in some ways even Washington. I loved the skyscrapers, the downtown underground, the culture and the ethnicity. It seemed like a great place to raise children, much better than New York City, another place where my husband had been job-interviewing.

People were so nice, so polite; they even lined up for buses and didn't shout on the subway. The city seemed so clean.

Before we would agree to move, I had to find a job. My husband's prospective employer hired an executive search consultant to help me. He told me that the investment community was "rationalizing" because institutional stock commission rates had just been cut. I met Arthur Vail, a business journalist and television personality, who told me that no one in Canada would be interested in a Fed economist. (We laughed about this years later.) I met one guy on a job interview who told me he liked to hire women because they worked harder and you didn't have to pay them as much. I went home to Washington quite discouraged.

Landing a Job

Back in my office the next day, a friend called to exchange news. Norman Mains was a former colleague of mine at the Fed and was then at Drexel Burnham in Chicago. I told him about my husband's job opportunity in Toronto. He said it was a great city and that he did business there with Nesbitt Thomson and Burns Fry. "I'll give them a call. I'm sure they would love to meet you," he said.

The next morning I was on a plane to Toronto. My first meeting was with Brian Steck, CEO of Nesbitt Thomson; my second meeting was with Jack Lawrence, CEO of Burns Fry. Brian put me at ease. He was warm and friendly, and introduced me to his Director of Research, who suggested I consider becoming a bank analyst; they were full up with economists. I had no idea what a bank analyst did, so I left armed with a copy of *Institutional Investor* magazine, the "All-Star Analysts Team" issue.

Getting off the elevators on the fiftieth floor of First Canadian Place, Burns Fry's head office, my inner voice told me that something very important was happening. The charcoal grey marble floors, cherry-coloured chairs, beautiful receptionists, all seemed so exotic, so impressive. Little did I know I would walk through those halls daily for the next twelve years. Mark Kassirer, Jack's protégé and head of the futures group, took me to lunch at Winston's, a Bay Street landmark.

We had a great lunch and a great talk about the Fed, Volcker and the bond market. Remember, it was late 1982 and bond yields were in the stratosphere. Indeed, they were peaking, but no one believed that then. I did, which generated a lively debate. After lunch, Mark ushered me through the trading room into Jack's corner office.

He didn't want to see my resumé; he just wanted to talk. Jack was a bond trader and, I discovered later, a closet economist. We talked about the markets, inflation, the deficits, Ronald Reagan's tax cuts, Paul Volcker, the inner workings of the Fed. At the end of it, he offered me a job: senior economist, start now. "Oh, by the way," he said, "have you got a master's degree or something?" I smiled. I liked his style. "A Ph.D.," I replied.

I was launched. I couldn't move up to Toronto fast enough. I was so excited. I loved the investment business, the trading-floor environment, the fast pace and the excitement. It was a far cry from Washington and a government job, and it suited me. The move to Toronto didn't save my marriage—we were separated less than three years later—but it took me to where I needed to be.

Living in a Foreign Country

It wasn't easy moving to a foreign city, indeed a foreign country. I knew no one, no old school connections, no contacts, family or friends. Yet in many ways it was liberating and energizing. I realized immediately the advantage of my Federal Reserve experience and the close links between the U.S. and Canadian financial markets. Fed economists were still very new on Wall Street, hired in the early eighties to divine the movements of the all-important weekly money supply numbers and the inner machinations of the Volcker Federal Reserve. Fed economists were unheard of on Bay Street. In fact, surprisingly, almost seventeen years later I'm still the only one.

I had expected Toronto to seem like another American city. It didn't, pleasantly so. Toronto was more European in tone and feel. We could live in the inner city and still feel safe. Quiet tree-lined streets with single-family homes were long gone in the cores of most American cities. I liked the dearth of mega-malls. Of course they're there in the suburbs, but it was a novelty for me to shop in small stores—the greengrocer, the butcher, the fish market. Toronto was much less plastic than other places I had lived, much less of an American fast-food-type culture.

But foreign it was. It took me six weeks to figure out how to store the open milk bags in the refrigerator, even longer to realize that "not too bad" in response to "how are you?" means "just fine." "Not too bad" in the United States means "I'm just getting over a cold" or "I'm finally back at work after a long illness." This summarized for me the difference between the Canadian and American psyches. Canadians are understated, reserved, constrained, willing to "make do." When the Toronto public transit system went on strike, sending the city into gridlock, I was astounded at how calmly people coped, sitting quietly in their cars for hours. In Baltimore, there would have been riots.

Canadian society is orderly and fair. Government is seen as good, profit as bad. Monetary success is suspect. A Robin Hood mentality exists, taking from the rich to give to the poor—or is it *noblesse oblige*? Doctors are government employees with pay ceilings, but medical care is free, sort of.

The tall poppy gets its head cut off. The kiss of death is your face on the cover of *Report on Business* magazine. While government is seen as good, patriotism American-style is bad. No yellow ribbons, no flags waving from houses on July 1 or Remembrance Day, no national unity celebration. Thanksgiving Day seems less of an event; it took me a while to figure out if it was Sunday or Monday.

The cities are cleaner, safer. The public transportation works. The rich array of immigrants haven't been swallowed up by the mainstream culture. There are foreign-language signs in parts of most cities (except Montreal, where it's French only). You can still find old-world craftsmen, artisans, tailors and chefs. The streets of Toronto look like a recently adjourned meeting of the United Nations; nearly half of the city's population are immigrants.

What a contrast for me in my early days in this country. In the United States, people are rowdy, loud, boisterous, exuberant. Authority garners no respect; as for government, Americans say "get out of my way." Profit is good and success is revered, particularly self-made success; Bill Gates, Oprah Winfrey, Michael Jordan and Warren Buffett are icons. Doctors earn fortunes and advanced medical care is costly, but it's also readily available without wait. Cities are not clean and safe, although the plunge in the jobless rate in the nineties improved the situation markedly. Society is anything but orderly; survival of the fittest reigns. New is better than old, new money is better than inherited money, and the can-do frontier spirit abounds. Americans are insular and parochial, and most of all proud to be Americans and proud to be proud. Thanksgiving and the Fourth of July are national holidays, celebrated by everyone, regardless of race or religion. Hard-driving, hard-working, dog-eat-dog, the tall poppy shines—at least until the next taller poppy pops up. Americans are optimists, rebels and lacking in snob appeal. Bank accounts rather than pedigrees and old-school ties determine status in society.

Good or bad is debatable; different is not. I've loved living in Toronto. My son has thrived, my career has blossomed, and I met and married a wonderful man. Canada has been very good to me. Today I hold dual citizenship, but Toronto is my home.

Part 1

You in a Rapidly
Changing World

ONE

The Evolution of Revolutions

My move to a new city for better job opportunities is far from unique. Leaving home for educational and job enhancement is rapidly becoming commonplace. Growth, adaptation and development are essential qualities for success. Innovation and knowledge are increasing at an accelerating pace, and households are more willing than ever to embrace new technologies.

It took almost fifty years after invention for a critical mass of households—roughly 30 percent—to benefit from electricity, thirty-five years to own automobiles or to install telephones, twenty-two years for radio and twenty-six for television. But it took much less time to adapt to computers, CD players, cell phones, e-mail and the Internet. IBM introduced the first personal computer in 1981. Apple Macintosh popularized the mouse and graphic displays in 1984, but Microsoft and IBM—not Apple—reaped the real benefits seven years later. In 1991, Microsoft launched Windows 3.1, a copycat technology similar to the Mac. It made computing much easier, breaking from the text-based design of MS-DOS in early IBM PCs that required you to remember often oblique keyboard commands. The Windows software featured a graphically oriented screen of small picture icons that could be accessed by clicking on a hand-held mouse. When Windows was introduced in 1991, the PC market took off. Apple had made a huge mistake in 1985: worrying that clone-makers would cannibalize its sales, it decided not to license its technology to others.

With Windows, almost anyone could operate a computer. In 1992, PC shipments jumped 20 percent to 32.4 million worldwide, compared with a 13.4 percent increase in the prior year, according to Dataquest, a U.S. tech research firm. Shipments reached about 50 million in 1994. Since then, the performance and versatility of the PC have sky-rocketed, and prices continue to fall. The driving force behind the PC industry's growth, Moore's Law—the doubling of computing power every eighteen months or so—will hold true through at least 2010, according to Intel. Dataquest forecasts that annual PC shipments will increase 54 percent by 2001 to 152 million units.

Initially, computers were for office and business use only. Today, they are commonly found in homes as well. The United States and Canada are global leaders in computer usage. The U.S. stood at the top of the 1997 rankings with 450 computers per 1,000 individuals. Australia was second with 366 and Canada a close third with 364. Norway, Iceland, Finland, Sweden and Denmark were next in line, with New Zealand and Singapore rounding out the top ten. It is interesting to see how far down the ranking core European countries fell: France and Germany were eighteenth and nineteenth. Japan was ranked twentieth, as PC usage in Japan is more difficult because the language does not lend itself easily to keyboard application. Moreover, non-tariff barriers to PC imports have been a huge impediment to change.

Acceptance and use of the Internet have been even more rapid. Not open for commercial users until 1994, the World Wide Web has trans-formed the PC from a productivity and entertainment tool to a com-munications and information resource. Moreover, e-commerce is taking off at an explosive pace. Judging from 1997 and 1998 data, Finland, Iceland and Norway had the largest number of Internet con-nections in relation to the size of their populations. The U.S., Sweden, Singapore and Canada were next.

While not nearly as ubiquitous as the VCR, the home computer is rapidly becoming a common sight. Roughly 50 percent of American households have at least one computer. The proportion in Canada is similar at an estimated 40 percent, and growing rapidly. Business use has skyrocketed to well over 90 percent in the United States and almost that high in Canada.

The Biotech Revolution

Advances in the life sciences are also dramatic and rapid, and will have a huge impact on our lives. Microprocessors have allowed the decoding of DNA. Very soon, all genes in the body will be mapped. The next step is to recode defective genes, substantively improving and increasing the quality and length of life for many. Biotechnology applied to agriculture is also boosting potential living standards, maximizing food production for a hungry world.

The application of the information sciences to the life sciences is leading to stunning breakthroughs in our understanding of the very source of life. Through genetic research, scientists are on the precipice of understanding and re-engineering life itself. The potential applications are head-spinning and will trigger major changes in the global economy.

The world's food and fibre supply will be increasingly grown indoors in giant bacteria baths at a fraction of the cost of today's farming on land. Food supplies will increase dramatically and prices will plunge. Millions of the world's farmers will be displaced, completing the movement of people from agriculture to the new sectors of the economy that began in the industrial age. This will lead to important and even wrenching social and cultural dislocations in many parts of the world.

Fibres with the strength of silk are being engineered in laboratories through the use of bacteria. These fibres will be used in the manufacture of hundreds of products. The U.S. military intends to use these in everything from airplanes to parachutes.

With the birth of Dolly the cloned sheep on February 22, 1997, animal cloning became a reality. Animal cloning will become commonplace, and human cloning (or at least artificial organ reproduction) cannot be far behind. While the possibilities are frightening, they are also potentially positive as well. New medical and pharmaceutical breakthroughs will undoubtedly extend and improve life. Developments in animal husbandry and marine biology will also further increase the world's food supply and reduce the number of livestock producers and fisheries. Monsanto Company, a U.S. agritech firm, has developed a product called Posilac that, when fed to dairy cows, greatly enhances milk production.

The ethics and regulation of genetic engineering are hotly debated. Recent research in Britain has raised concerns about the health risks of genetically modified food products, although others have suggested that their research is flawed. The British people are particularly vulnerable to these fears because of their horrible experience with mad cow disease. Europeans generally are quite concerned about the integrity of the world's food supply and they supported an early-1999 United Nations initiative to regulate the export of genetically altered crops and animals. The United States, Canada and a few other countries were opposed to these initiatives, suggesting they would curtail one of the fastest-growing industries in the world.

We still know little about the long-term impact of biogenetics on our food supply, but we do know that it is big business. Canada in particular has a strong vested interest in agritech. Roughly 38 percent of the canola grown in Canada in 1999 was genetically modified; so was 19 percent of the corn and 5 percent of the soybeans.

Human beings have long worried about the dangers of tampering with life forms, a situation fictionalized by Mary Shelley in the early nineteenth century through her character Victor Frankenstein and his engineered creature. These fears have haunted biology through the twentieth century, and the ethics of cloning and genetic alteration will continue to be a key area of analysis and debate in coming years. When first developed, transplant surgery, in vitro fertilization and genetically modified bacteria that are used to produce a number of important drugs were all seen as unnatural and frightening. In these cases, scientists and doctors were able to dispel fears by showing the value and safety of their work. In the minds of many, today's genetic researchers have yet to do that.

Biotech and the Resource Sector

Scientists are creating substitute products for the world's nonrenewable resources. They are also improving the extraction and production process, significantly reducing costs and increasing supplies while protecting the environment. Traditional natural resource producers are already going the way of the farmers and fishermen.

Increased global supply and falling prices have driven many to cut production or simply close down.

The potential payoff of the application of technology to the surviving nimble resource companies is staggering. Mining companies are already using bacteria and micro-organisms to extract ores from the ground. These organisms eat away salt and other unwanted substances in the ore, leaving pure metals. Low-grade ore bodies will become economical, increasing the world's supply of base and precious metals and reducing the price.

Research is moving ahead in the energy field to create renewable resources as a substitute for oil, coal and natural gas. An example of this would be ethanol, which comes from sugar and wood or grain crops, and could provide the fuel for automobiles in the coming century. Scientists are working on breakthrough developments in biofuels in an effort to replace fossil fuels altogether. The chemical industry is conducting research to replace petroleum with bioengineered products in the production of plastics. There has already been some success in creating plastics from bacteria.

Forestry companies are searching for genes that can be injected into trees to make them faster-growing and more resistant to disease, bad weather and environmental conditions. Artificial substances and bioengineered forest products will massively increase supply in this sector as well. Here too, prices will fall and all but the new innovators and leading-edge researchers and producers will be driven out of business.

It is very clear that economies like Canada's, which still depend significantly on agriculture and resources, will suffer serious restructuring. The shifts in the marketplace will be stunning as commodity prices continue their long-term downward trend and productivity in food production rockets higher. Traditional low-skilled, high-paying jobs in these sectors will continue to disappear—a process that began in the mid-1970s with the oil crisis and the resulting worldwide economic restructuring. New jobs will be created in the laboratories of the great surviving natural resource companies. Biotech companies, already burgeoning in Canada and the U.S., will continue to grow.

The economic restructuring will, as always, be as painful as it is unavoidable. Canada will continue to suffer negative economic consequences if it attempts to stand in the way of progress by subsidizing obsolete pulp mills, mines and fisheries with no fish. The government must accept the inevitability of the changes and redeploy funding for training and research, assisting people to relocate and re-educate if necessary to share in the enormous prosperity that will be created by these breakthroughs. Very real success stories are already happening in Canada, as we will discuss in detail in chapter 13. Technology companies are flourishing in the suburbs of Ottawa and in the technology triangle around Kitchener-Waterloo. Saskatoon has become a hotbed of biotechnology, creating a centre of excellence in the life sciences in the university. Calgary and Edmonton also boast a growing number of hi-tech companies specializing in research and development related to the oil industry, information technology and medicine. Software and biotech companies are spotting the Vancouver landscape, abetted by the researchers at the University of British Columbia. This sector will be increasingly important for provinces like Saskatchewan, Alberta and British Columbia, which have traditionally relied so heavily on agriculture and resources.

The Early History of Change— Seems Like a Snail's Pace

It is useful and interesting to put today's revolutionary changes in historical perspective. Change has always been with us, but never before in history has it been so rapid or had so much impact. Dramatic shifts in social and economic development are upon us. This is not new—the history of humankind is a history of innovation and change—but progress used to be a lot slower. From one century to the next, the rate of technological advance and the rate of growth in per-capita income have been accelerating.

Paul Romer, an economist at Stanford University who specializes in growth theory, believes that the fundamental ingredient for economic progress over the ages has been ideas or knowledge. He asserts that the rate of progress in the past one hundred years has surpassed that of the previous one thousand years because of what economists call "increasing returns" to knowledge, to the process of discovery. Sir Isaac Newton once said that it was easier for him to discover because he could stand on the shoulders of giants. The point he was making, and that Romer refers to, is that knowledge builds on itself. Ideas create new ideas, and the speed of innovation accelerates over time. The use of the computer, augmented by the development of the transistor, has led to breakthrough developments in many fields, which in turn create other breakthroughs in other fields, and on and on. The long sweep of human history shows that the more we have learned and discovered, the better we have become at learning and discovering. This suggests that there is no limit to the things we can develop.

It took thousands of years to move from foraging tribes—hunting and gathering societies—to horticultural villages. The big technological innovation then was the primitive hoe or digging stick. Several more millennia passed before the introduction of heavy animal-drawn plows shifted the economy from light horticulture to agrarian empires. Life moved beyond subsistence for the first time as farming on this scale created enough of a surplus of food to free up some to pursue other tasks. Mathematics was invented. So were writing, metallurgy and specialized warfare. The first contemplative endeavours such as philosophy evolved, and the great military empires began.

The First Information Revolution

The Sumerians are credited with developing the first efficient writing system, in about the third millennium BC. Clay tablets were the medium—heavy and fragile—cumbersome to say the least; yet it was another two thousand years before the Egyptians figured out how to use papyrus instead. It too had its drawbacks (it cracked), but it was much lighter and therefore made long-distance communication possible. The Greeks later made parchment out of animal skins, which could be folded into pages, encouraging the development of the book format. It took scholars years, however, to handwrite books, and mass production was virtually impossible. Monks spent lifetimes handcopying the great works of European literature. Paper entered Europe from China through Byzantium in the twelfth century, but it was a lot more fragile than parchment. Hand copying was too tedious and time-consuming to be wasted on something as perishable as paper.

Breakthrough technological innovation occurred around 1455 when Johannes Gutenberg invented the printing press. The impact was spectacular, and the speed of change began to accelerate. By 1500 there were more than a thousand presses in Europe producing millions of copies of books. Literacy and knowledge no longer belonged solely in the realm of the Church or the elite. Without the Gutenberg bible, the Protestant Reformation might never have happened. Books finally became accessible to the common man, allowing for the Scientific Revolution in the sixteenth and seventeenth centuries. As a sign of how innovations feed off each other, the importance of eyeglasses was not fully realized until after Gutenberg's invention of the printing press.

This was the period of the Renaissance—da Vinci, Copernicus, Galileo and Newton—the discovery of America and the adoption of Arabic numerals in the West. The Enlightenment thinkers in the sixteenth and seventeenth centuries, from Descartes to Locke to Kant, encouraged rational scientific thought and advocated the supremacy of human rights. The forty years beginning in 1776 witnessed the American and French revolutions, the invention of the steam engine, the publication of Adam Smith's *Wealth of Nations* and the beginning of the Industrial Revolution in Europe.

Industrial States—Change Accelerates

This was a period of spectacular change, an age of reason and of revolution. Autocratic monarchist governments were dismantled with bloody ferocity. Hallmarks of this era were the rise of democracy, the abolition of slavery, the first stirrings of the feminist movement, and the development of the empirical and technical sciences. Church doctrine no longer dictated scientific belief. Mary Wollstonecraft's *A Vindication of the Rights of Woman* was written in 1792, and was the first major feminist treatise in history.

The Industrial Revolution brought with it an increase in urbanization and a growth in population fostered by improvements in medicine and public health. Until the Industrial Revolution most of the world's population base was rural, but by the mid-1800s half the people in England lived in cities. By the end of the century the same was true in other European countries. Industrialization required a concentration of the workforce. Factories often had to be located where coal or other essential materials were available. Marketing of products required access to waterways or railways. London, Paris, Berlin and New York—established political centres—became centres for banking, finance and advertising.

The structure of society was also substantively affected. This was a time of widespread social upheaval and the massive movement of people away from their ancestral lands. A new factory-owning bourgeoisie came into being, as well as a new class of industrial workers—men, women and children in the factories, mills, pottery works and mines. Many skilled artisans found themselves degraded to the status of routine process labourers as machines began to mass-produce items formerly made by hand.

Wages were low, hours were long and working conditions were very unpleasant and often dangerous, giving rise to the labour-union movement. Unions were created to improve safety, to reduce the working day to ten hours and to raise the minimum working age to twelve. Strikes became more common, and by the turn of the century unions were growing more militant as big business continued to flex its muscle.

We think we suffer the ravages of change, the societal costs of technological innovation, the human costs of downsizing and restructuring. My great-grandmother, my namesake, immigrated to the United States in the first decade of the twentieth century from a shtetl, a small village, in Russia. She had three young children; the eldest, my grandmother, was seven. My great-grandfather had come to America earlier to make his way. He was supposed to send for his wife and family, but he never did. All alone in a strange country, my great-grandmother went to work as a seamstress in the sweatshops of the New York garment district. Hers was a world of twelve-hour days, unbearable noise and heat, no ventilation, fire traps. She put her children in an orphanage—the 1910 version of daycare—and visited them on weekends until she could afford to rent a place large enough and arrange for someone to look after them while she worked. She understood even then about "knowledge workers," a term coined by Peter Drucker in 1993 to describe people whose jobs require analysis, innovation, synthesis, insight and lateral thinking—educated people who command the highest salaries in the new information age. She knew that the way out of the east-side New York ghetto for her children was the same as today, through education. Her eldest child, my grandmother, only finished Grade 9, but her middle son finished high school and her youngest, miracle of miracles, finished law school. My father followed in his footsteps.

Back to the Future

In the future, education and training will be more important than ever. Knowledge workers are already paid the most and enjoy the greatest labour mobility and flexibility. The knowledge-based economy rewards interpretation and insight. Computers process data, but humans interpret and synthesize that data to provide information and knowledge. Interpretive and innovative capabilities will be disproportionately rewarded. Gone are the days when physical brawn was the critical factor for success. In the modern world, mental stamina and innovative spirit determine the big earners and winners. Education becomes increasingly important as computers perform all the rote left-brain activities and humans are elevated to using intuition and non-linear thinking skills. Theoretically, neither sex has an inherent competitive advantage in this world.

The twenty-first-century economy will be one of rapid real growth, low inflation and low interest rates. Past periods of major innovation have wrought profound increases in living standards; think of the early days of the steam engine, the railway, mechanized production and electricity. In each of these cases it took time for productivity gains, the gains that spark real income growth, to show through. Old technologies had to be replaced and a new infrastructure to be built. Eventually, huge gains in household purchasing power bubbled up.

In today's world, the dislocations are immense. Job security is an old-time concept. Businesses are forced by global competitive pressures to minimize costs, and people are usually the biggest cost item. Even local businesses are affected. Local merchants and service providers—corner stores, schools, hairdressers, restaurants, supermarkets, dry cleaners, sports and entertainment facilities and the like—account for 60 to 80 percent of the economy. With the rapid growth in Internet shopping, even some of these businesses are subject to global price pressures and enhanced competition. Consumers are more discerning, more aware of international standards than ever before. Whether we travel literally or through the media, we understand differences in quality and performance like never before. The array of entertainment and educational alternatives is broadening, and all fields of endeavour and bodies of knowledge are influenced by global developments, research, fashion and style changes. Have you noticed that teenagers all over the world dress alike?

Even our food tastes have become more global, and local restaurants and food stores must respond. In the fifties, ketchup was exotic; today we use salsa. We eat kiwi, tuna—fresh, not from a can—jalapeño peppers, quesadilla, pad thai noodles and dim sum. Radicchio and arugula, goat's cheese and pecorino are menu staples. We drink vintage wines from all over the world, and expect to buy tropical fruits and flowers in the winter. Clearly, even the most local of businesses are influenced by the growth in global trade and competition, the increase in consumer sophistication and awareness.

Computers have made many people dispensable: behind every Automatic Teller Machine breathe the ghosts of two or three living tellers. At the same time, service has improved and people are redeployed to other areas, where human talent is needed. The fact that the U.S. unemployment rate fell to near-thirty-year lows in the late nineties even as layoffs hit record levels shows that creative destruction—the replacement of old industry with new—does not necessarily mean jobless workers. To minimize unemployment, though, we need to increase the economic pie and enhance opportunity, innovation and entrepreneurial spirit.

Businesses in the United States are hiring high-school dropouts and training them on the job because labour is in such short supply. The social benefits of this have been huge, as welfare rolls have dwindled and crime rates have fallen to twenty-year lows. The times are tough, but the opportunities are huge. Taking advantage of these opportunities is the key.

Only You Can Take Care of Yourself

Most families are stretched like never before, with endless chores and commitments leaving barely any time to relax together. Mom and Dad are spending more time working and commuting, while the kids run from school to sports to a multitude of extracurricular activities. Women are working outside the home in unprecedented numbers. Time and money are in short supply. Innovation and technological change have increased the speed of communication and made instantaneous response an expectation. No longer can we wait for snail mail. Pagers, voice mail and e-mail have made many of us far too accessible. Globalization has shifted the work and marketing day to twenty-four hours. We are suffering from an information and work overload.

Without doubt, this has put strains on family life, personal time and general peace of mind. Stress levels are very high as we all try to juggle too many roles, too many commitments. Whether by choice or economic necessity, we have less and less leisure time and far less ongoing contact with our families—very little time to smell the roses and recharge our batteries. We are burdened by fears of an uncertain future with an unknown degree of financial security.

Gone are the days when we could count on lifetime employment, on big business and big government to take care of us. There is no guaranteed job security any longer, even in the public sector, regardless of how good a job we are doing. Even those with successful careers in strong companies run the risk of layoff, downsizing and merger. Business is under increasing global competitive pressure. The world-wide surge in mergers in every sector is a reflection of this. Mergers attempt to capture economies of scale and scope, spreading costs over a broader revenue base.

The Internet will intensify this process. Internet commerce shifts the balance of commercial power to consumers, who demand a very individual shopping experience. On the Net, the competition is just a click away. If you have trouble finding the book you want at Amazon.com, you can go to ChaptersGlobe.com. The Internet makes it easy for consumers to find the least-cost source for many products. The Net eliminates the geographical protections for local businesses. Car dealers selling online, for example, have drawn buyers from hundreds of miles away. The same is true for online mortgage providers, insurance agents, financial planners and many more.

The European Monetary Union has had the same effect, increasing cross-border price competition. As eleven European countries (and more to come) have given up their individual currencies for the euro, pricing has become transparent across these country lines, making comparison shopping easier for businesses and consumers both. Mergers have surged in all business sectors, consolidating activity and raising productivity. Within-country, cross-country and even cross-continent mergers are now common. The Daimler Benz–Chrysler and Deutsche Bank–Bankers Trust mergers announced in 1998 are examples of what is to come. With intensified price competition, businesses must continuously improve efficiency and productivity. This means reducing their labour bills as much as possible; labour is, after all, two-thirds of the cost of production for the economy at large.

Highly paid, low-skilled jobs have been disappearing since the mid-1970s; jobs in mining, other resources, fishing, farming and basic manufacturing have either moved to cheap-labour foreign locales or been replaced by technology. This process is only going to accelerate with the ongoing information and biotechnology revolution.

People will retain the opportunity to drop out of the corporate structure. Record numbers of people are choosing to be self-employed, to work from home, to try mid-life career changes. Technology has helped to make these shifts more feasible, allowing for telecommuting and business outsourcing to independent providers.

In this period of rapid change, everyone's skills obsolesce at an unprecedented pace. This requires each of us to devote time and energy to remaining up-to-date in our area of expertise. The body of knowledge in every field is growing at an astounding rate. If we don't continue to grow and learn, we fall behind. Education can no longer end with a high-school or university degree; six months out of the University of Waterloo's computer science department—one of the best in the world—even the top students will be behind the times if they haven't kept up with developments in their field. And the pace of change is not likely to slow in the foreseeable future. It is difficult and stressful, but constant learning and adaptation to new technologies is essential to outpace the productivity gains of our competitors.

Me, Inc.

The traditional relationship between employer and employee is dead. No longer is lifetime employment with regular pay increases guaranteed for competent, conscientious workers. My college friend Neal had been with a very large multinational food and wine corporation for twenty-three years. He had risen through the ranks at lightning speed in the early years, then transferred abroad for extended stretches to see the world. He ultimately headed two large divisions. At the age of forty-eight, he was unceremoniously fired. No real reason was given, but his company had just acquired a smaller competitor and the two operations were being consolidated. Neal was having trouble getting along with his counterpart at the new company, and evidently the other guy won. Neal was devastated. Sure, he got a pension, but the damage to his ego and sense of self-worth were huge. He, like many, defined himself by his career success, enjoying the perquisites and societal status of a corporate executive.

For the first time in his career, he had to fend for himself. He tried outplacement counselling and networking but was unable to land another job at anywhere near his skill level. In fact it became obvious that firms were not interested in hiring forty-eight-year-old executives. Neal changed his attitude and stopped looking for a "job." Instead, he began to see himself as the president of his own personal services company. He started consulting for small companies and start-up operations in the food and wine business. He offered advice to venture capital firms and merchant banks, accepted board appointments—both profit and non-profit—and traded his time and expertise for stock in a number of new and promising businesses.

Today, Neal is happier than he has been in years. He now is more the master of his own destiny. He would like to continue working in this way indefinitely. He likes the challenge, being busy and adding value. He needs to feel that he still has great potential, and he does. In addition, he needs the money. Even a good company pension isn't enough to insure financial security in the future. He has four children; the two youngest are still in university and the two oldest are working but living at home. His dad is elderly and might ultimately need extended nursing-home care. His wife has a part-time job, but it doesn't pay very much. As the currency continues to fall, he and his wife don't want to be denied the opportunity to travel.

The lessons here are very real for all of us. None of us is safe. None of us is immune to downsizing, restructuring, layoffs. In the tightest U.S. labour markets in years, layoffs are still up more than 50 percent. Not a day goes by that we don't see a major layoff announcement in the U.S. and Canadian press, and this is not likely to change soon. Indeed, it's a reflection of economic buoyancy and growth, not of recession and decline. U.S. job layoffs surged in the nineties, yet so did employment growth. As U.S. job layoffs rose sharply in 1998, 2.8 million net new jobs were created. Layoffs continue to mount in Canada as well, largely as a result of cutbacks in the resource sector and rationalization in the retail sector. Even so, job growth has been strong. More than 450,000 net new jobs were created in Canada in 1998, bringing the gain for the decade thus far to 1.5 million.

Reflecting the ongoing revolution in the labour market, each of us must change our mind-set. Like Neal, each of us must become the President of our own personal services company, Me Inc., whether we have a job or not. We sell these services to the highest bidders with the greatest potential. We all have enormous competition: our competitors are anyone anywhere who provides the same service. The risk is that there will be someone, sometime, somewhere, who will provide it better, faster, cheaper or more effectively. We can reduce this risk by committing to never-ending improvement of our service. If we don't, we will inevitably fall behind. It's very tough; we can't ever rest on our laurels. Excellence today does not mean excellence tomorrow—it is a "what have you done for me lately" world. The body of knowledge in every field is increasing at an exponential rate. Computers and the Internet have made this possible. Business methods are also improving at lightning speed, and we must adapt constantly to keep up.

Guaranteed Job Security— A Thing of the Past

Recognize that the corporate world has changed. It may be painful, even sad, but business no longer has the luxury to guarantee work for anyone, from the top of the organization to the bottom, and it is never going to revert to the old ways. *Never*—and no amount of government intervention or union power is going to change that. In fact, the more the government or the unions attempt to stand in the way of the process of restructuring, the lower the standard of living for everyone. This was painfully evident in the Soviet Union and China, where governments tried to protect unprofitable and non-competitive state-owned enterprises; overall economic growth waned and living standards fell. The demise of Japanese economic supremacy in the past ten years has put the final nail in the coffin of lifetime employment guarantees. The core European countries are discovering that excessive labour market rigidities and union power—as in Germany, France and Italy—ultimately lead to higher, not lower, unemployment.

Competitive pressures are immense, and the stock market is heartless. Corporate stock prices plunge on weaker-than-expected earnings reports. The cost of capital—borrowed money—then rises, and it becomes more difficult for businesses to finance inventory and payrolls. Cash-flow squeezes occur. Smaller businesses feel the pinch quicker.

Corporate boards, now more accountable to shareholders than ever before, demand adjustment: reduced costs and enhanced revenues. Often that requires restructuring. Profit margins are razor thin and narrowing in many sectors, and most businesses have no pricing power. They cannot pass higher labour or materials costs on to the consumer in the form of higher product prices, especially if they compete with imported products. Even if they don't, there is almost always someone down the street or on the Internet that will take their customers if they attempt to raise prices. Many companies have tried, only to lose business and ultimately roll back failed price hikes. Indeed, price wars are not uncommon—look at the gas stations.

Non-competitive businesses lose customers and market share. When that happens, they lose money. Money-losing companies freeze hiring. Then, if they can't turn it around, they lay off workers and close outlets and branches. (A recent Canadian example of this syndrome is Eaton's.) If that still doesn't work, they hope for a white knight, another stronger business, to come in and buy them out. If none is forthcoming, they ultimately go out of business, everyone loses their job, and shareholders and creditors lose their money. That is why profit is not a dirty word. Without profitable business, new jobs and share-holder value will not be created.

The "Quit Your Job" Mentality

In these enormously competitive markets and rapidly changing times, the way you think about your work life must shift. Think of yourself as a consultant providing services to your company. Your boss now becomes your client. The more value you add, the more likely you are to keep your client; but, through no fault of your own, things could change. If they do, you move on and find new clients. Always polish your skills, stay current, look around and keep your options open.

Stephen Pollan referred to this mind-set as "quitting your job" in his book *Die Broke*. He recommends you quit your job—not literally, but in your mind. Don't think of it as a career any more but as your current assignment, your current consulting project. He likens it to the situation of a professional athlete: expect to be traded, maximize your income, give your best to the team, but move to the next team if necessary. Psychologically, this attitude might help deal with the uncertainty in today's world. Through no fault of your own, you might be put on waivers.

In my world the change has been dizzying. Sixteen years ago, a chief economist at a major Canadian investment dealer had to be expert in Canadian and U.S. economic and financial market developments. Reports were written by hand, typed by secretaries, sent to reprographics for hand-drawn charts, then to the print shop and mailroom, to reach clients within a few days. Today, we follow developments all over the world, not just in Canada and the United States. Overnight movements in Asian and European markets regularly have an impact on Canadian markets, and we are responsible for twenty-four-hour-a-day monitoring. We type all reports ourselves online, charts are computerized, and dissemination is instantaneous via the Internet. For those that prefer hard copy, we fax. Only long reports are mailed or sent by courier, and even those are produced internally, using desktop publishing and data-charting software.

Gone are traditional secretaries and reprographics personnel. The print shop and the mailroom have been re-engineered. The service is better, broader, cheaper and faster. My competitors are not just economists in Canada, but economists worldwide—those who work for other financial institutions and those who are self-employed, providing our clients and our colleagues with analysis and insight via fax and e-mail. The proliferation of financial news networks—like CNBC, CNNfn, CTV-N1, CityPulse and Newsworld—has increased competition dramatically. Our clients are bombarded with information. A lot of it is hype—breathless reporters giving the latest earnings report as though it were urgent late-breaking global news. Nevertheless, it is clear in my world that if we don't add value, we're gone.

The consolidation in the financial services industry in Canada is representative of what is happening everywhere, in every industry. The former four pillars—the banks, trust companies, insurance companies and investment dealers—have broken down; banks bought trust companies and investment dealers, dramatically reducing the number of economist jobs. Even without bank mergers the consolidation has been appreciable, and more is no doubt to come. Looking around the world, we see a growing number of mergers in every field. Layoffs are surging as never before. No wonder people feel insecure about their jobs. While layoffs will continue and many will fall victim, there are ways to reduce the potential career damage.

Neglecting to keep up with the times is the kiss of career death. What is worse, the general presumption is that the younger you are, the more current you are. There is well-documented evidence of age bias in the corporate world. A late-1998 Exec-u-net survey of 400 thirty-five to sixty-year-old job-seekers in the United States showed that the older they were, the fewer interviews they got and the longer it took to find a job.

Difficult at Any Age

"Over forty" is a euphemism for "over the hill," "beyond your prime," "not quite as energetic." Being referred to as "seasoned" or "mature" is regarded as an insult in the corporate world, sending you looking over your shoulder for the twenty-eight-year-old wanting your job. Never mind that it takes twenty years to learn a business well, to learn a discipline well. Never mind wisdom, experience, judgment, maturity. This is a tough world. We need to work longer and save more for retirement, but the business world wants us to retire early. Incomes peak in the fifty-to-fifty-five age range, which explains why so many companies look to this group as a target for downsizing: they are expensive.

In early 1999, *Fortune* magazine ran a cover story called "Finished at Forty," describing a new trend in corporate America. Forty is starting to look and feel old. No longer is seniority rewarded. Companies in Canada and the U.S. have less and less tolerance for people they see as earning more than their output warrants. It is a cruel world. In a few years, there will be more workers over forty than under, owing to the postwar baby boom, and this helps to compound the problem. The Boomers are competing for a limited number of top jobs. For those who have made it, OK; but for the legions of decent, ordinary performers— watch out. They cannot rise to the top, because there is no room. Right behind, moving into the passing lane, is another generation, a generation seen as more energetic, flexible, technically savvy and willing to work gruelling hours. In an economy where the rules seem to change every day, it's the risk-takers who are being rewarded. A forty-six-year-old with a mortgage and two kids in university is less likely to take risks than a thirty-year-old with nothing to lose. It is not only the high-tech firms that are closing the doors on people over forty; older industries also find that their product life cycles are getting shorter and shorter, and as the speed of change accelerates, it is awfully hard to keep up unless you have the stamina of a twenty-five-year-old.

In 1998, when U.S.-based management consulting firm Watson Wyatt Worldwide asked 773 CEOs at what age they felt people's productivity peaked, the average response was forty-three. The signs of age that employers complain about are less enthusiasm, less creativity and less productivity. These are all signs of boredom. Psychologists have found that there is a trajectory in a traditional career: it rises, then peaks and declines. Once you get everything there is to know about a job down pat, you run out of challenges and everything becomes a little too easy. The solution is to find new challenges. Take on more responsibility, innovate, improve what you are doing, learn new skills. Quit your job if you have to, switch disciplines, get on another path before the boredom saps your energy.

Older workers will get some respect in the future—when they are needed. By about 2003, more than half the workers in Canada and the U.S. will be over forty. The next younger generation, Generation X, are far fewer in number, and the Boomer children will not meaningfully hit the labour force for at least another decade. At some point, probably around 2011, when Boomers start turning sixty-five, companies will be in need of workers, even older workers, according to the Hudson Institute's Richard Judy, a co-author of *Workforce 2020*.

It is not easy for the twenty-eight-year-olds either. Baby Boomers and their elders have clogged the corporate ladder. Education inflation is rampant. A bachelor's degree has become increasingly more expensive and it is worth less and less in salary payoff. Many entry-level positions in large corporations require a university degree even for the most menial tasks. Promotions are harder to get, and many will have to wait years more than today's fifty- and sixty-year-olds to be given their opportunity to shine.

So, what should you do?

- Stay current. Invest the time needed to keep up with developments in your field, company and industry worldwide. Read, read, read—at least one hour a day. Read relevant periodicals (newspapers and magazines) in your field from all over the world. Read general business publications to understand the landscape and how it is changing. Read books.

- Create new challenges. Look for new opportunities and endeavours in order to ward off career boredom.

- Take courses, go to seminars, attend lectures, listen to audio programs. Universities are now offering courses on the Internet and on television. Many firms are offering training opportunities in a wide array of fields and technologies. Take advantage of these, many of which are online and can be done in your own time frame.

- Use new technology to the fullest. Use your computer; it's easy now. Transmit and communicate electronically. Use the Internet; it's a resource for both communication and research. Everyone in every field publishes their ideas on the Net. Most newspapers and periodicals are there as well.

- Network. Maintain and expand your contacts in your field and related ones. Keep in mind that you might be selling your services independently in the future, so actively develop a potential client list.

- Keep fit, look good. Exercise regularly, eat healthily, get enough rest, have fun—it's great for your mental outlook. The older you are, the more important it is to stay fit. The twenty-eight-year-olds have an edge if you look tired and unhealthy; you have an edge if you look energetic and fit. We all admire fifty-year-olds who run, ski, lift weights. This is even truer for sixty-year-olds. How about seventy?

  Looking good is important for both men and women. Whether we like it or not, we are judged by our appearance; it's our first foot in the door. Good-looking people, regardless of age, have an advantage. I don't mean movie-star good looks, which might actually be a disadvantage. I mean looking like you care about your appearance: good grooming, attractive and appropriate clothing, making the most of your natural attributes. It's a sign to the world of self-esteem.

Even if you do stay current, keep fit, adapt to new technologies, you may find yourself downsized out of a job. With the surge in mergers worldwide, many formerly very successful people have been rendered redundant. Some will find jobs in other companies; some will change fields, open small businesses, take on entrepreneurial opportunities.

More and more are literally opening their own personal services company, selling the same services they used to provide to their employer to a host of companies that prefer to outsource the service. Some of these companies have decided it is more cost-effective to out-source, shutting down their own internal operations; others are too small to support the capabilities in-house, but still have need of the talent or expertise. Self-employed consultants are a growth industry. It's not easy, and it takes guts—no guaranteed paycheque, no big business benefits, no job security. But then, no one has true job security any more. And the flexibility of being your own boss, making your own decisions, exploring sky-is-the-limit possibilities can be exhilarating.

Others are voluntarily making mid-life career switches for quality-of-life enhancement, following long-lost dreams—opening bistros on the beach, running bed-and-breakfast homes in the mountains, tele-commuting from remote locations. Small businesses are springing up at a rapid rate as many extend their working careers, potentially well beyond age sixty-five.

Don't Forget the Children

Sons and daughters too must be trained to ultimately take care of themselves. Learning to handle money at an early age is invaluable. Understanding what things cost, recognizing the responsibility to earn money and saving for something special create tremendous self-esteem in young people. Children have jobs too—chores around the house—and responsibilities to other family members.

Their number-one job, however, is to get an education in the broadest sense possible, from academic excellence to social skills. The demands on students today are enormous. The importance of educa-tion has never been greater. Even entry-level jobs in business today require a bachelor's degree. We all know educated Generation Xers—

those born between 1966 and 1976—with McJobs, hamburger-flippers with no hope of advancement. It is a tough world out there, but it doesn't have to mean underemployment or unemployment.

At the same time that youth unemployment is high, there are labour shortages in many sectors. Some graduates are receiving multiple job offers, signing bonuses and loan repayments. In about a decade and beyond, as Boomers retire, many sectors will be clamouring for workers. There are insufficient numbers of engineers, computer scientists, programmers and Internet designers in Canada today, and those shortages are likely to intensify. Help your children find out where the shortages are, and match them with their skills and interests. Impress on them that, after graduation, on-the-job training is the best training of all. They should invest in their own human capital by taking the job with the most learning potential, not necessarily the highest starting salary.

Education is never-ending and never wasted. Basic liberal arts study, speaking skills and writing skills are essential for all educated people. Teach your children to study independently, to read the newspapers, indeed to read generally and broadly. You can only do that by example and by turning off the television. The outlook in so many fields is staggeringly positive. Share this optimism with your kids, and encourage them to maximize their talents and attributes. Teach them to excel, to settle for nothing but their best possible performance. Teach them that a positive attitude, hard work and perseverance—not intellect, pedigree or money—are the differences between winners and also-rans. My son and I had a special saying when he was a little boy: "If you think you can, you can." Many times over the years we have repeated that saying to each other, him to me as much as me to him. Today, my son is at Harvard; a positive attitude, hard work and perseverance got him there.

One final word that should go without saying: please don't shortchange the girls. They need to become financially independent every bit as much as the boys. They deserve the tremendous joy of self-actualization through work and achievement. Even if one day they choose to stay home with their families, give them the skills to excel financially; you never know when they will be needed. Assume that we all have to take care of ourselves.

A New World of Financial Independence

I n this world of rapid change and growing insecurity, traditional means of financial planning will no longer work. Gone are the old rules of work hard, keep your nose clean and retire comfortably at age sixty-five on a government and corporate pension. Those really were the rules for only one or two generations—today's Matures, born before the 1946 Boomer divide. These are the people that have, and will benefit most from, the Canada Pension Plan and government and private employee pensions as well. They had reasonable job security. They retired at age sixty-five or younger and have lived reasonably comfortably on pensions and their savings ever since.

Unlike the Boomers, the Matures did save. They grew up during depression and world war; they understand frugality, self-denial, saving for a rainy day. They are the financial beneficiaries of the Boomer bulge. They gained from the rise in interest rates in the seventies and early eighties, having already paid down much of their debt; many were net savers by then. They earned sky-high rates on their Guaranteed Investment Certificates and bank deposits. Their homes became their retirement nest egg, increasing many times in value thanks to the Boomer-induced housing inflation. And finally, they have benefited from the Boomer-led surge in some stock markets, particularly in the United States.

Boomers face a different situation. It takes two incomes today to pay for the same lifestyle their parents enjoyed on one; and for many, two isn't enough. Government old-age benefits are relatively small, and they may be reduced by the time Boomers retire. Corporate pensions are changing, and most people will not spend the requisite thirty years in one job to maximize the corporate retirement payout. House prices plunged in the early nineties, wiping out housing equity for many. Boomers are up to the gills in debt, and savings rates are at the lowest levels since the 1930s. This generation, born to prosperity, never learned self-denial, never learned to save. Many will not be able to retire at sixty-five or younger. The good news is that many, if not most, will not want to.

Retirement at sixty-five was the idea of Prince Otto von Bismarck, Chancellor of Germany, who established the first old-age-pension system in 1889. At the time, Germany's life expectancy was only forty-five years; so Bismarck did not expect the average worker ever to receive a pension. Sixty-five was also the age chosen by President Franklin Roosevelt in 1935 when he created the U.S. Social Security System. It was the New Deal Depression era, and average life expectancy at that time was only sixty-three years. Most people who collected did so for a relatively short period of time.

Life expectancy will hit eighty and more by the time the bulk of the Boomers retire. Most work today requires intellectual and reasoning skills rather than physical strength. This will be increasingly true even for factory jobs and other blue-collar work. Scientific research suggests that knowledge and reasoning capabilities need not wane until well into the seventies or later. Norman Vincent Peale was still writing books at age ninety-four. The ruling clique in Beijing never seems to hit its prime until eighty. Li Ka Shing, the Hong Kong tycoon, is seventy-one and going strong. Alan Greenspan, Chairman of the Federal Reserve Board, will be seventy-four when his current term ends in 2000, and he has made it clear to the administration that he would like a third four-year term. Alice Rivlin, former Vice-Chairman at the Fed, is sixty-nine and still accepting new government appointments.

Even in big business, there are now some seniors running companies. Sandy Weill, the co-chairman of Citigroup Inc., the firm created by the Travelers–Citicorp merger, is sixty-six. Andy Grove, the chairman of Intel, is sixty-two; and Paul Desmarais, the head of Power

Corp., is seventy-two. Alan "Ace" Greenberg, chairman of U.S. invest-ment dealer Bear Stearns, recently celebrated his fiftieth anniversary with the company, at age seventy-one. He still sits at his raised desk on the firm's trading floor, actively managing his clients' money, and has one of the biggest pay packages on Wall Street. Money management gurus Warren Buffett and John Templeton are sixty-eight and eighty-four, respectively. Toronto retailer and theatre magnate Ed Mirvish is eighty-five. Lee Iacocca, formerly of Chrysler, is seventy-four and not too long ago made a bid to take over his former company. The former chairman of the National Trust Company, Henry (Hal) Jackman, is sixty-seven years old and still going strong. The list goes on. Working well beyond age sixty-five is not new. The concept that our professional and business life must end at some predetermined age is what is new; retirements extending for twenty or thirty years have only been in evi-dence for one or two generations at most.

It is crucial to understand the new reality and to plan for it. Playing by the old rules will get you nowhere. Financial security is possible, but it will take adjustment.

Don't Bank on the Government to Be Your Safety Net

Unless you could be comfortable with a family after-tax income of about $28,000 a year in retirement, government pension money will not be sufficient to ensure financial security. The rule of thumb today is that the Canada Pension Plan, Old Age Security and Guaranteed Income Supplement combined will provide a couple with at most about $28,000 a year after tax in 1999. If one of you dies or if you are single at retirement, the household benefit may well be insufficient to cover household expenses.

Keeping in mind that you probably need less income in retirement to maintain your pre-retirement lifestyle, this may be close to enough income for families making below the average annual household income of $55,000 to $60,000 in Canada. When you are retired, your taxes will be lower, you will no longer need to make Canada Pension

Plan and Employment Insurance contributions or to save for retirement, and your general expenses will likely be lower. Children will be grown and gone, mortgages will hopefully be paid off, and incidental expenses will be lower for things like parking, transportation, clothing and lunches when you're not working. On the other hand, emergencies do occur. Some very expensive long-term care may be needed, and more and more retirees still have parents to care for.

In addition, there are no guarantees that the government support at today's level will be there when the bulk of the Baby Boomers retire in 2011 to 2030. We may see a reduction in government retirement benefits and an increase in the eligibility age. Many believe that generational warfare could break out in the political arena. The relatively small percentage of the population in the workforce could refuse to fully support the retired Boomers. The aged Boomers, in turn, could refuse to support schools. Canada's dependency ratio—the percentage of old people relative to those of working age—will rise from 12.7 percent in 1960 to 26.3 percent in 2020 and to a whopping 35 percent in 2030. This, everyone knows, is going to put a huge burden on the government pension system. Expect cutbacks in government retirement benefits; it's the safest expectation.

Corporate Pensions Have Been Cut Back As Well

Many corporations are shifting away from traditional defined-benefit pension plans, the ones that guaranteed annual retirement income of up to 70 percent of your top yearly earnings, depending on years of service. The move has been to defined-contribution plans and group RRSPs (Registered Retirement Savings Plans), which allow you to contribute 18 percent of your income up to a maximum of $13,500 each year. The maximum kicks in at annual income levels of $75,000. Often your company matches your contribution, usually up to about 3 percent of income.

With RRSPs, your financial security in retirement depends on how much money you save over the years and how well it has been invested.

This is an extremely unnerving reality, because most people do not have the time or inclination to become investment gurus. We are bombarded by investment information, from newspaper how-to columns to financial television news networks to hot tips from friends and family. The number of mutual funds is growing faster than the number of retirement accounts. The myriad investment opportunities are dizzying, even for someone in the investment business. No wonder people are stressed out about managing their own money. There are ways, however, to keep it simple.

The amount contributed to your RRSP each year is deducted from income for tax purposes. So, for example, if your annual income is over roughly $60,000, you are in the top tax bracket, which means the government reimburses close to 50 percent of your RRSP contribution (or a bit more in some provinces; top marginal tax rates vary from province to province). With lower incomes, say $29,500, your marginal tax rate is about 40 percent, and the government would return $2,124 of your $5,310 maximum allowable contribution each year. You can invest up to 20 percent of your RRSP in foreign securities. Given the underperformance of the Canadian stock market relative to the U.S. since 1980, you should maximize your foreign-content exposure.

There is no bigger tax break in Canada, yet according to government statistics only about 13.5 percent of the maximum allowable RRSP room was used in 1997. Revenue Canada does allow unused contributions to be carried forward into later years, so people no longer have a "use it or lose it" mind-set.

Most people, therefore, are not taking full advantage of their only real means of ensuring future financial security. Indeed, Canadian savings rates have been falling for much of the past seventeen years. And yet we know we must save for the long term. Government will not take care of us in our old age—certainly not in a manner that will satisfy many of us. We can no longer rely on corporate Canada either. Even if your employer continues to offer a defined-benefit pension plan, your job is probably no longer as secure as it once was. And if you work for one of the growing number of firms that offer group RRSPs, or if you are part of the rapidly rising proportion of the population that is self-employed or works for a business too small to offer any matching RRSP contributions, you are on your own. The fact is, you must take care of yourself.

Create a Financial Game Plan

Start saving today. In an ideal world, you should save 15 percent of your gross income each year. You should do it consistently, week by week or month by month. I know it is difficult, maybe even impossible, for many. But according to Thomas Stanley and William Danko in their best-selling book *The Millionaire Next Door: The Surprising Secrets of America's Wealthy*, financially secure households—high-net-worth households—got that way in overwhelming numbers not by massive income windfalls, but by saving on a regular basis. That's right: good old-fashioned frugality. Sure, high incomes help, but it is all relative. Households that are comfortable today on $75,000 a year don't need to amass as much wealth as those needing $150,000 a year to maintain a desired lifestyle.

Stanley and Danko found that high-net-worth families generally saved 15 percent of gross income, and some saved even more. Surprisingly, the authors found that affluent people lived well below their means. Stanley and Danko have a very particular way of defining "wealthy." It does not involve having a lot of material possessions: expensive homes, cars, country clubs, jewelry, clothing and vacations. They say that many families with these things have very little in the way of investments, or income-earning or appreciable assets. The families they describe as wealthy typically place a higher value on accumulated investments than on a high-consumption lifestyle.

Stanley and Danko determine whether or not a family is wealthy solely on the basis of their net worth: the current value of accumulated assets (including real estate) less liabilities (debts and bills owed). There were roughly 3.5 million American families with net worth of $1 million or more in 1996, when they completed their study; this group represents about 3.5 percent of all American families. Roughly 95 percent of them had net worth of $1 million to $10 million. The authors focused on this group because most of them earned their own money, rather than inheriting family wealth.

A person's expected net worth depends, of course, upon his or her age and income. The older you are, assuming you are not yet retired, and the higher your income, the higher your expected net worth. Stanley and Danko used their survey data of wealthy American families over many years to determine the level of net worth that is consistent with a high-wealth, low-consumption lifestyle.

The authors found that high-net-worth families achieved their financial security by operating on a budget, limiting their extravagances relative to their income and looking for value. These were the families that did not consume conspicuously relative to their income levels. While many enjoyed at least some of the finer things money can buy, these expenditures were well within the limits of their savings parameters. They socked their money away, month after month, and invested conservatively and often in their own businesses.

Stanley and Danko came up with a rule of thumb to assess if your household has, by their definition, high net worth. Remember, it is relative to your income and age. Their rule says:

> *Your net worth should be your gross (before-tax) family income from all sources except inheritances multiplied by your age divided by ten. This, excluding any inherited wealth, is what your net worth should be, given your age and income.*

It seems to me that this rule has greater validity in mid-life than early in a career. But, even early on, there are examples of young entrepreneurs creating small businesses in university, investing the money early and getting off to a head start. Clearly, starting your first job with a load of student loans sets you back. The answer is to live as modestly as possible, maybe returning home to your parents or taking in a few roommates, and pay off that debt as soon as possible. If your net worth meets the requirements of the rule by the time you turn fifty, your family is truly wealthy. It has been more difficult for Canadians to accumulate wealth in the past twenty years than Americans as our relative tax burden has risen and our economic performance has lagged. Our broader social safety net justifies only a part of this relative shortfall, as older Canadians often find unpaid medical expenses burdensome.

What was fascinating about Stanley and Danko's study was the number of very high-income families that did not have high net worth by this measure. These families belonged to multiple country clubs, drove expensive late-model cars and spent a lot of money on entertainment, restaurants and travel. Clothing and jewelry were also big-budget items, as were home upkeep and redecoration. These families were usually heavily in debt, with very large mortgages (often on multiple homes), car leases and car loans.

In contrast, take the example of the Johnsons. Earl is a fifty-five-year-old auto mechanic for a Pontiac dealer. He makes $43,000 a year. His wife, Jean, is a legal secretary and earns $40,000 a year. With their combined gross income of $83,000, their net worth according to Stanley and Danko should be $456,500. In fact, they have a net worth close to $600,000. The Johnsons are wealthy by any reasonable standard. They know how to live on a mechanic's and secretary's income.

The other side of the spectrum is the Costello family. Don is a forty-seven-year-old senior executive for a large publicly traded company. His gross annual income is $650,000. His wife, Ellen, does not work outside the home. Don has a group RRSP; he has no other pension. The Costello family net worth should be more than $3 million; instead it is just under $1 million. Although their income and net worth are sizable by anyone's standards, the Costellos are not wealthy given their income. They are a high-consumption family with relatively little to show for their huge income. If they continue this way, they will suffer a substantial decline in living standards when Don retires.

Most of the millionaires next door—the high-net-worth, low-consumption families—do not appear outwardly to be as rich as they are. Often their children don't realize their parents are wealthy. Generally, both husband and wife are relatively cost-conscious given their income levels. They take advantage of sales, drive the same cars for many years, spend relatively little on restaurants, eschew most traditional status symbols and paid down their debt early on in their lives. They bought a home consistent with saving at least 15 percent of their gross income, and they used those savings to pay down debt.

They do not buy on credit except for homes and, maybe, cars. Many paid cash for cars. They pay off their credit card balances in full each month, and did so even when they were just starting out. Most of these millionaires next door are relatively ordinary, self-made people. Many are small-business proprietors, salespeople and professionals. Interestingly, a disproportionate share of the spendthrifts are senior executives at large companies and doctors. (Remember, this survey was conducted in the U.S., where doctors' incomes are not controlled by government as they are in Canada.)

Lessons to Be Learned

- Start a regular savings program now. Work up to saving 15 percent of gross income from each paycheque. If necessary, start with 1 percent and gradually increase it. Get into the habit of paying yourself first. Work up to maxing out your RRSP contribution to take advantage of the tax break.
- Use the tax money saved by maximizing your RRSP contribution to pay down debt. Pay down the highest-interest-rate non-tax-deductible debt first—probably credit card debt, personal and car loans, and then mortgages. Get out of debt as soon as you can.
- Stop using your credit card as a line of credit. The interest rates are too high, and it is important to develop the discipline to postpone purchases you can't afford today. Save your credit card receipts and keep track of what you owe; this will help you to limit your purchases. If necessary, use only one credit card; it's easier to keep track of only one. You don't want to fall into the credit trap. If you are in it now, get out. I know it is difficult, but there are professionals who can help you. Ask your banker, investment adviser or financial planner. Credit counselling services are available free of charge in most provinces.
- Create an investment strategy for your portfolio based on your age, risk profile and future plans. A core portfolio usually consists of broadly based equity and bond mutual funds. Once your portfolio is large enough, you can consider professional proprietary

money management rather than mutual funds. The mix between stock and bond funds will depend on your age and risk profile. Canadian stocks have substantially underperformed those in the United States and most other countries, so a heavy weight of foreign-equity mutual funds is important. Don't try to time the market in your core portfolio; very few people are consistently successful. You can enhance your core returns by investing in particular sectors or companies, but this is more risky; keep this to a relatively small component. There are many investment vehicles that will reduce volatility and diversify your portfolio. This will be described in more detail in a later chapter. Get professional advice and follow your common sense.

- Contribute to this portfolio monthly through automatic payroll or chequing-account deduction. This allows you to dollar-cost average, that is, *to buy mutual funds*, individual stocks and bonds month in and month out, when prices are up or down.
- Do not mortgage your house to buy stocks—not if you like to sleep at night.
- Segregate your savings by purpose: children's education; down payment on a house; car or vacation; and retirement. *Never* dip into the retirement fund except to buy a first home; in this case, the withdrawn RRSP money must be repaid in equal instalments over a fifteen-year period.
- If you are already retired or close to it, you still need to be invested in a diversified portfolio. Life expectancy is rising and you don't want to run out of money. There are interesting investments available today that guarantee your principal but give you some meaningful upside potential returns. We will discuss these in the last chapter.

Expect volatility. Periodically, we will see major stock market corrections. View sell-offs in stocks and bonds as buying opportunities, and invest for the long term. Excessive churning of your account will result in unnecessary commission fees. Buy and hold good-quality diversified investments. Save the speculative stocks and high-flyers for only a small portion of your portfolio or your entertainment fund. You can play with some of your money, but see it for what it is: gambling. Sure, have fun with it, but only if you can tell yourself that losing it all wouldn't materially affect your long-run financial security.

Tough for Boomers

All of this frugality and self-denial will be particularly difficult for Boomers. I know; I am a Boomer. We are a generation born to economic prosperity. We don't see a rainy day coming—it is not part of our psyche—so we don't save for it. We believe we are entitled to the good life, privileged from birth. Unlike our parents, we never learned to sacrifice. In our formative years, Canada was a global growth leader. Times were good. We hoard experiences, not money.

Many of us, maybe even most of us, will never save. We will work as long as we can and hope for the best. That is OK in some ways. Many Boomers thrive in their work. They live to work rather than work to live. Nevertheless, even Boomers can work only so long, and financial security in old age is crucial to all of us. Our behaviour in old age will be very different than our parents'. I will explain this in detail in chapter 6. This will have important implications for the economy and financial markets in the future.

Individual Preferences

No one can tell you how to spend your money. Economics is the science of choice. Every individual and household maximizes its happiness or satisfaction—or as economists would say, you maximize your utility—subject to budget and wealth constraints, subject to how much money you have and how much things cost. There are always trade-offs. A fabulous restaurant dinner costing half my weekly grocery bill might seem worth it at some times and a terrible waste of money at other times.

Choices and satisfaction levels are individual and unique. You have experienced that if you have a life partner. What is an extravagant waste of money to me might be a necessity to my husband, and vice versa. What gives me great utility, joy or happiness might not turn his crank at all. That's why variety is so important, why there are so many flavours of ice cream, so many choices on a menu.

There is no ideal basket of goods. I find it fascinating to watch what other people buy in the grocery store. My basket is so different from theirs. I try to imagine what kind of people they are, what kind of life they lead, from what is in their basket. It helps to pass the time in the checkout line, but it also tells me a lot about human nature. While most of my food bill is spent on fresh fruits and vegetables, seafood for me and beef and lamb for the men in my family, others prefer prepared foods and boxed snacks. Our treats are Swiss chocolate and premium ice cream. Others hit the bakery counter. There are whole aisles I never bother walking down, while others frequent them regularly.

Each of us wants the freedom to choose what makes us happy. That is what toppled the Communist system; someone else was making the choices. My dream vacation is not yours. My ideal abode is mine alone. It is hard enough to mesh desires for a couple or a family—city versus country, townhouse versus ranch-style, ski slopes or the beach. We make these choices every day, often without thinking.

Houses are Consumption, not Investment

Too many people confuse a lifestyle choice with an investment choice. Yes, older generations today, the Matures, made a killing on their residences. For many it was their most successful investment, their retirement nest egg. My parents bought their first house in Baltimore in 1953 for $13,500 and sold it for $16,500 eleven years later. They bought their second and last house for $28,500 in 1964, a huge step up. Their mortgage rate was 4 percent (and it was tax-deductible). My mom sold that house after my father died in 1992 for $165,000. Most of the money had originally been borrowed, so the rate of return on my parents' capital was very high. Baltimore house prices are still relatively low compared to other big cities. The gains in cities like Toronto, New

York, Los Angeles, Boston, Calgary and Vancouver would have been even greater.

In the early nineties we saw the price of residential real estate plunge. Though house prices have recovered a bit, the demographics suggest that we can no longer count on meaningful appreciation in our homes. That doesn't mean that house prices are likely to plunge either; Boomers won't do what their parents did because they have very different values and attitudes about lifestyle.

Nevertheless, housing should be seen as a consumption good, a lifestyle decision, not an investment. Your choice of house should maximize your personal satisfaction given your budget and wealth constraints. Boomers more than Matures will look at it that way. My husband and I moved three years ago from a downtown townhouse to a larger single-family house, even though our son was already sixteen at the time and would be going to university in a few years. I know the demographics and the economic prospects, but ours was a lifestyle decision. We use the extra bedrooms as home offices and a gym. Our out-of-town friends and relatives visit regularly, often for a week at a time. My son and his friends have plenty of room to hang out in privacy, and we enjoy the garden and trees.

The demand for good single-family properties in cities like Toronto is unlikely to evaporate, as many predict, despite the aging of the population. Many of my neighbours are older, with grown children. Many have recently bought or built their homes. Lifestyles are varied and changing.

In any event, don't confuse consumption with investment decisions. It may well turn out that a traditional family home is a bad investment, but it may be the only way to maximize your lifestyle satisfaction and, after all, that is what this is all about. Enjoy it—but don't assume it to be your retirement security. Make sure you are amassing sufficient other assets to take care of yourself in old age.

Part 2

The Technology Revolution

The Upwave is Coming

With all the uncertainty in all our lives—reduced job security, gyrating financial markets, no guarantees of retirement security—there is good news out there. I believe we are in the early days of what will prove to be a twenty-five-year uptrend in global economic prosperity, triggered by the technology revolution. We are on the precipice of stunning developments in applied technology, the use of the computer in all aspects of the sciences and business. The Internet, biotechnology and other computer-driven scientific breakthroughs will hugely enhance productivity—output per unit of input, both labour and capital—and global living standards.

There will no doubt be dislocations, winners and losers. For the losers, it will be painful and difficult, as it always is during periods of rapid change; but even they can, and will, find opportunities in the new growth areas. The net gains will be stunning for Canada and for the world. Just as Canada was a global growth leader in the thirty years following World War II, an era when the resource sector, agriculture and manufacturing led the way, Canada could once again assume the role of a global growth star. To do this, however, we must allow the diversion of labour and capital away from the declining sectors and towards the high-growth areas. We must encourage the collaboration of business and government to provide the training and re-education necessary to redeploy people to areas where jobs abound. We must also protect intellectual property rights: patenting and copyrighting ideas. The critical success factors will be research, education and deregulation—the removal of impediments to innovation and change. We already have the educational muscle power in place. We already have advanced capital markets that could provide the seed capital needed for new enterprises. Coupled with this, and essential to our success, must be a revamping of the incentive structure to encourage entrepreneurial spirit, risk taking and innovation. That, plain and simple, means a cut in tax rates—corporate and personal—so that people and companies can reap the rewards of their successes.

The technology revolution will increase world trade and globalization, enhancing competitive pressures. It will lead to strong productivity gains and improve the standard of living for much of the world. The middle class in Canada will share in this boom as many avail themselves of the burgeoning and varied educational opportunities at community colleges, corporate training sessions, schools and on the Internet. The demographics of Canada and the U.S. will add to the prosperity as Boomers hit their peak earning years, ensuring that expansions are strong and long-lived and recessions are short and mild. Volatility will remain, recessions will occur, but the trend will be up.

The Long Cycle

Economists have always analyzed cycles in economic activity, the ups and downs of economic growth and their relationship to consumer and business behaviour. The business cycle is well known. We read about recessions and expansions every day in the popular media. We scrutinize the incoming economic data to read the signals for slowdown or acceleration. We call on the government or the Bank of Canada to adjust tax rates, program spending or interest rates based on our sense of where we are in the business cycle. The problem is that we generally don't know exactly where we are until well after the fact. Economists have a disappointing track record in predicting turning points in the business cycle.

We make our forecasts based on the incoming economic statistics, which means we observe the economy through a rear-view mirror. The incoming data are lagged; they tell us what has happened, not what is happening, and often they give us very little useful information about what will happen. Some economic statistics, like employment numbers and bank loans, are lagging indicators of economic activity, describing more about where we were than where we are going. Others are considered leading indicators, like the stock market, interest rates and consumer confidence; they help to predict the economic outlook. Many of these indicators, however, are subject to wild gyrations because of temporary factors like politics, individual company news and general irrational exuberance.

Making matters worse, the data may not be accurate. There is a good deal of "noise" in the numbers—random fluctuations reflecting sampling error, weather distortions or human error. Remember, most economic indicators are based on telephone surveys of a relatively small, randomly chosen sample of households or businesses. Some data series are notoriously volatile and subject to huge revision. Statistics Canada, the government data collection and processing agency, does its best to remove seasonal distortions from the numbers, but an unusually mild winter or a late spring can wreak havoc on the data; so can labour disruptions like strikes, ice storms, elections and referendums.

While short-term movements in the economy are important and will continue to dominate the workday of most economists, more attention should be focused on the long term as well. After all, we invest for the long term. We make education, career and lifestyle decisions for the long term, and we advise and encourage our children based on the long-term outlook.

While the economy moves in short-term business cycles, lasting five to ten years or less, the economy also exhibits a much longer cycle of roughly forty-five to sixty years, around which the business cycles fluctuate. This long cycle was first discovered by Russian economist Nikolai Kondratieff in the 1920s and is sometimes referred to as the Kondratieff wave. It remains controversial, because the exact dates of peaks and troughs in long-term economic activity are difficult to pinpoint, especially when looking back hundreds of years. To see a recurring pattern of sixty-year cycles, you need an awful lot of historical data—data that go back well before government statistics bureaus were set up. Even with these technical difficulties, however, a discernible long cycle in economic activity can be mapped out. Kondratieff caused such a stir with his cycle research in post-Revolution Russia that he was arrested and banished to Siberia. His work implied that downturns in capitalist economies were ultimately self-correcting, a conclusion that the Bolshevik government was not prepared to tolerate.

A flamboyant Austrian-born Harvard economist named Joseph Schumpeter carried on Kondratieff's work between 1932 and 1950. Interest in Schumpeter's analysis has blossomed in recent years because of his emphasis on the importance of technological innovation. Paul Romer, the Stanford University economist, has continued Schumpeter's work in his new growth theory, an analysis of the importance of knowledge and ideas in the growth process. Schumpeter believed that long periods of economic prosperity—upwaves in the long cycle—were triggered by the widespread acceptance of breakthrough technologies. These new innovations, according to his studies, lead to "creative destruction"—the burying of old technologies to make way for new. For example, the stagecoach industry was supplanted by the railroad; the buggy whip industry contracted with the shift to automobiles; kerosene and coal-oil usage plunged with electricity; vinyl record albums were replaced by CDs; and mainframe computer demand waned with the advent of personal computers.

Schumpeter saw this as a natural process of economic evolution, painful for those in the declining industries but essential nonetheless. Alan Greenspan, respected Chairman of the U.S. Federal Reserve, often mentions the importance of creative destruction in the U.S. economic expansion of the nineties. In a March 1999 speech he said:

Competition and innovation breed the continuous churning in ways that, on balance, result in more efficient production of goods and services and enhance our standard of living. New businesses are formed and existing businesses fail or contract, new products and processes replace old ones, new jobs are created and old jobs are lost. I never cease to be amazed at the ability of our flexible and innovative economic system to take advantage of emerging technologies in ways that raise our productive capacity and generate higher asset values. Technological advance is a process that combines the best creative thinking of entrepreneurs and research scientists in business and academia. It is a process that thrives in a competitive market environment in which risk taking is valued and in which prices and asset values signal how ideas and resources can be applied most productively.

Standing in the way of this process stalls economic progress and reduces an economy to second-class status.

The Upwave

The long cycle is the strongest of all economic cycles. Shorter-term cycles act only as brakes or accelerators on the long wave, strengthening or weakening, but never diverting its major path. In the upwaves, expansions are long and strong, while recessions are short and mild; in the downwave, recessions are deep and long, while expansions are fleeting.

Today, we are in the early stages of an upwave, a period of general prosperity that is likely to last into the third decade of the new millennium. There will still be economic downturns, but they will be surprisingly short. As we move into the twenty-first century, the United States is experiencing its ninth year of economic expansion. This has been the longest expansion since 1850. Even in a long-cycle upwave there will be volatility, often dramatic, but sell-offs in stocks and bonds should be seen as buying opportunities: the bigger the sell-off, the bigger the opportunity. An example of the kind of volatility we are likely to see is the 1987 stock market crash in the U.S. Within two years, stocks were back up to record levels—and that was in a downwave.

The general trend over the next twenty-five years will be up. Not everyone will win. Not every company will win. The new, innovative economy will show enormous growth, but obsolete, uncompetitive businesses will die. Creative destruction will be evident in robust and growing economies. If governments attempt to protect declining industries, the process of change will slow for everyone. Painful as it is, the obsolete or uncompetitive must give way to the new. This is not to suggest that all old companies are obsolete. Many are reinventing themselves, innovating, investing in technology, and improving customer service, product design and delivery. These too will flourish.

Not all new companies will be sustained winners. Technology companies will come and go, some burning brightly for a short time and then falling by the wayside. The new-product life cycle will be very short. Some will misstep, emphasizing the wrong technologies. Many of the top technology companies of the early eighties are long gone from the ranks of winners: Wang, Commodore, Control Data and Coleco. New competitors will enter the markets quickly, turning formerly high-tech products into mass-produced commodities. Great ideas will be copied, and ongoing innovation will be key. Prices will tumble, as they always have in leading-edge technology sectors. Competitive pressures will continue to mount.

The Role of Defence Spending

The ups and downs in the long cycle are often tied to major military events as well as to private-sector technology breakthroughs. As shown in figure 4.1, a stylized picture of the long-wave cycle (where the dates are meant to be suggestive, not exact), turning points in the long wave have often been associated with major wars. Some long-wave theorists suggest that the end of the more popular wars have triggered the beginning of an upwave, and the devastation of unpopular wars mark the start of a downturn. While this view is controversial, there is little question that war has had a profound effect on economic activity and technical innovation. The massive buildup of the military industrial complex during and after World War II had very positive spinoff effects for the civilian economy after the war. Military defence establishments around the world have conducted much of the advanced technological research.

FIGURE 4.1

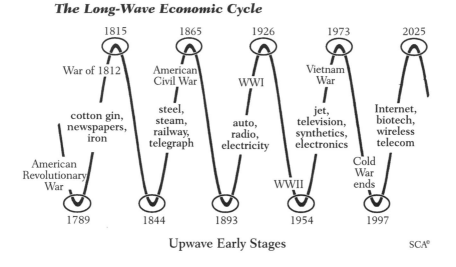

The Long-Wave Economic Cycle

Upwave Early Stages   SCA©

Today, we see the positive technological implications of the end of the Cold War. Since the breakup of the Soviet Union and the opening of the Berlin Wall in 1989, substantial resources, in terms of both people and capital, have been redeployed to civilian use all over the world, most notably in the United States. This has certainly helped spur today's technology revolution. The Internet itself is an outgrowth of a U.S. government network called the ARPANET, which was created in 1969 by the Defence Department so that defence contractors and researchers could continue to communicate in the event of a nuclear attack. The network quickly caught on with computer scientists and engineers in industry and universities. It became a vital communications link for far-flung research collaborators, but it was virtually unknown elsewhere. In 1989, with the end of the Cold War, the U.S. government decided to stop funding ARPANET. Its users quickly devised plans for a successor, called the Internet.

We see the importance of redeployed defence technology elsewhere as well. With the beginning of the peace process in the Middle East, Israel's major defence capabilities have been put to civilian use, creating an extremely successful high-tech sector in that country. High-tech and related industries now account for over 60 percent of Israeli

TABLE 4.1

ANATOMY OF THE LONG WAVES

	Inventions	Leading Industries	Infrastructure
1780s–1815	Cotton gin, water power	Textiles, iron	Canals, turnpike roads
1840s–1870s	Railway, steam engines, telegraph, telephone	Steam engines, steamships, machine tools, railway equipment	Railways, shipping
1890s–late 1920s	Electricity, automobile, radio, first office machines, first aircraft, photography	Steel, autos, aircraft, telephones, radio, plastics, cable and wire	Electricity
1950s–mid-1970s	First computers, transistors, jets, rockets, lasers, television	Consumer durables, synthetic materials, petrochemicals	Highways, airports, airlines, television networks
1990s–2025	Microchips, fibre optics, cellular phones, Internet, biotechnology	Semiconductors, PCs, telecom equipment, biotechnology, computer software	Internet, digital networks, satellites, wireless telecommunications, genetic engineering in farming, livestock and fisheries

SCA©

exports, and this component of the economy has been growing by a full percentage point every two years. Israel boasts the world's largest number of engineers, scientists and doctors per capita (one-quarter of the population has a university degree), augmented by the influx of Russian immigrants with the end of the Cold War. Israel has become a global leader in the technology revolution. Tel Aviv has recently been ranked one of the top ten technology hubs in the world.

A History of Upwaves

Every upwave in the long cycle has been preceded by a multi-year period of breakthrough innovation (table 4.1). Oftentimes there are several innovations in a number of fields, synergistically improving one another. Typically, basic scientific advancement is accompanied by improvements in communication and transportation. It generally takes years for these new technologies to have their full positive effect on economic well-being and productivity. This time is no different.

Upwaves in the past two centuries have been generated by the breakthrough discoveries of the time. They may also have been associated with military developments. For example, in the latter years of the eighteenth century, the new technological wonder was the threshing machine and cotton gin, which dramatically enhanced productivity and lowered prices in food production, textiles and iron working. This was the early mechanization period, which lasted from just after the American Revolution to the end of the War of 1812—the late 1780s to roughly 1815. This was a period of massive building of transportation routes, canals and roadways.

The next upwave began around the time of the U.S.–Mexico war in roughly 1844 and lasted until the U.S. Civil War in 1864. The breakthrough technological developments then were the steam engine and the railway, which increased productivity and lowered prices in the production and distribution of virtually all goods. The railway and steamships precipitated a dramatic decline in transportation costs. The actual infrastructure required for a nationwide railway system was a spectacular creator of construction jobs and consumer of basic commodities such as lumber, coal, iron and, later, steel and oil. Cities and towns sprang up where none had existed before; existing towns flourished when the railway came. Food prices fell with the easy transport from agricultural areas to cities far away. The telegraph was also invented, dramatically improving communication.

The next upwave began with the end of the Spanish-American War in 1893 and lasted until after World War I, to about the mid-1920s. This was the electrical wave. The mass shift to electricity, the automobile and the development of plastics all contributed to substantial growth, infrastructure building, natural resource demand, massive productivity gains and reduced prices. Communication breakthroughs included the telephone and radio. This was a period of falling prices and rapidly rising living standards. Real family purchasing power surged with the growing number of improving products. The automobile led to the building of highway systems and ultimately to the development of roadway businesses and suburbs.

The real move to the suburbs did not occur, however, until the upwave that followed the end of World War II—the upwave during which the Baby Boomers were born. The war effort itself led to the development of many new technologies: radar, jet engines, electronics, synthetics, nuclear technology and computers. Consumers rapidly embraced jet travel and television, which dramatically improved the speed of transportation and communication, reducing their costs. The nationwide highway and airport infrastructures were built. Developments in synthetic materials and petrochemicals were coupled with improvements in mass production of all manufactured products. The computer began to see its way from military to civilian use. Canada benefited from a boom in the commodity and natural resource sector that didn't end until the oil-crisis-induced U.S. recession in 1973, the same year the U.S. finally pulled out of the very unpopular Vietnam War.

The current upwave follows the end of the Cold War and is led by the Internet, wireless telecommunications and biotechnology breakthroughs. The Internet—including e-mail and e-commerce—has allowed for the promise of instantaneous communication worldwide. Already the Internet's surging popularity is the biggest breakthrough in the world of computing since the introduction of the IBM PC in 1981.

The day has nearly arrived when, sitting in their own homes, a critical mass of households will be able easily to conduct business, undertake research, call up great entertainment, explore the world, communicate globally and make friends in far-flung places. The Internet is still just a baby, however. Some 160 million people around the world are logged on the Net now, according to International Data Corp. By 2003, IDC expects that figure to mushroom to 500 million. Online spending is also in for a considerable bump. IDC predicts that businesses and consumers, which spent a combined $50 billion online in 1998, will fork over $1.3 trillion in 2003. This is why traditional bricks-and-mortar retailers like Sears and Safeway are clamouring to develop Internet sites, cannibalizing their own businesses.

The biotechnology revolution—the application of genetic engineering facilitated by computers to the life sciences—will revolutionize medicine, agriculture and natural resource production, to name just a few. These developments will be accompanied by advancements in alternative energy and nanotechnology—the production of miniature machines molecule by molecule, which will revolutionize medicine, manufacturing and many aspects of daily life. Nanotechnology is taking place at the crossroads of physics, biology, chemistry and electrical engineering. Many believe that over the next five years a whole new breed of miniaturized machines called microelectromechanical systems (MEMS), currently in the planning stages, will take the place of more expensive components in factories, computer hardware, automobile engines and many other processes and products. MEMS combine sensors, motors and digital capability on a single sliver of silicon. They open the way for the re-creation of human organs and the internal monitoring of blood counts, insulin levels and organic functions. The possibilities are breathtaking.

Productivity Gains are Always Slow at First

It generally takes years for a new technology to realize its full potential benefit. The experience with the advent of electricity and the automobile are good examples of this. Many believe that Thomas Edison invented the light bulb in 1879. The little-known truth is that a Canadian, Henry Woodward, a medical student in Toronto, patented the first incandescent lamp with an electric light bulb in 1874. He sold a share in the patent to Thomas Edison in 1875. In 1879, Edison invented a more practical lamp that efficiently transmitted electricity into a light bulb. He built the first electric utility in 1882. However, it wasn't until the 1920s that factories began to use electricity to full advantage. It took that long for the electrical infrastructure to be built and for business to reconstruct the factory workspace in order to maximize the productive potential of the new technology.

Alan Greenspan has referred to the early days of electricity usage when pondering the surprisingly slow growth of productivity in the U.S. service sector until late 1998. This sector comprises about 65 percent of the economies of Canada and the U.S., including the relatively high-tech areas of health care, education, business, and personal and financial services, as well as lower-tech retail and wholesale trade and government. The potential productivity gains associated with the personal computer and the Internet have not yet come to full fruition, especially in the service sector, where it is very difficult to measure output.

Bob Davis and David Wessel explain the phenomenon in their book *Prosperity*. They analyze in detail the case of the Maytag company in Newton, Iowa, the first producer of wringer washing machines in 1907. The Maytag company is an interesting example of the early problems of electricity for two reasons. Firstly, the Maytag factory had to wait years for a reliable source of electricity to enhance productivity on its assembly line. Secondly, the early motorized washers had to have a Multi-Motor—a built-in gasoline motor with an exhaust hose you put through a window—because most houses were not wired for electricity.

This is no different from the infrastructure problems associated with full household usage of the Internet today. Nearly all residential connections to interactive networks like the Internet use telephone lines, which are not capable of rapidly transmitting a lot of information. This is the reason the world is moving away from narrowband analog networks, which were designed to carry voice, towards digital networks, which carry much greater amounts of information per second. Telephone and cable companies are now upgrading their networks with new digital switches and fibre-optic cable, which has far greater bandwidth than copper wire. Once the new infrastructure is in place, the full value of the Internet will be evident; the information highway will have arrived. It is still a few years away in Canada and the U.S.

Automobiles—Slow to Take off

The auto story is similar. The Duryea Brothers designed the first gas-powered automobile in the U.S. in 1893. Henry Ford started his company in 1896, but it wasn't until cars became relatively cheap and easy to use in the 1920s that a critical mass of households bought one. At first, only a tiny fraction of the population owned vehicles, and road and highway construction was in its infancy. By 1913, Henry Ford revolutionized the auto production process with the mass assembly line, allowing him to increase the speed of production and cut the cost of the final product. By 1914, Ford was able to double the wages of his workforce while continuing to cut auto prices. For example, the price of the Model T fell from its original cost of $825 in 1908 to below $290 in 1927. At the Model T plant, built in 1913, an automobile was completed every 93 minutes, down dramatically from 728 minutes. When Ford ceased Model T production in 1927, they were producing a car every 24 *seconds*.

Falling prices encouraged widespread automobile ownership. Over 15 million units of the Model T were sold by 1927. The success of the automobile led to increased competition, as a whopping 485 companies entered the business between 1900 and 1910. A few big players like General Motors Corp. and Ford Motor Company survived and even continued to be profitable, but many others, like Auburn, Franklin and Pierce-Arrow, disappeared in the following years, along with most of the money that people invested in them.

The effect in the twenties was spectacular. The single biggest force for growth that decade was the tripling of auto production, along with a similar expansion of capacity in related industries such as steel, gasoline, glass, rubber and highway construction. The S&P index for car-maker stocks more than quintupled between 1925 and the spring of 1929. During the same period the market as a whole rose 144 percent.

When car sales hit their peak in April 1929, it was the end of the boom time for automobiles and the rest of the economy. In the next four years, carmakers' stock prices dropped as far and as fast as they had risen, with only a few big players surviving the rout. The 1920s was the top of the long cycle, peaking in about 1926 and sliding mercilessly through the 1930s, the Great Depression.

Despite this, the widespread ownership of automobiles ultimately led to the countrywide highway system, the development of trucking, the move to the suburbs, and everything from fast food to drive-in movies to mega shopping malls. Paved-road mileage rose sixfold from 1920 to 1956, and the Interstate Highway Act of 1956 was the largest U.S. public sector project to that time. By the mid-1950s, about three-quarters of American families owned a car. This began to revolutionize society by pushing city living into suburbia and ending rural isolation.

The excesses of the 1920s, the overproduction, the stock market mania—much of which was financed on credit—might seem comparable to the U.S. economy today. The *Economist* magazine called it the bubble economy and Alan Greenspan has referred to the "irrational exuberance" in the U.S. stock market.

The Internet Stock Mania

No doubt there is a good deal of irrationality in the stratospheric rise in Internet stocks, most of which have no earnings. Similar manias have occurred in the past. During the 1830s, shares in canals and Eastern railways sold like hot Internet IPOs (initial public offerings) today. Mark Twain and Charles Dudley Warner tellingly chronicled the post–Civil War railway booms in *The Gilded Age*. A series of mini-booms accompanied the introduction of the telegraph and telephone. These booms did their job; they got the transportation and communication systems built. Likewise in the 1920s, there were Internet-style manias in radio, motion pictures, automobiles and aviation. The greatest of all was the meteoric rise of RCA Corp. of America, the star of the market in 1928.

While the Internet stocks will correct, maybe even plunge, as they did intermittently in 1999, we should not expect a 1929-style stock market crash and depression. The huge government policy errors of the late 1920s are unlikely to be repeated. Economists now understand that a major contributing factor to the Depression of the 1930s was the decision by the Federal Reserve Board to stand idly by and watch as the financial system in the United States hemorrhaged. Between 1930 and 1933, the money supply fell by about one-third as the banking system collapsed. That would not happen today. In late 1998, central banks around the world eased monetary policy, by lowering interest rates, when global financial turmoil mounted. The International Monetary Fund and the World Bank today stand ready to assist countries in crisis. These institutions played an active role during the Asian crisis in the late 1990s. The banking systems of Canada and the U.S. are far more sound today, with deposit insurance and strict government regulation. Banks and investment dealers around the world worked together in 1998 and 1999 to help institutions and countries damaged by the Russian default and instability in Latin America.

Maybe most importantly, global trade is increasing rapidly today with the creation of free-trade blocks—the European Union (EU) and the North American Free Trade Agreement (NAFTA)—and the development of cross-continent trade deals. In contrast, the biggest policy error of the earlier period was the 1930 passage of trade barriers under the Smoot–Hawley tariff. It raised prices, dramatically slowed global economic activity and seriously worsened the economic distress during the Depression. Trade restrictions, while possible politically when unemployment rates are very high, are less likely now when the jobless rate in the U.S. is so low. Today's commercial markets are a lot more difficult to restrict as electronic commerce continues to surge.

Nevertheless, as the 2000 presidential election campaign heats up, protectionist rhetoric mounts. U.S. trade restrictions on Europe in early 1999—the so-called banana war—are an example of the risks to business and household confidence of an increase in protectionism. So are the punitive tariffs on Japanese hot-rolled steel and softwood lumber quotas on Canada. This, if sustained and escalated, would be very negative for global economic activity. I agree with Alan Greenspan in urging the U.S. Congress to refrain from protectionist measures. They are a threat to growth, confidence and the stock market. In a very intense political period, anything can happen. The fundamentals don't warrant it, but mounting trade restrictions are a risk.

Volatility will remain. Recessions will occur, and stock markets will correct and move into temporary bear (or down) phases. The risks are there, and the more speculative companies are very risky, but unlike 1926—the peak of the long cycle—we are in the very early days of an upwave, leading to what will be a surge in productivity-driven growth and economic prosperity. Inflation pressures will continue moderate and, in the technology-related sectors, falling costs will lead to price declines. Income per capita will rise and the shift to knowledge-based growth will lead to an explosion in educational opportunities. The potential gains in the new knowledge-based sectors are mind-boggling and will continue to be reflected overall in their stock market valuations, at least for the companies that can maintain their lead.

The Productivity Boom

In a few years, a substantial proportion of households in the United States and Canada will have easy, inexpensive access to the Internet using television and personal computers. This will accelerate the productivity takeoff—a surge in output per worker that has already begun in the United States, and will truly revolutionize the way we communicate, research, shop, invest, bank, play and work. Electronic commerce has already been growing at a spectacular pace, but the real acceleration is imminent. Electronic malls include everything from travel to groceries to books, music and toys. You can buy virtually anything on the Net, with better variety and service than in traditional stores. Gone are the days when you had to deal with the hassles of traffic, parking, public transportation, crowds and unhelpful salespeople. Traditional stores and malls will not disappear, however. People will still choose the social and physical contact of traditional retailing for some of their purchases; but these businesses will be forced by e-commerce to improve service, reduce prices and make shopping a more positive, entertainment-like experience. Today, you can order products over the Net for next-day delivery almost anywhere in the world. Products can even be customized to your measurements or specifications, and ordered on a predetermined regular basis.

Price competition has never been greater, and it will increase. There are now consumer-shopping Web sites that deploy automatic computer programs to hunt down the best price for everything from cars to books to airfares. The new shopping robots, or "bots" as they are called, are capable of searching for goods on hundreds of Web sites in seconds, putting unprecedented pressure on Web merchants to beat their competitors' prices. These bots could set off vicious price wars, reducing margins to razor-thin levels. With profit margins under so much pressure, Web merchants need large-volume markets, and they get them on the Internet. The entire world is fast becoming the marketplace.

The Internet, not surprisingly, has made huge inroads in consumer-goods retailing, beginning with the online bookstore pioneer Amazon.com in 1994. When the commercial use of the Internet first arrived just over five years ago, it was dismissed in many circles as a quirky communications device with a cloudy future. It has since permeated almost every segment of society. Sales of goods over the Web in the 1998 Christmas season totalled almost $3 billion, more than double the year before. Web users topped 102 million in 1998, up from 57 million in 1997, and growing fast in 1999. Soaring Internet usage and the explosion in e-commerce have, in turn, expanded opportunities for the search-engine companies—the Internet gateways or portals, like Yahoo! Innovation is feeding on itself.

The computer industry has benefited as well, with companies like online pioneer Dell Computer Corp. and Beamscope Canada Inc., a Toronto-based distributor of software and consumer electronics that gets 22 percent of its annual sales from the Internet. Beamscope vice-president Ephram Chaplick told the *Wall Street Journal* that being online brings down costs considerably through reductions in labour and long-distance telephone charges. He calculated that his company spends just 75 cents to service an order over the Net, compared with $12 apiece to handle phone orders.

Financial services is another area revolutionized by the Internet. Americans can in a matter of minutes get a mortgage, shop for insurance, trade stocks and pay bills online. Increasingly, these services are becoming available in Canada too. Discount brokerage sites are booming, and traditional brokers like Merrill Lynch are offering free access to their research on the Net on a trial basis. Even full-service brokers are forced to respond to the e-trade sites: Merrill Lynch announced in mid-1999 that it would offer discount e-trading by the end of the year.

The Net is also increasing productivity in traditional manufacturing, as it has become a powerful tool throughout the supply and
production process. Retailers are using the Net to manage inventories
and orders, ensuring that they deal with the lowest-cost suppliers anywhere in the world. The Web is also used to book and track shipments.
The potential for this supply-chain management to reduce costs in the
future is spectacular, particularly as privacy issues are addressed and
the world at large becomes wired.

Pricing Power Pinched

Globalization was in train well before the Internet. In fact, every
advancement in communication and transportation has spurred
international commerce. But the end of the Cold War, which opened
up more than a billion people to free markets, has had a profound
effect. This, coupled with the Internet and other advancements in science and biotechnology, will increase trade and global competitive
pressure like never before. Global price comparisons are now possible.
As Internet usage increases outside the U.S., Scandinavia, Australia,
Canada and Israel—the early leaders—and spreads through Europe,
Asia and the more remote parts of the world, the implications are huge.

There is no doubt that this will be a highly disinflationary or even
deflationary development. Few companies can increase their prices
and hope to compete. Price pressures are already enormous, forcing
businesses continuously to minimize costs in any way possible: shorten
production time, innovate, invest in technology, squeeze suppliers and
reduce labour costs. Productivity has been rising in the U.S., and
strong productivity growth will continue to be evident in coming years.

Canada, on the other hand, has been a global laggard in the productivity race owing to continued relative reliance on low-tech manufacturing and resources—low-productivity growth sectors—as well as
to non-competitive tax rates and a depreciating currency. Relatively
high tax rates, especially in comparison with the U.S., have reduced
foreign direct investment for start-up operations in this country—
investment that would create jobs, increase growth, enhance real

estate values and transfer technology. We suffer a meaningful technology gap with the U.S. The ever-falling Canadian dollar leads to rising import prices, which reduces household purchasing power while protecting Canadian business from global competitive pressures. As a result, Canadian business has not felt the incentive and market-driven need to restructure and invest in technology to the same degree as most other major industrial countries, particularly the U.S. Elsewhere in the world, the competitive pressures have been immense, and even in Canada many of the multinational companies have responded.

Producers worldwide, in their effort to capture market share, have increased the supply of their products and cut prices. Commodity prices, for example, fell to twenty-plus-year lows. Some have since rebounded, but the sustainability of the price rises is questionable. Manufacturing capacity in the automobile sector is about 35 percent greater than prospective demand, driving down car prices. This overcapacity was one of the underlying causes of the Asian crisis in the late 1990s. Excess supply and price cuts resulted in a dramatic plunge in corporate earnings. Asian stock markets collapsed under the pressure of egregious overbuilding and real estate development—see-through office towers, roads leading to nowhere and shopping centres in remote locales—all funded on bank credit. Real estate companies and banks dominated most of the equity markets of Asia. Prices began to topple, corporate bankruptcies surged, already weak banks collapsed under the pressure. Japan, the second largest economy in the world, went into a deep recession and commodity prices fell further. Weak commodity-producing nations like Russia and Brazil were devastated. Russia defaulted on its debt in August 1998, and the crisis intensified as Latin America threatened devaluation of its currencies. The International Monetary Fund (IMF) and a consortium of global banks and investment dealers came to the rescue by providing Brazil, the largest economy in Latin America, with huge credit lines. The Federal Reserve and other central banks around the world eased monetary policy, reducing interest rates and relaxing credit restrictions. Even so, Brazil was eventually forced to allow its currency, the real, to depreciate substantially in January 1999.

The strength of the U.S. economy in the face of considerable weakness in the rest of the world is testimony to the American leadership in the technology-driven upwave. The U.S. has been the oasis of prosperity acting as the importer of last resort, triggering a rebound in most of the rest of the world.

Much of the global economy is in, or is coming out of, a painful period of adjustment. The leader and former leader among the Communist nations—China and Russia—are making very difficult transitions to more market-oriented economies. Asian economies are adjusting as well, shifting away from so-called "crony" capitalism, a controlled system where the power elite in the government, banks and business determine where money should be invested rather than allowing market forces to make those decisions. Crony capitalism has proven to be highly inefficient and has led to excesses in some countries; market capitalism is once again gaining ground. Painful as market capitalism is, with all of its Schumpeterian creative destruction, the world is increasingly recognizing that markets work. As Adam Smith pointed out in the eighteenth century, the invisible hand of supply and demand sets the appropriate price to clear markets.

All will share in the economic prosperity. For the first time since 1973, American workers are experiencing an increase in real income growth. This trend has not been much in evidence in Canada, however, because the nominal wage gains here have been offset by a falling Canadian dollar, exceedingly high tax rates and an underperforming stock market. But that too will change. I believe that as people understand the potential opportunities, they will force a change. A great Canadian tax revolt—no doubt a very understated, peaceful one—will foster the change and the prosperity.

Increasing Returns and Decreasing Costs

The very process of technological innovation leads to falling costs and reduced prices. As we described earlier, knowledge builds on itself. The more we learn, the easier it is to learn. Discoveries beget discoveries and the pace of innovation accelerates. In other words, there are increasing returns to the process of discovery, to knowledge; and because of increasing returns, costs fall and prices decline. There are no limits to ideas; ideas are not scarce, they cannot be used up, they are not a finite resource.

This is very different than the physical world—the world of physical hours worked, capital expended and natural resources used up—where scarcity is the overwhelming fact we have to deal with. The physical world is characterized by diminishing returns. One hundred farmers on twenty acres of land produce a certain amount; but one thousand farmers would not produce ten times as much, even if you gave them one thousand additional tractors. In fact, if you were to increase the number of farmers on tractors sufficiently, production would actually decline as they got in each other's way. This is because the land is available only in limited supply. Diminishing returns lead to rising costs and increasing prices.

Examples of Increasing Returns

Now imagine that you send the unneeded farmers for training at Innovation Place at the University of Saskatchewan in Saskatoon. Innovation Place is one of the world's leading education, research and production facilities in the application of biotechnology to agriculture. Included in their list of credits has been the first genetically manipulated crop and the first genetically engineered animal vaccines. Teach these farmers the new technology of growing crops indoors in crop factories and you no longer are faced with diminishing returns; no longer is scarce land a concern. Instead, you create increasing returns from the application of knowledge. Costs decline and so do prices.

Take another example, this time in the computer software world. Microsoft invested hundreds of millions of dollars in research, development and testing to make the first copy of Windows NT. But once Microsoft got it right, it could produce the second copy for about 50 cents—the cost of copying the program onto a CD-ROM. Since then, all copies have the same cost or less. Windows NT is now distributed over the Internet; the cost of making additional copies is virtually zero. This keeps the cost of new software very low. What it means, however, is that to provide incentives to companies like Microsoft to foot the bills on the original research, you have to give them a patent or copyright on their product, and thereby give them what amounts to monopoly power, at least temporarily, to sell their product worldwide. They have to get broad enough distribution to warrant the initial investment and to encourage further innovation. Microsoft, of course, will take advantage of this monopoly power and create other systems, like Internet browsers that are included with Windows NT. This is exactly what another browser-software producer, Netscape, objected to in their path-breaking legal trial against Microsoft.

In the world of technology, the increasing returns to innovation and discoveries will ensure that many prices keep falling. Not only have computers been getting cheaper and cheaper, but they have been getting better and better—lighter, easier to use, much more powerful. This turns traditional economic theory on its head. Strong demand and improved product quality are supposed to increase price; but deflation, not inflation, is the rule in the technology world. Traditional economic theory is based on the presumption of diminishing returns to inputs in the production process, not increasing returns. Traditional economic theory presumes all resources to be scarce, so that when labour markets are tight and unemployment is low, inflation will rise. Just the opposite happened in the United States in most of the nineties. Many economists got it wrong, expecting inflation to rise quickly as unemployment fell. With investments and advancements in technology, U.S. productivity growth surged. While wage rates have gone up faster than prices, increasing real household purchasing power, this has not been inflationary. The prices of many tech-related products are falling. Couple this with substantial global competitive pressure and the surge in supply, and you see why price inflation declined worldwide.

With the prospects of an Asian economic revival in early 1999, oil and base metal prices began to surge. Commodity-related currencies benefited, the Canadian dollar among them. So did some resource and cyclical stocks. This led to widespread inflation fear in the U.S. bond market, enhanced by the stronger-than-expected inflation figures for the April consumer price index (CPI) released in May. Rising interest rates and tighter monetary policy are negatives for the U.S. stock market and could well correct some of the overvaluation. Even so, however, this will not derail the longer-term disinflationary process. Expect volatility in inflation, stocks and bonds. Inflation scares are likely late in an economic expansion; especially so given the two-year decline in U.S. inflation in the face of enormous economic strength. Inflation in the United States is likely to rise to just over 2½ percent in 1999, compared to under 2 percent earlier. But the double-digit inflation rates of the seventies are behind us.

The technology-driven disinflationary process is still in its early days. The potential purchasing-power gains are enormous. Central to this process will be a focus on ideas, knowledge, research and, of course, education.

The Knowledge Revolution

Peter Drucker, in his 1993 book *Post-Capitalist Society*, coined the term "knowledge workers" to refer to people who create, innovate, synthesize, strategize, analyze, instruct, integrate and interpret. These people will be in huge demand in virtually every field: information technology, entertainment, banking and financial services, retailing, health care, law, management consulting, research, market analysis, telecommunications, recruitment, biotechnology, pharmaceuticals, all of the sciences, the humanities, farming, animal husbandry, linguistics, the creative arts, design, engineering and many more.

The great retailing success stories of the past decade have been those companies that reorganized their old-economy businesses around information. Companies like Wal-Mart, Nordstrom, Home Depot, Canadian Tire, Loblaws and Toys "R" Us use information technology to reduce supply costs, manage inventories, maintain accounting systems, monitor the competition, service the customer and garner important market intelligence. All of the traditional industries that managed to grow during the past decade did so by restructuring around knowledge and information.

In the early 1950s, people working in traditional jobs in manufacturing, natural resource production and agriculture represented roughly 50 percent of the labour force in most developed economies.

By 1998, their numbers had been reduced to 16 percent of the U.S. workforce and 20 percent in Canada, and by 2015 they will likely represent no more than 10 percent of the workforce of any country in the developed world. The productivity boom helped to cause this shift. It takes far fewer people to produce the world's food supply than ever before, and that number will continue to shrink fast. The same is true for the production of natural resources and manufactured goods.

When the Canadian government subsidizes hog and grain farmers, or decrepit pulp mills, or depleted fisheries, it is diverting capital to unproductive use. It is standing in the way of progress, of the natural evolution of economic systems, and of the Canadian competitive advantage in the future. It is a painful but unassailable fact that the commercial base of Canada must shift to the knowledge-driven sectors or Canada will continue to fall further and further behind in relative economic prosperity. This does not mean that farming and natural resource companies will disappear. What it does mean is that new technologies will be applied to these areas, dramatically reducing costs and prices as supplies rise sharply. This situation will come about as a result of genetic engineering of existing products and processes, as well as the introduction and discovery of new products to replace the old. For example, the replacement of fossil fuels by biofuels replaces a scarce resource with one in potentially infinite supply.

The government should assist by creating a policy environment where innovation and creative destruction are fostered, not stifled; where people and businesses are not afraid to fail; where capital is readily available for new ventures and entrepreneurial spirit is encouraged. The government can ensure that intellectual property is protected, just as physical property has been in the past. Canada's regulations regarding drug patents and other intellectual property have been a deterrent to capitalizing on innovation here. The government must ensure that businesses and schools work together to create the talent and research needed to succeed in the marketplace. There need to be appropriate incentives for students to study in areas of high demand, and to encourage them to take jobs in Canada so that our economy may reap the benefits of their state-of-the-art training. Too often today, the top graduates of our best schools hightail it to the U.S. upon graduation. There are shortages of highly skilled workers in engineering and in all of the information technology (IT) fields. These are the challenges we must face; if we do, the outlook for Canada is extremely positive.

Education is Key

The world leaders in the technology revolution will be those countries with the best educational, training and research capabilities and with the right incentives to maximize their value. The U.S. has had a leading edge in knowledge because the U.S. is seen to have the top universities and graduate schools in the world. People come from all over the planet to study in the United States. The U.S. therefore attracts and keeps the best professors, researchers and scholars, and the most Nobel Prize winners. Of the eleven Nobel prizes awarded to Canadians in the past twenty years, eight were for work carried out in the United States. Nevertheless, other countries are rivalling the U.S. in advanced technical education. Singapore, Israel, Romania and India have developed particular specialties. The computer science program at the University of Waterloo in Ontario is considered one of the best in the world, and programs are burgeoning in Canada in all technology-related fields.

The innovative education programs popping up all over Canada in both the private and public sector are very exciting. Many people will take advantage of these programs and share in the rising wealth. Businesses by the hundreds are offering on-the-job training. Learning centres are springing up everywhere, and online courses are available through many employers. Increased corporate support for training is good business, and more will follow. Highly skilled workers are in great demand. Technical skills of all sorts are needed, and the schools can't pump trained people out fast enough. Many employers are offering signing bonuses and finders fees for information technology personnel. But the demands go way beyond IT workers; expertise in design, engineering, the sciences, finance, biotechnology and the skilled building trades are in huge demand as well, and the list goes on.

Among the new educational offerings are a part-time MBA on the Internet offered by the University of Athabasca in Alberta. You can get an MBA in enterprise development from the University of Calgary, designed to help graduates start their own businesses and to play entrepreneurial roles in larger companies. Carleton University in Ottawa offers a variety of courses on television and the Net. Sheridan College in Oakville, Ontario, is an acknowledged leader in animation and computer graphics education. A private company called ITI gives an intensive eight-month full-time course towards a post-graduate degree in information technology. While expensive, this course is extremely popular because it is designed to meet the IT demands of the marketplace. Graduates are often regaled with multiple job offers, bidding wars and prospective employers that are willing to cover the costs of their program. See my Web site at **www.sherrycooper.com** for a list of innovative educational programs in Canada.

Educational excellence must also extend well below the university and graduate levels, and that is where the U.S. falls short. It is estimated that 30 percent of students leaving U.S. high schools in 1998 were not fully literate or proficient in basic arithmetic skills. Remedial courses are offered at community colleges and many universities, but the basics in grades 1 to 12 are lacking, especially compared to Europe, Asia and Canada. The Japanese system of disciplined rote learning is not the answer either; what you gain in basic memorized learning, you lose in creativity and innovation. Non-linear, out-of-the-box thinking is not encouraged in Japan, and for this reason Japan has not, for the most part, led in idea creation. Their expertise has been in the efficient and low-cost manufacture of products created elsewhere.

Profiting from Knowledge

Education and innovation are just part of the economic success puzzle. The follow-through in the marketplace—the use or application of knowledge for commercial purposes—is also essential. This is where the United States has excelled. After World War II, you might have expected the British to take the lead. They, for example, are credited with the development of antibiotics, the jet engine, the computer and the World Wide Web; but they were unable to capitalize on these innovations, to turn knowledge into productive use. The U.S. surpassed them in what Peter Drucker called "knowledge productivity"—the application of knowledge for economic gain.

Often in the past, the U.S. has led in the innovation process only to see the product development dominated by others, most notably the Japanese. While technological innovation is difficult, time-consuming and costly, copying innovation is relatively easy. In other words, technology is expensive to produce but cheap to reproduce. Examples of products that are easily reproduced are microchips, photocopiers, fax machines and cash registers—all innovations created in the U.S. but produced more effectively in Japan. For this reason, governments are increasingly trying to provide strong intellectual property rights for those who develop new technologies.

The history of West Germany before the 1990 reunification is fraught with examples of knowledge breakthroughs without major productive gain. Germany was extremely proficient at re-engineering old knowledge sectors like basic industries, chemicals, automobiles, banking and finance, but it was unproductive in new knowledge areas like telecommunications, computers, software, advanced materials, biogenetics and pharmaceuticals. Even though Germany produced a reasonable amount of new knowledge, it was not translated into successful commercial use.

Canadian Commercial Disappointments

Canada has had a few missteps in this regard as well. Insulin was discovered in 1922 by Sir Frederick Banting and Dr. Charles Best at the University of Toronto, but the commercial use of insulin was exploited by the U.S. pharmaceuticals industry. Alexander Graham Bell, the inventor of the telephone, was a Canadian. He once said, "The telephone was conceived in Brantford in 1874 and born in Boston in 1875." John Manley, minister of industry in the Chrétien government, reported that the list of products created in Canada but commercialized elsewhere also includes: Microsoft mail, the proportional assistance ventilator, the electron microscope, the Alzheimer's gene and the Playtex bottle.

Commercial disappointments in the Canadian aerospace industry have been legion. The first commercial jet plane to fly in the Western Hemisphere, the Jetliner C-102, was designed in Canada by James Floyd and built by Avro of Toronto. It was first flown in 1949. In a record-breaking flight from Toronto to New York on April 18, 1950, the Jetliner transported the first airmail ever carried by a jet-powered aircraft and made the first international jet flight in North America. According to Ralph Nader in his book *Canada Firsts*, a U.S. syndicated column at the time reported the following about the event:

> This should give our nation a good healthful kick in its placidity. The fact that our massive but underpopulated good neighbor to the north has a mechanical product that licks anything of ours is just what the doctor ordered for our overdeveloped ego. The Canadian plane's feat accelerates a process already begun in this nation—a realization that Uncle Sam has no monopoly on genius, that our products are not necessarily the best simply because we made them.

With all of this fanfare, the plane was never produced commercially in Canada. The outbreak of the Korean War in 1950 convinced the minister of defence production, C.D. Howe, that Avro should concentrate on producing fighter planes instead. The Jetliner was sold for scrap in 1956.

This wasn't the only Avro aviation nightmare. The Royal Canadian Air Force commissioned Avro to design and build a fighter plane that was later dubbed the Arrow. Its first flight took place on March 25, 1958, and it was immediately hailed as the most advanced jet interceptor in existence. Finally, Avro would put Canada in the lead in aviation technology. This was not to be, however, as Prime Minister Diefenbaker announced on February 20, 1959, that the Avro Arrow program was cancelled, stating the government's view that the aircraft was obsolete. The six Arrow aircraft that had been built were demolished, the Avro plant in Malton was shut down, and the company's researchers were dispersed to other companies and occupations.

Fortunately, some of the aviation heritage of Avro was collected in de Havilland and saved from government destruction by privatization.

Canadians Go South

A huge negative for Canadian development in a multitude of fields has been the historical lure of our talent to the United States. So many Canadians with world-class capabilities choose to live and work in the U.S. Canadian knowledge transfers include countless actors, singers, musicians, scientists, mathematicians, medical and legal professionals, and athletes who moved south to pursue work in the better-established U.S. industries.

Here the list is very long. Emigrating actors include Mary Pickford, Norma Shearer, John Candy, William Shatner, Dan Ackroyd, Donald Sutherland, Raymond Burr, Glenn Ford, Margot Kidder and Michael J. Fox. There is a tremendous irony in this because Canada is credited with many firsts in the motion picture industry. The first film advertisement was produced by a Manitoban farmer, James Freer, in 1897. It described an idyllic life on the Prairies and was used in the United Kingdom to promote immigration to Canada. The first documentary film—*Nanook of the North*—was produced by an American in Canada in 1921. Canadians were responsible for the first public motion-picture presentation in North America. Two brothers who worked as photographers in Ottawa opened the world's first Kinetoscope Parlour in New York City in 1894. The first deluxe movie theatre was opened on Ste. Catherine Street in Montreal by Leo Ernest Ouimet in 1907.

One lasting success in the Canadian film industry has been IMAX, invented in 1968 by Graeme Ferguson, Roman Kroitor and Robert Kerr. An IMAX motion picture was first shown at the Canadian pavilion at Expo 1970 in Osaka, Japan. The first permanent IMAX theatre was Cinesphere, opened the same year in Toronto's Ontario Place. Films are produced by IMAX Corporation of Toronto, and the specially designed film projectors are manufactured in Oakville, Ontario, although most of the senior management are now American. The company continues to be a leading innovator in the field of large-screen high-tech filmmaking.

While many movies have been made in Canada in recent years, they are most often American productions, attracted by the low Canadian dollar.

The list of others who have left Canada for opportunities in the U.S. is long, and it includes singers (Joni Mitchell, Gordon Lightfoot, Diana Krall), athletes (over half the National Hockey League) and a whole host of race-car drivers. In the world of economics and finance we lost John Kenneth Galbraith, William Vickrey and Myron Scholes, to name only three of the more famous ones. Scientists who emigrated from Canada to the U.S. include Nobel Prize–winning Rudy Marcus, Henry Taube, Richard Taylor, Sydney Altman, Arthur Schawlow and Dr. David Hubel.

The challenge for Canada is not only to train our people appropriately to excel in the upwave of this technology revolution; we must also keep the people we train. This is a huge and complex issue. Some people leave because they feel the commercial opportunities are better in the U.S. The United States is, after all, the global leader in the entertainment business, in finance, in pharmaceuticals, in medical, science and technology-related research. But there is a chicken-and-egg problem here. One reason Canadian industry is underdeveloped in many fields is that the talent leaves. Canadians leave because they perceive that the opportunities are better in the U.S. and because they can reap the rewards of their success. Canadian companies such as Bahaus and Coopers leave for the same reason. Others, like Varity, Northern Telecom and Seagrams, shift most of their core activities to the States to draw on their talent pool and consumer, capital and entertainment markets.

Tax rates play a huge role in this. American personal, capital gains and corporate tax rates are substantially below those in Canada, and the top tax rates kick in at much higher income levels. Moreover, the Canadian dollar—the money we earn and the money we invest—has been in secular (or long-term) decline for the better part of twenty-four years. Our dollar today stands at less than 69 percent of the value of the U.S. dollar, and two-thirds the value it held in the Canadian heyday.

We will discuss why we have fallen behind and what we can do about it. Before we do, though, let's look at one more piece of the economic puzzle: the population. The economy is in the very early days of a long-cycle upwave, driven by breakthrough technological innovations that will have a dramatic effect on the way we live, work, play and do business. Canada has a huge advantage in this upwave—our people. Compared to all other major industrialized countries besides the U.S., we have a relatively young population. Couple that with our knowledge-generating capabilities and our highly skilled labour force, and we have every reason to shine in the twenty-first century.

Demographics

The age distribution of the population has a role to play in the long cycle. Edward Cheung in his book *Baby-Boomers, Generation-X and Social Cycles* suggests that each long wave is associated with a baby boom. He believes that generations alternate from high birth rates to low birth rates, creating the ups and downs in the wave. I think it's a stretch to attribute economic ups and downs in the long cycle to population alone, but we know from the postwar period in Canada that meaningful population shifts affect the economy in dramatic ways.

The postwar baby boom in Canada was spectacular. More than 9 million people were born between 1946 and 1965. Today, the Boomers represent an eye-popping 31 percent of the population and therefore dominate the economic landscape. In the U.S., the Boomers are somewhat less dominant: there are 79 million of them and they account for 29 percent of the total.

As we enter the next millennium, the leading edge of the Boomer generation is in their mid-fifties. Their incomes may well have peaked, and their children have left home, at least temporarily. Household expenditures have probably peaked as well, and they are now saving for retirement, or trying to. The bulk of the Boomers, however, are still much younger, just over forty. For them, income will grow, spending will continue robust, and money will be funnelled into financial markets. These will be good times.

Part 3

Generations and the Spending Cycle

A Colour Picture of the Canadian Population

I am a Boomer, a member of that vast group of people born in the span of time between the end of World War II and the middle of the 1960s. I was born in Baltimore in late 1950. Most middle-aged women won't tell you their age, but what the hell. I turn fifty at the end of the year 2000—my millennial birthday gift. But I promise you, turning fifty won't be nearly as traumatic as turning thirty. I spent too many formative years believing the sixties radical Abbie Hoffman's slogan, "Never trust anyone over thirty." I too am a product of my times.

Age is a funny thing; it's always relative. In some groups you feel young, in others old. What should fifty look like, feel like, I ask myself. Like my parents when they were fifty? Heavens no, they were old, they had a thirty-year-old daughter and grandchildren. My son is still a teenager. I won't be them at fifty. Over fifty are Raquel Welch, Jane Fonda, Cher, Ann-Margret and Sophia Loren—icons of my coming-of-age. Fifty is not so bad, I conclude, especially if you don't take yourself too seriously. Boomers will always see themselves as young, even as they experience middle-age spread and don reading glasses, because they grew up in a time that celebrated youth.

Generation Markers

The demographics of a population are its vital statistics: age, births, deaths, household formations and the like. Many now appreciate more fully the impact of demographics on spending patterns in the economy. It is useful to look at Canadian demographics and see how they compare with those of our trading partners and competitors. But demography alone is not enough. We need to understand the real dynamics of our current and future economy. As Michael Adams points out in *Sex in the Snow*, we need to understand the values and attitudes of the people and how they shift from generation to generation. We need a colour moving picture of the population, not just a black-and-white still photo.

Demographic analysis as applied to economic forecasting usually assumes that age determines all; that knowing the age distribution of the population allows you to fast-forward twenty years and see the coming economic landscape. While demographics is a useful tool, the foregoing model is overly simplistic. It assumes that people in any generation behave the same way at the same age. If that were true we would simply observe the spending and saving patterns of today's seventy-year-olds to determine what the Boomers will do in twenty years. Call your parents, see what they're up to—their concerns, dreams, goals, investments, lifestyle and you will see yourself two decades from now. Simple?

No, it is not that simple. People are affected by the times in which they live, by current conditions—economic, political and societal—and most importantly, by the key set of collective experiences that shape their values and attitudes. These experiences are called generation "markers." They define, unify and differentiate generations. They set the tone and provide a sense of cohesion. They create the attitudes and values through which all of life's experiences are seen, all economic decisions made.

For the generation of people born before 1946, the Matures (comprising Traditionalists and Veterans), some of the most significant markers—the key collective experiences—were the Depression, World War II and the postwar economic boom in Canada, which lasted until the mid-1970s (see figure 6.1, a diagram of the generations in Canada and the U.S.). The Boomer markers were very different. Whereas Matures experienced depression and war in their formative years, Boomers experienced general economic prosperity and the movement to the suburbs. Other markers that influenced and defined the attitudes and values of this generation included: Mom at home, Quebec nationalism, Expo '67, Canada's Centennial, Trudeaumania, the FLQ crisis, television, Vietnam, Martin Luther King, Watergate, the pill, sex, drugs and rock 'n' roll. For the Generation Xers, born between 1966 and 1976, the markers include economic recession and restructuring, bilingualism, Meech Lake and the fall of Canada as a global growth leader, Mom at work, divorce, AIDS, Live Aid for Ethiopian Famine Relief, the death of John Lennon, *Sesame Street, The Bill Cosby Show,* MTV, grunge music, the 1987 stock market crash, CNN and computers. The Millennials, born after 1976, have seen a resurgence of family values, free trade, globalization, diversity, the end of the Cold War, the Gulf War, the Oklahoma City bombing, the death of Princess Diana, Monica Lewinsky and the impeachment of a president, cable TV, *The Simpsons,* rap music, Game Boy and the Internet. Millennials take the world of technology for granted.

FIGURE 6.1

North American Boomer Bulge
(number of births)

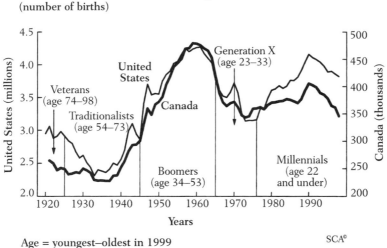

Age = youngest–oldest in 1999   SCA©
Sources: U.S. Census Bureau; Statistics Canada

The members of a generation are linked by the shared life experiences of their formative years. This includes things like pop culture, world events, economic conditions, politics and technology. These common experiences create a bond among the people of a generation that makes them different from other generations before and after. Social scientists have called these bonded groups "cohorts." Because of their shared markers, cohorts develop similar values and attitudes, which they retain throughout their lives. These values and attitudes are very different from those of their parents or their children. The past, therefore, is not prologue.

Boomers today look nothing like Matures twenty years ago. When Boomers retire, they will not mimic the lifestyle and spending patterns of their parents. Xers are not just young Boomers; they do not behave like Boomers twenty years ago and they will never follow Boomer patterns, because their attitudes and values are so different. From a marketing perspective, these differences are essential. If they weren't, today's middle-aged Boomer women would be wearing girdles and their husbands would be sporting fedoras.

Not all people in a particular cohort or generation are alike, however; no individual defines a generation. Michael Adams delineated some of the differences within Canadian generations. There are nuances and differences, religious and cultural, socio-economic and geographical. But the broad core values are representative and crucial in forecasting economic behaviour.

There are also no pre-set dates to determine exactly when one generation starts and the other leaves off. The delineation is more subtle, generations fade into one another. I have tried to pick dates that are more or less conventionally accepted, but a year or two in either direction doesn't change the conclusions materially.

Finally, the Canadian and U.S. experiences are very different. The cultural, economic and political backdrops are deceptively dissimilar in the two countries. I say deceptively because at first blush they would seem to be nearly the same. But the differences, though sometimes subtle, are very important, especially as we apply them to economic forecasting. As a born-American living in Canada, I am quite cognizant of these differences, and I will attempt to point them out where they are relevant.

The Matures—Veterans and Traditionalists

The Matures are often divided into two groups. Those born between 1901 and 1925 are the Veterans, the fighters of world wars, either literally as individuals or figuratively as a nation. Those born between 1926 and 1945, the Traditionalists, although some were Depression babies, were too young to fight in the war. What these groups share is a core set of very traditional values: discipline, self-denial, hard work, teamwork, obedience to authority, and financial and social conservatism. There were 6.7 million Matures in Canada in 1998, representing 22 percent of the population.

The Veterans, Born 1901–1925

These were Canada's confident and fearless warriors, men and women who were influenced by the Depression and the war that followed. Triumphant in Europe, they returned to a peacetime Canada that had become a global leader in economic growth. Their generation had conquered transatlantic travel with Charles Lindbergh's 1927 flight; they won two world wars and watched a man walk on the moon. They created the big-band sound. Guy Lombardo, a Canadian, was a member of the Veteran generation, as was movie actress Fay Wray and economist John Kenneth Galbraith. They had unstoppable energy, immortalized in the comic-strip hero Superman, created by Canadian Joe Shuster along with his American co-author Jerome Siegel.

Veterans came of age preferring clear and distinct gender-role definitions. They produced the largest one-generation jump in educational achievement in Canadian history. They held the highest office in the land for fifteen years with Pierre Elliott Trudeau, born in 1919. In the United States, the Veterans occupied the White House many times—most notably John Kennedy, born in 1917, and Ronald Reagan, born in 1911. They enjoyed enormous upward mobility and rising home ownership, more than any other generation this century. Statistically, they fared better financially then their parents, and benefited from the baby boom explosion in house prices and interest rates.

In retirement, they have gained from the 1960s development of the social welfare system; they are the primary benefactors of the Canada Pension Plan. They are activist senior citizens with a large and vocal lobbying power. Having defeated the demons of two world wars, they saw the value of an activist government. Unlike their generation in the U.S., they did not see a pro-business government as the ideal model. Right and wrong—like black and white—were easily discernible for this generation. The Veterans, in many ways, have been rewarded for their stalwart commitment to traditional good.

The Traditionalists, Born 1926–1945

The first wave—Norman Jewison, Paul Desmarais, Maureen Forrester, Jean Chrétien and John Turner—were children of the Depression, when birth rates plunged and the unemployment rate in Canada surged to 20 percent. They knew hardship and self-denial. They came of age too late for war-era heroism, but their teenage heroes were soldiers. The last wave—John Cleghorn, Conrad Black, Joni Mitchell, Joe Clark and Brian Mulroney—graduated from college just ahead of the great Boomer onslaught. These were the days before the pill, abortions on demand and drugs. They got there first, but they missed all the fireworks. Indeed, getting there first was their greatest strength, allowing the Traditionalist generation to climb the corporate and political ladders with relative ease, in relative solitude.

They have produced four prime ministers (and more may come) and countless corporate leaders. Interestingly, there has never been an American president from this generation; presidential aides, yes, but no presidents. This was a very small generation and, though they would not like to admit it, they received the maximum reward for the minimum effort. For them, the Woody Allen maxim was correct: "80 percent of life is just showing up." My sixty-year-old friend Don—a very successful investment banker and alumnus of the University of Western Ontario's MBA program—quipped at a university dinner honouring his achievements that back then all it took to get into the program was a signed cheque.

The Traditionalists benefited from a long period of economic growth and relative social tranquillity. The expectation of good times became ingrained in society. They enjoyed the century's steepest rise in real family income and wealth. They were the earliest-marrying and earliest-babying generation. Birth rates surged in Canada; large families were in vogue. These were the "traditional" folks that the Boomers rebelled against with alternative lifestyles and women in the workforce.

Having suffered economic hardship and sacrifice as children, the Matures, both Veterans and Traditionalists, enjoyed adulthood in the glory days of Canadian economic supremacy. From the end of World War II until the mid-1970s, Canada's real economic growth rate outpaced that of the United States by an average annual rate of 1.3 percentage points, at a time when the U.S. was doing well. In the period from 1947 to 1976, real GDP growth in Canada averaged 5.0 percent per year, compared to 3.7 percent in the United States. Canada enjoyed booming commodity markets and a dramatic rise in standards of living. Family purchasing power surged, and this was a world of one-income families. Mom was still at home with the kids.

Thanks to C.D. Howe and the industrial buildup during World War II, the Canadian economy enjoyed enormous strength. GDP doubled during the war years, and strong growth continued after the war as military innovation was put to civilian use. The baby boom also triggered an unprecedented run-up in consumer spending. The surge in the birth rate and a wave of immigration, largely from Europe, led to a 40 percent rise in Canada's population from the end of the war through the late 1950s.

The federal government became increasingly proactive, and as early as 1942 it implemented path-breaking social welfare measures like unemployment insurance and family allowance legislation. The government also provided assistance for home ownership for the veterans returning from World War II. Canadians took great pride in their country's ability to provide these social programs, and still do. A fundamental underpinning to Canadian culture is a society that is seen to be far more equitable and caring than in the U.S. The social safety net is a part of the very fabric of the Canadian psyche—the pride in being Canadian. Without question, Canada has provided a higher standard of living for low- and lower-middle-income families than the United States by any measure—health, education, welfare and old-age support.

Canada in the Sixties

In many respects, Canada came into its own in the sixties. A sense of boundless optimism was fuelled by the Centennial celebrations and supported by a roaring economy. Real growth averaged over 5 percent annually during the decade. The Canadian dollar was almost at par with the U.S., and personal disposable incomes more than doubled. While Canada basked in the United States' achievements during this period, including a man on the moon, they felt comfortably removed from its many problems: inner-city riots, the Vietnam War and political assassinations.

In a nutshell, it was a time when almost everything was going right for the country. However, not surprisingly when conditions were so favourable, complacency set in and long-term policy mistakes were made. In Canada's case, the "mistake" was the creation of overly generous social programs, which even the richest in the country could take advantage of. These included medicare, the Canada Pension Plan, the Guaranteed Income Supplement (for seniors), family allowances and the Canada Assistance Plan (for have-not provinces). While these programs have been the pride of many Canadians for the better part of thirty years, their huge cost rendered them unsustainable, and many were dismantled or scaled back in the nineties.

What made the sixties such a period of optimism? Essentially, it was a time of promises fulfilled, of long-term projects completed, holding out the prospect of an even more robust economy. The St. Lawrence Seaway was completed in 1959, the Trans-Canada Highway in 1962; the Auto Pact was signed in 1965. It was also a time of intense national patriotism—rare in Canada—following the adoption of the new flag in 1965, Expo in 1967 and the Centennial celebrations the same year. Almost all schoolchildren were taught to sing "O Canada" in both official languages in 1967, and many can still hum Bobby Gimby's Centennial song to this day. Mini-flags and Centennial pins were handed out freely, while special Centennial coins circulated across the country. The Centennial symbol was omnipresent (a stylized maple leaf, constructed with ten triangles, representing the provinces). Montreal's Expo was seen as a huge success, and will be remembered for the futuristic architecture, notably Buckminster Fuller's massive geo-desic dome.

Following hard on the heels of the feel-good factor of 1967, Pierre Trudeau emerged in 1968 as the leading candidate to replace Prime Minister Lester Pearson as the leader of the Liberals. Trudeau's flaw-less bilingualism and the stark contrast between his flamboyance and the decidedly grey Pearson captured the Canadian imagination. Treated almost like a rock star through the 1968 campaign, Trudeau easily won the election and heightened the sense that Canada was on the forefront of a brave new world.

The sixties were also a time before cable TV was widely available, and most viewers had access to only a few channels, one of which was the CBC. Accordingly, Canadians developed some strong national cul-tural symbols during this period. *Front Page Challenge, This Hour Has Seven Days* and *Don Messer's Jubilee* probably garnered much larger audiences than present-day CBC shows could ever hope to attain in the hundred-plus-channel universe.

In sports, the 1960s icons were Nancy Greene (gold and silver medalist in skiing at the 1968 Winter Olympics); Russ Jackson (the last Canadian starting quarterback in the Canadian Football League); and, in hockey, Jean Béliveau (Montreal) and Dave Keon (Toronto). The quality of the CFL approached the NFL in the sixties, and the Canadiens and Maple Leafs dominated the National Hockey League. Canada also got its first major league baseball team—the Montreal Expos—late in the decade.

Socially, Canada certainly did not ignore or totally avoid the pro-found changes that were taking place in the U.S. and the rest of the world in the sixties. Yorkville in Toronto and Gastown in Vancouver were seen as the centres of youthful unrest, roughly akin to Haight-Ashbury in San Francisco. Peace demonstrations were commonplace, especially around Queen's Park late in the decade. The influx of U.S. draft dodgers throughout the sixties gradually had a heavier influence on the Canadian political scene. Many youthful Canadians were proud to be part of the anti-war movement, hiding their guests well.

While Canada was undoubtedly a more socially conservative, staid society than the U.S. in the sixties, the same cultural revolution (sex, drugs, rock 'n' roll) swept through Canada in the decade, with only the briefest of lags. Parents didn't know what hit them. Boomer sons and daughters were beyond their control, and worse, they were moving in together!

The percentage of the Canadian population caught up in the hippie anti-war movement was small, but because the Boomers were such a large and visible proportion of the population, their numbers seemed big. A friend of mine named Jackie, hailing from Vancouver, described it this way:

> "Free School" appeared in the public school system, new thoughts were coming out of the universities. Local politicians fought and lost a desperate battle, from the "hippie-a-day-wash-away" (fire hoses washed away loiterers in front of the Hudson's Bay department store each day) to the infamous Gastown riot. Greenpeace sprouted in a Shaughnessy basement. The outspoken *Georgia Straight* rolled off the alternative press. Although sympathetic, we weren't fighting the war of blood like our American neighbours. We didn't have brothers dying or returning home addicted and deranged. Ours was a much more peaceful revolution of social order and social conscience. The end of the sixties focused our attention even closer to home, as we had found our greatest ally in the prime minister of Canada.

> Pierre Trudeau's message was loud and clear. Travel your country, meet your countrymen. The federal government set aside funds for a major youth-initiative project. Grants were given to youth to set up and run businesses that would benefit culture and communities. Youth hostels sprung up in almost every community, and the highways were lined with Canadian kids. Train cars were full of guitars and backpacks. We met each other, travelled with each other, and saw Canada in a way that should be the envy of anyone feeling the lack of a Canadian identity. We ate French bread and honey on the Gaspé. We dug for clams and made chowder for everyone on the *Newfie Bullet*. We slept in abandoned prison cells of Quebec's bastille. We worked on farms in Alberta and picked cherries in the Okanagan. French beside English. We relied on the kindness of strangers and we shared generously whenever we could.

The sixties gave me my Canadian identity, of that there is no doubt. I often wonder if I'll ever see a decade with more force. What a shame for those who missed it!

The Matures Prospered and Pondered the Changing World

The Matures approached adulthood and middle age during this period of immense economic prosperity and optimism. They benefited mightily from the Canadian social safety net. As the first recipients of the Canada Pension Plan, established in 1966, their return on investment has been huge. Moreover, Matures have had the benefit of other pension plans as well: defined-benefit plans that guarantee roughly 60 to 70 percent of your top annual earnings in retirement if you worked thirty years for a company or government agency. Happily for this generation, thirty-year tenures were not uncommon.

Adding to Canada's affluence was the Auto Pact. Signed in 1965— the same year as the adoption of the maple leaf flag, a symbol of heightened Canadian nationalism—the Auto Pact eliminated all trade barriers with the U.S. automobile industry. This touched off a manufacturing boom in Southern Ontario. The Canadian dollar was strong —very strong—the economy was unmistakably prosperous, and the adult population, the Matures, were enjoying the fruits of their labour. Tax rates in Canada were below those in the U.S., and the stock market had been substantially outperforming the U.S. market. Savings rates in the sixties were beginning to rise, and household debt levels had not yet taken off. (Household debt as a percentage of income was at half of today's level.) The federal budget was in balance, which was not to change much for another ten years.

The only fly in the ointment was the growing nationalism in Quebec. The victor of the 1960 Quebec election campaign, Jean Lesage, had as his campaign slogan "Maîtres chez nous"—masters in our own house. This ushered in a new era. Quebeckers increasingly turned away from the Church and looked towards the state for a new sense of identity. Birth rates fell sharply. The intelligentsia fuelled hopes for an independent state. This process later became known as the Quiet Revolution. Ironically, the 1967 Centennial year for Canada also coincided with Charles de Gaulle's infamous visit to Quebec, when he bellowed from the balcony of Montreal's city hall, "Vive le Québec libre!" René Lévesque celebrated Canada's one hundredth birthday by forming the Mouvement souveraineté-association, later to become the Parti Québécois.

But all of this was yet to hurt the financial standing of Matures. The dollar remained strong until the mid-1970s, and the financial markets remained calm. The Matures' careers continued to blossom. They had their children, moved to the suburbs, paid off their mortgages and lived in prosperous contentment. This generation was well served by the traditional values of family, thrift and charity. They could afford to share the wealth, taking care of those in need, because they were so few in number. They were a loyal bunch—no job hopping for them—and their loyalty paid off: big business was loyal in return.

They saved for retirement and it wasn't that difficult; their homes were their retirement nest eggs. They enjoyed the Boomer-induced surge in house prices and benefited from the skyrocketing interest rates of the 1970s, which improved the returns on their favourite investment, guaranteed investment certificates (GICs), fully insured bank certificates. With company pensions and the Canada Pension Plan, they have done just fine.

The youngest Matures, coming in at the tail end of this boom, have suffered the consequences of the corporate downsizing of the nineties. Many were targets for the cuts, as fifty-somethings always are. However, with severance packages and paid-up pensions, many are off to start new careers.

The Boomers, Born 1946–1965— A Very Different Cohort

A postwar baby boom didn't happen everywhere, only in Canada, the U.S., Australia and New Zealand. War-ravaged Europe and Asia did not share the experience. The Boomer countries have an advantage today over Europe and Japan: they have a younger population. The Canadian baby boom was spectacular and lasted a year longer than in the U.S. There are 9.3 million Boomers in Canada. The birth rate peaked in 1957 at 3.7 children per family, much higher than in the U.S. Times were very good here.

The Boomers in both Canada and the United States grew up in times of economic bounty. From 1946 through to the mid-1970s, economic prosperity and progress were evident everywhere. One-income families did very well. Boomer kids lived in a *Leave It to Beaver, Father Knows Best, Donna Reed Show* world. Youth was celebrated, and the world was good. That is why nostalgia is so big among Boomers, why they continue to listen to the Rolling Stones and the Beatles.

Boomers shared a confidence that progress and prosperity would never end. Unlike our parents, we had never seen anything else. This created a sense of expectation and entitlement that is common to the generation. Older Boomers especially—Bill and Hillary Clinton, Abbie Hoffman, Kim Campbell, John Candy, Dan Akroyd and all of my college classmates—thought that we could change the world, overcome all odds. The idea of unending prosperity shaped all members of the Boomer generation. With the notion that the future was secure, Boomers, unlike Matures, felt free to focus on themselves, on experimentation and on fulfillment. They are still doing just that, and always will.

This was the generation raised by Dr. Benjamin Spock, the famous, permissive pediatrician whose book became a classic for mid-century moms. Thanks to Spock, Boomers grew up pampered and spoiled. Aging Boomers will not be anything like the Matures we will replace. Businesses that assume that Boomers will take on the characteristics of Matures as we age will find themselves failing. As we have throughout our lives, Boomers will create a new image, a new marketplace.

Profound economic optimism was a hallmark of Boomers' formative years. We believed that robots would one day do all the work, and that leisure time would extend indefinitely. Atomic energy would replace limited fossil fuels, families would have their own helicopters, people would vacation on the moon and have second homes in outer space.

We were confident that more was always to come. We could volunteer for the Peace Corps and ask our parents to give all their money to help the needy, because more would always be there.

Matures, having experienced depression and war, learned to save, to deny themselves for greater security tomorrow. Boomers never learned that lesson. Boomers know how to spend—spend for today, for instant gratification, because we are entitled, because more will come.

American Boomers were great at breaking the rules. It started with the drugs, sex and radical movements of the sixties, and carried on into the marketplace of the eighties and nineties. Canadians, even Boomers, have always been more rule-abiding, but the spillover from the U.S. is undeniable. The U.S. has just had its first Boomer president in Bill Clinton. Canada has had only a fleeting experiment with a Boomer prime minister, Kim Campbell in 1993.

Leading-edge and Late-end Boomers

Boomers are often divided into two distinct groups: the early or leading-edge Boomers, born 1946 to 1954, and the late-end Boomers, born 1955 to 1965. Some actually define another group called the Trailing Boomers, born 1960 to 1965. David Foot calls the Trailing Boomers Generation X, after Douglas Coupland's famous book of the same title. Most, however, use the term Generation X to refer to the next younger cohort, born 1966 to 1976. All of this can become needlessly complicated. What is important is that all Boomers shared a prosperous childhood and the sense of optimism, expectation, privilege and entitlement that creates. The distinction between the older and younger Boomers is useful, however, in describing what happened to them.

The great divide between the two groups in the United States was the coming of age during the Vietnam War versus the coming of age during the Watergate period. In Canada, the front-end Boomers came of age during the positive atmosphere of the Centennial celebration in 1967, while the late-end Boomers were coming of age in the aftermath of the negative atmosphere surrounding the imposition of the War Measures Act during the 1970 FLQ crisis and the Parti Québécois victory in 1976.

Post-Centennial Hangover

Separatist tensions were mounting in some circles in Quebec, despite the passage of the federal Official Languages Act in 1969, which recognized both English and French as official languages and required federal institutions to provide services in both. The late 1960s was marked by violent demonstrations and riots, culminating in the October 1970 kidnapping of James Cross, the British trade commissioner in Montreal, and Pierre Laporte, the provincial Liberal labour minister, by the Front de Libération du Québec. In the end, the implementation of the War Measures Act did nothing but create heroes in Quebec, despite the murder of Pierre Laporte. This was a dark period in Canadian history, in deep contrast to the Centennial celebration only three years earlier.

Pierre Trudeau, as the new prime minister, quickly began the process of what he called "economic equalization," the creation of a "just society." In 1969 he established the Department of Regional Economic Expansion, which within a decade was pumping more than half a billion dollars annually into Quebec and Atlantic Canada. Social welfare spending increased dramatically. Unemployment insurance, which was enacted in the 1940s in response to the Depression to help job seekers through temporary tough times, was expanded into a vast income support program. Benefits were raised repeatedly.

Policy began to take on a decidedly anti-business, anti-American tone. Concerned about the increasing U.S. ownership of Canadian business, the Canada Development Corporation was established in 1971 to strengthen Canadian ownership. In 1973 the federal government set up the now infamous Foreign Investment Review Agency (FIRA) to "protect the Canadian economy from foreign domination." FIRA was charged with approving all new direct foreign investment in Canada, and did so only if it were deemed to be of benefit to Canadians. This was equivalent to hanging a "Not Open for Business" sign outside the country. The net inflow of foreign capital dried up.

This was the beginning of the end of Canada as a global growth leader—a leadership we had enjoyed for the thirty years following World War II. This was the beginning of the decline in the Canadian economy relative to the U.S., a decline that has accelerated in the nineties and has now lasted for more than twenty-five years.

The anti-business climate continued to intensify. Inflation pressures mounted worldwide and oil prices surged, capped by the OPEC oil crisis in 1973. Rather than let the oil patch enjoy the fruits of the price surge, the government intervened to restrict exports. It froze Canadian oil prices at less than 40 percent of the world market price, and brought in a wave of tax increases and royalties to ensure that producing firms would make little profit. The notion that profit was a dirty word in Canada became clear; once again, foreigners saw signs that Canada was anti-business. From 1972 to 1979, the total government share of oil industry revenues soared from 30 percent to over 50 percent.

Not surprisingly, the Western provinces were at great odds with this policy. Western alienation from Ottawa continued to mount. Moreover, in 1976 the separatist Parti Québécois under René Lévesque defeated the provincial Liberals led by Robert Bourassa. Support for the Trudeau government was waning, undermined by the uncertain future of Quebec, Western alienation and continued rampant inflation.

Canada Heads into the 1980s in Rough Shape

By 1980, Canada was faced with a heavily regulated economy, huge government intervention, burgeoning budgetary deficits and political uncertainty. Trudeau was voted back in that year after briefly losing to the Tories' ill-fated Clark government. Trudeau's comeback could not have come at a worse time; he turned the clock back in Canada just as Margaret Thatcher was setting it forward in the U.K. and Ronald Reagan was doing the same in the U.S. Both were introducing structural and systemic changes that would benefit their economies for decades to come. Canada failed to catch on to the new mood of lower taxes, privatization, union busting and pro-business entrepreneurial spirit. Canadians were proud to be different, seeing ourselves as a kinder, gentler nation than the U.S. or U.K.

The 1980 election of the Trudeau-led Liberals gave them a mandate to continue the government's intrusion into the private sector. They introduced the National Energy Program (NEP), billing it as a program to raise Canadian ownership of the oil and gas sector, making the country self-sufficient by 1990. What the NEP really amounted to was a move to regulate an integral part of the economy. It succeeded in alienating the business community, both here and abroad.

The program provided extensive government subsidies for exploration and development to oil and gas companies that were at least three-quarters Canadian-owned. In response, foreign oil companies quickly dismantled their Alberta operations. Resentment of the NEP ran deep in the West—so deep that the federal Liberals, already devoid of representation in Alberta, would not hold a seat in the province again until the 1993 election.

Trudeau plowed ahead on the constitutional front as well, despite the severe economic recession in the early 1980s. Despite all efforts, Quebec was not represented when Queen Elizabeth II proclaimed the new Constitution Act in Ottawa on April 7, 1982. Trudeau had tried to soothe sovereigntist sentiment by enacting the Charter of Rights and Freedoms. This entrenched bilingualism in areas of federal jurisdiction and provided for minority-language education across Canada. Appease the separatists this did not.

The U.S. Boomer Experience

The assassination of President John F. Kennedy, followed by that of Martin Luther King and Robert Kennedy, signalled an end to the status quo and galvanized the large leading-edge Boomer cohort in the United States. This was the group that marched against Vietnam and in favour of civil rights. The effort in the U.S. to avoid service in Vietnam was a more pervasive generational bond than service in the war itself. We burned our bras and our draft cards and shut down university administration buildings, and then the universities themselves. We were a major and vocal force in the 1968 presidential election, and considered ourselves responsible for Lyndon Johnson's decision to withdraw his candidacy for re-election.

Even with all this political turmoil, some of it very painful—the inner-city riots following the murder of Martin Luther King and the Kent State shootings of students by the National Guard—the leading-edge Boomers maintained a sense of optimism and belief in the possibilities of change. We experimented with drugs and sex, but were anything but apathetic. Ironically, in later years, many of these Boomers, even the radical ones in the Black Panthers movement and SDS (Students for a Democratic Society), found themselves in MBA programs and carrying briefcases on Wall Street. The yuppies were in full bloom by the 1980s.

The members of this cohort experienced economic good times and wanted a lifestyle at least as good as the one they had as children in the fifties. The early Boomers in both Canada and the U.S. got there first. They were the first to enter the schools, the universities, the job market and the housing market. They outpaced their parents in educational and economic achievement, although much of the economic performance was the result of two-income families.

They have now had their first bout in the White House with Bill Clinton. In many ways he is the quintessential front-end Boomer. He evaded the draft and thereby avoided Vietnam; he experienced the sixties drug culture, even if he didn't inhale; and he believed he could change the world. Many of his political problems may also be a reflection of the times in which he was groomed. Pushing the envelope, testing the rules, blurring the distinction between right and wrong— Boomers do not exhibit the black-and-white morality of the Veteran and Traditionalist generations. The early Boomers will likely occupy the White House for years to come.

1979—A U.S. Turning Point

Just as late Boomers in Canada came of age during a more negative environment of threatening Quebec nationalism and massive, ill-conceived governmental intrusion into what had been a booming economy, late Boomers in the U.S. grew up to a deteriorating picture as well. It began with the shock of Watergate and the ultimate resignation of the president in 1974, but it went beyond that period. The year 1979 was an important turning point. This was a year of inflation and economic slowdown—stagflation and rising unemployment; the year Muslim fundamentalists in Iran took sixty-three hostages at the American embassy in Tehran, the year the Soviets invaded Afghanistan. Gasoline lines returned once again.

Boomers realized that the notion of permanent economic prosperity was in grave question. President Jimmy Carter described it as a national feeling of economic malaise. Cynicism abounded. The Boomers moved into the eighties with a new-found determination to win—in the marketplace, in business. We hung up our love beads and tie-dyed shirts, cut our hair and went to work. The yuppies were born—compulsively accumulating, compulsively achieving, compulsively climbing the corporate ladders. The excessive conspicuous consumption of the U.S. yuppies in the 1980s was in full swing.

Jimmy Carter was replaced by Ronald Reagan, who swept into office on a wave of neo-conservatism and tax-cut fervour. He implemented the largest personal and corporate tax cuts in history, and by the time the Reagan recession was over in 1983, people had money to spend—and spend they did. But yuppiedom unravelled too. Ivan Boesky and Michael Milken—former junk-bond kings and financial superstars—were hauled off to jail in 1988 and 1990. The leveraged buyout craze died when the stock market crashed in 1987. Although the stock market in the U.S. reached new record highs less than two years later, the tides had turned. Sentiment had changed, and more and more Boomers were dealing with the financial and emotional responsibilities of parenthood. The excesses of the eighties shifted to the value-consciousness of the nineties.

Divergent Political Climates Lead to Divergent Economic Growth

When the British and Americans went to the polls as the eighties were beginning, they were driven by much the same philosophy. It was time to dismantle big government and the social welfare state. It was time to create a pro-business environment and to put tax dollars back into the hands of the people. It was time to break the back of union militancy, and improve the prospects for profits and productivity. Thatcher took on the coal miners while Reagan took on the air traffic controllers. No longer was labour able to hold management hostage with excessive and inflationary wage demands and long work stoppages. Many state-owned businesses were privatized. Foreign direct investment was encouraged. A decidedly pro-business atmosphere was created in both countries, as tax rates were slashed—an atmosphere that remains today. This has led the U.S. and the U.K. to the position of growth leaders among the G7 countries, the world's largest industrialized nations (United States, Japan, Germany, France, United Kingdom, Italy and Canada). Canada, in contrast, has fallen markedly behind in economic terms.

The United Nations, however, ranks Canada as the best place to live, and Canadians are rightfully proud of this. Their ranking is based on what they call the Human Development Index, which measures GDP per capita adjusted for purchasing power parity, life expectancy and educational attainment. Our cities are clean, crime rates are relatively low, the poor and the elderly are guaranteed a basic lifestyle. Health care is free, education is free through high school and relatively inexpensive thereafter, and the income distribution is more equal than in many other countries. The problem since the mid-seventies, however, is that middle- and high-income Canadians have experienced a marked decline in relative living standards. This can be reversed without jeopardizing the support for lower-income families by creating an environment conducive to stronger growth in the overall economy.

Late Boomers Feel the Crunch

Members of the late-end Boomer cohort in both Canada and the U.S. had a very different experience of life than their older sisters and brothers. Rather than being first in line in the booming fifties, they were last in line in the sixties. They entered elementary schools already crowded by their older siblings. Their American experience of bomb shelters and air-raid drills as children was daunting, but the real distinguishing factor came with the Watergate trauma. Watergate changed the outlook of people who were coming of age in America; Canadians, through the wonders of the media, could not help but be affected as well. And Canadians had their own problems, with Quebec separatism, Western alienation and continued stagflation. The idealistic fervour of youth disappeared. The late-Boomer cohort exhibited an apathy and cynicism towards politics and changing the world, and a narcissistic preoccupation with themselves. They became the "me generation."

Changes in the economy had a profound effect on this group. Debt as a means of maintaining a lifestyle made sense. They were the first generation in years to make less than their parents, and many were forced by economic necessity to return home after university. They experienced the job-clog created by the front-end Boomers and the unaffordable housing of the 1980s. These were the alienated young people described as Generation X in Coupland's classic book.

Most of their parents were from the Traditionalist generation, who could not understand why their children were having so much trouble finding their economic bearings. Remember, the Traditionalists were a very small cohort with relatively little job competition, at least in comparison with their children. They were the ones who married early, and by the time they were twenty-five they had jobs that supported a family—a family with a single breadwinner. How different from the experience of their children!

Generation X, the Baby Bust Cohort— Born 1966–1976

What is usually called Generation X is the cohort born just after the late Boomers, representing almost 4.5 million people in Canada, 14.5 percent of the population in 1998—the same proportion of the population as in the U.S. They came into a world far different from the *Leave It to Beaver* world of the early Boomers. Mom was at work, and Mom *and* Dad often became Mom *or* Dad, as divorce rates surged. These were the original latchkey kids. Raised on *Sesame Street* and music videos, introduced to computers at an early age, they span the beginning of the technology revolution. They remember television before cable, vinyl records and life without a PC. The defining developments for this generation, according to authors Robert Barnard, Dave Cosgrave and Jennifer Welsh—all Gen Xers themselves, or as they prefer to be called, members of the Nexus generation—were the computer and cable television; hence the title of their book, *Chips & Pop: Decoding the Nexus Generation*.

Xers were the first generation to see the world in real time, thanks to the wonders of CNN. They watched the Gulf War in their living room, and most know where they were when they saw the Los Angeles police chase O.J. Simpson's Bronco on CNN. They have been affected by the growing diversity of the Canadian population and are comfortable with friends of varying nationalities and alternative lifestyles. Diversity is a key fact of life for Xers; they have experienced good and bad in many things, and are willing to accept trade-offs and options. They are not judgmental of other people's choices. Xers are vigilant and adaptable. They know nothing lasts forever, so they are ever ready to adjust.

As kids, they were familiar with disappointment. Suicide rates among teenagers surged in the U.S. They were searching for anchors with their seemingly contradictory "retro" behaviour: the resurgence of proms, coming-out parties and fraternities. Their political conservatism was motivated by a "what's in it for me?" cynicism. Their apparent alienation was reflected in the violence and brutal sex of their popular culture.

Their disappointments were real; divorce, recession and economic restructuring, Chernobyl, Tiananmen Square, Meech Lake and the *Challenger* disaster were markers for this generation. The early eighties recession put their parents out of work, and the early nineties recession, the longest in the Canadian postwar period, ravaged them just as they were starting their careers. Unlike the early Boomers, who believed that economic prosperity would last forever, Xers are more pragmatic and skeptical, less trusting. Boomers believe we can change the world; Xers work within a world over which they feel they have little influence. Xers have a survival mentality. In direct contrast to the early Boomers, Xers have a "don't expect too much" attitude, born of hard personal experience. Xers are the generational cohort that has never been able to presume success.

Even a university degree did not assure them success; many saw it as a guarantee of nothing. They suffered the consequences of education inflation. Today, a bachelor's degree is often required for the most menial entry-level positions, and a degree costs far more than it used to. Sharp cutbacks in federal money to the universities has increased the cost of tuition, and many Xers are left with crushing school loan payments.

This generation has not had a higher standard of living than their parents at the same age. They have been hurt by restructuring, as the last in are often the first to go. The answer for many is their technical expertise. Better trained technically than Boomers, this is their competitive advantage, and the demand for tech skills is huge.

The Canadian Backdrop for Xers— Successes and Failures

The decade of the eighties, with all its successes and failures, was a harsh training ground for the Xers. It was kicked off in Canada with the return of Trudeau economic interventionism and a win for the federalist forces in the 1980 Quebec referendum. The mix of good and bad continued throughout the decade, throughout the Xers' lives. Unlike the Boomer childhood, when all was seen as good and hopeful, Xers knew that marriage could mean divorce—almost one-third were in divorced families—sex could mean AIDS, drugs could mean addiction, even John Lennon could be murdered. Canada gained a new constitution and Charter of Rights and Freedoms in 1982, only to have Quebec refuse to sign it. Xers have always lived with the threat of Quebec separation.

By mid-1981, the economy was mired in a deep recession, hitting Western Canada particularly hard. Interest rates had surged to kill inflation, but the economy was the unintended victim. Massive economic restructuring and layoffs ensued. Even the banks, a Canadian icon of stability and strength, were hit hard by the 1981 Dome Petroleum failure and the subsequent Latin American debt crisis. Nothing was sacred, nothing was for sure. By the end of Trudeau's last government, Canada was in dire need of change.

The Mulroney Years

Following in the footsteps of Trudeau, the Mulroney government was distracted by constitutional issues. The failure of the Meech Lake Accord was a political disaster for Mulroney, as it played into the hands of the separatists and paved the way for the founding of the Bloc Québécois. The country remained focused on Quebec in the years following Meech.

The ever present separatist threat in the late eighties and early nineties wreaked intermittent turmoil on financial markets, causing interest rates in Canada to rise, the currency to fall and the stock market to languish. While the U.S. stock market had already hit new highs following the 1987 crash, the Canadian stock market was underperforming—in direct contrast to the earlier postwar experience. Canadian interest rates rose appreciably relative to those in the United States, dampening economic activity and driving foreign investors elsewhere.

The government continued to push ahead on the constitutional front. The ensuing years were marked by numerous federal-provincial conferences to recognize Quebec as a distinct society, culminating in the Charlottetown Accord, a new federal-provincial agreement reached in August 1992. When a national referendum was held on October 26, 1992, the Charlottetown Accord was rejected by 54.8 percent of the voters.

By and large, the Charlottetown Accord was viewed cynically by most Canadians as little more than a series of behind-the-scenes compromises cobbled together by the country's elites. The separatists were in a position yet again to drive home the point that the rest of the country was impeding Quebeckers' aspirations. This was obviously a successful strategy. The Bouchard-led Bloc, a party dedicated to the separation of Quebec from Canada, won enough seats in Quebec to become the Official Opposition following the October 1993 federal election.

The continued uncertainty regarding Quebec's place in Canada had an important negative impact on the perception of Canada in the eyes of foreign investors. They demanded higher and higher interest rates relative to the U.S. to hold our bonds, and by 1990 many were selling.

Deficits Further Damaged
Mulroney Government

Another important area of Mulroney-government failure was the budgetary deficit. By the time he left politics in 1993, the deficit had skyrocketed to a record $40 billion-plus, despite the repeated efforts of his finance ministers to get the budget under control. Even with the introduction of the very unpopular Goods and Services Tax (GST) in 1991, budgetary red ink continued to rise as the bills kept mounting for the universal and overly generous social safety net. Canadian voters expressed their dissatisfaction with the Mulroney government by annihilating the Conservative party in the 1993 election. The federal Tories, under the leadership of Kim Campbell, lost party status, winning only two seats—a crushing defeat.

The Chrétien Government—
Move to Budget Surplus

The Liberals under Jean Chrétien have as their crowning achievement the move to a budgetary surplus for the first time in almost three decades. It is consistent with the lessons of history that the party that got us into fiscal trouble is the party that ultimately got us out of it. Most Canadians began to realize that we were in serious financial trouble when the credit-rating agencies stripped the nation of its coveted triple-A debt rating in the early 1990s. And to most Canadians, the "kind-hearted and caring" Liberals could be trusted to make the move to budget surplus less painful than the "hard-hearted," fiscally prudent Tory or Reform parties. In addition, the Reform party provided the political cover needed to get the job done, demanding that the deficit be eliminated even faster.

While some of the move from budgetary deficit to surplus in the second half of the nineties was due to fiscal restraint enacted by the Liberals—tax hikes and spending cuts—at least some reflected the flow-through from policies enacted by the Tories in the late 1980s. The reviled GST finally began to spin off sizable revenues as consumer spending revived after a long hibernation. The Free Trade Agreement also began to pay big dividends. With exports to the United States accounting for over 33 percent of Canadian GDP, the economy was closely hitched to the world's locomotive in the latter stages of the nineties. However, the tide in the long-standing deficit fight finally turned for good with Ottawa's watershed 1995 budget, which implemented deep, but necessary, spending cuts. Even with this, over 80 percent of the improvement in the budget balance since 1995 has been the result of tax increases rather than spending cuts. In contrast to the most dire predictions, these tough measures did not pump up unemployment. Instead, the belated shift to fiscal sanity allowed the Bank of Canada to slash interest rates, which in turn spurred job growth to a tremendous pace over the next few years. As the decade drew to a close, the unemployment rate dropped below 8 percent for the first time in almost ten years, and though it ticked up with the return of many formerly discouraged workers to the labour force, it will move much lower if the North American economies remain on track.

A Generation of Pragmatists—
Adaptable and Diverse

Having lived through the economic turmoil of the period, it is not surprising that Generation X has doubts about the future. Xers postpone marriage and child-bearing, and have less connection to traditional institutions—religious, political and financial. They are very different from the Boomers at the same age. They are not compulsive achievers and accumulators; they are not yuppies; they work to live, not live to work. They do spend money, however. They love small extravagances, are experiential shoppers, value entertainment and leisure activity. Even their notion of fitness differs from the Boomers'. The Boomers make fitness work—they work out; but Xers have fun—they are into camaraderie and excitement. That is why the extreme sports have become so popular: mountain biking, rock climbing, skateboarding, rollerblading, snowboarding. They are avid experiential travellers—

travel as a mind-opening enlightenment—and the more remote the place, the better.

Many Xers are hunting for opportunities that will free them from the career imprisonment that confined their parents. They are open to non-traditional career options, and are typically suspicious of big business. They like the flexibility away from the traditional corporate lifestyle. Many are showing enormous entrepreneurial spirit and are among the leaders in the technology revolution. Thirty-year-old billionaires like Michael Dell and Jeffrey Bezos, founder of Amazon.com, are in direct contrast to the stereotypical notion of the Xers as slackers or deadbeats with hamburger-flipping McJobs. This generation has experienced disappointment and challenge. Unlike Boomers, they are not starry-eyed Supermen and Superwomen, thinking they can conquer the world and fix everything. They are adaptable, pragmatic, fun-loving, daring and open-minded. They understand, however, that you have to save for a rainy day.

The Millennial Generation— The Echo Boom, Born After 1975

The echo baby boom has been proportionately much smaller in Canada than in the United States, owing to the sharp drop in birth rates in Quebec (see figure 6.1 on page 102). Nevertheless, the Millennial generation is sizable at more than 8 million young people, representing over 26 percent of the population. In the U.S., the Millennials are now rivalling the Boomers in size, claiming 78 million people today and growing fast, largely through immigration. Like the Boomers, the American Millennials account for 29 percent of the population. America will have a bigger pool of young workers to replace retirees than Japan, Germany, France, Italy and much of the Eastern bloc. The United States will have an advantage over most other industrial nations owing to the relative youth of its population.

The early Millennials—the oldest of which have just turned twenty-two—have the lowest child-to-parent family ratio in history. In contrast to the Generation Xers, these children frequently arrived to parents who desperately wanted them. The abortion rate peaked in 1980 and has since declined gradually. Infertility treatment has boomed in the past twenty years, as many Boomer women found they had postponed motherhood too long and desperately sought help.

The number of children in American schools has hit a record high and the diversity of these children is unprecedented. Only 66 percent of this generation is white, non-Hispanic. The number of kids under the age of eighteen in the U.S. is now higher than in 1966, when a wave of Boomers pushed the figure to a then record 69.9 million, and that number is growing fast.

What makes this growth trend different from the surge in the late 1960s is that the trend in the U.S. is a long, slow, rising wave, and there will be no immediate fall-off. The number of births is projected to remain fairly stable at around 4 million or more, in contrast to the decline after the previous baby boom, when births fell to 3.1 million in the early seventies. Long-range projections by the U.S. Census Bureau indicate the number of births rising to 4.2 million in 2010 and 4.6 million in 2020.

The growth now is driven largely by immigration. This is a reflection of two trends: more children are coming into the U.S., and immigrants generally have higher birth rates than the native population, especially Hispanic immigrants. There is another key difference from the 1960s Boomer-driven jump: the share of kids in the population is much smaller today as the country's population rises to 270 million. Youth comprised 36 percent of the population in 1966, but only 29 percent today. By 2020, that percentage will dip even further.

Canada's youth are a proportionately smaller cohort than in the U.S. and are not quite as ethnically diverse. Roughly 86 percent of the Canadian population under the age of eighteen is white (non-Hispanic), twenty percentage points higher than in the U.S. Nevertheless, immigration here has also played an important role. Today's big-city classrooms look like meetings of a United Nations youth group, with a multitude of cultures and races represented. Kids today are colour-blind more than ever before, and increasingly they are becoming citizens of the world. They are more racially and ethnically diverse than their parents' generation, and therefore more tolerant and accepting of differences. Millennials are divided into "haves" and "have-nots" according to their access to technology and their ability to acquire important technical and traditional reading and math skills early in life. This technology gap will tend to exacerbate the widening gulf between rich and poor among children and teens in both Canada and the U.S.

Millennials are the children of the computer age, cable television, Nintendo, the Internet, free trade, globalization and multiculturalism. They are the best-travelled, most sophisticated youth in history. Television and videos have expanded their horizons. While many have seen a return to traditional family values, all have been exposed to the realities of life at a very early age. The details of the Lewinsky–Clinton affair on prime-time television led many ten-year-olds to ask their parents about oral sex. Television tells them everything, and this knowledge is augmented by the Internet.

It was the anxious and protective Boomer parents that raised this generation, nurtured them, car-pooled and tutored them. I know; I was one of them. Middle-class Boomers, true to our generational values, made a project of our children. Boomer moms went to Lamaze classes and studied breast-feeding. In fact, we studied everything about our children. We knew the appropriate age for walking, talking and toilet training. We endlessly discussed our children at cocktail parties and at the office. We wanted them to have everything we had and much more. The privileged among these kids were wait-listed at the best nursery schools as soon as they were born, tutored for entrance exams at age seven, and primed and pampered with a multitude of varied experiences from birth. This is the most "coached" generation in history. Swimming lessons at nine months, computer classes and gymnastics at four years—no kidding, the Science Centre in Toronto offers computer classes for three-year-olds—skating, skiing, tennis and soccer before the age of ten. Throw in a little karate, horseback riding and ballet and it's a wonder these kids were not exhausted.

In fact, they were enervated. They are the most competitive kids in history. Their standardized testing scores for university are actually going up, even as the lower-level basic-skill test results are going down for underprivileged kids. This is another example of the widening gap between have and have-not children and teenagers, particularly in the

United States. This generation will do more because more has always been expected of them. Growing up with such high expectations, Millennials will be more civic-minded, with a greater sense of their own power.

Susan Mitchell, author of *The Official Guide to the Generations*, says the Millennials will be more self-confident than their parents. Comparing today's university freshmen to the Boomers twenty-five or thirty years ago, Mitchell found today's group twice as likely to rate themselves highly in social self-confidence. According to a 1997 *American Demographics* magazine survey, 43 percent rated themselves above average in leadership, popularity, and intellectual and social confidence. They are less worried about nuclear war, unencumbered by guilt or doubt over Vietnam or civil rights, but more worried about AIDS, pollution, street violence and terrorism. They are equally distrustful of government, health care and the media, but possess a greater determination to become active and change things.

Neil Howe, co-author of *The Fourth Turning*, believes that this new generation will "escape the nihilism and cynicism of Generation X. They will be very focused on the outer world, on science, math, economics, politics—not the inner world, the questioning and value-searching of the Boomers and Xers."

The Millennials will be hard-eyed, realistic and independent-minded. They have grown up with downsizing, restructuring and rapid technological innovation, and consider them the norm. They have experienced the end of the Cold War, the unification of Germany, and the creation of NAFTA and the European Monetary Union. They are, therefore, freed from left-right political oversimplifications. They will support third-party politics, environmentalism and egalitarianism. They will be gender-neutral, but appreciate traditional family values—the values that their parents only rediscovered twenty years ago. They put more value on team play than their parents ever did. They have not been raised to rebel. As Susan Mitchell says, "expect them to be straight arrows." They have been affected by the images of the Oklahoma City bombing, the Colorado high school shootings, global conversations on the World Wide Web and the sex scandal in the Clinton White House. The millennial celebrations of the year 2000 will be their coming-out party.

They have a closer affinity to their parents than their Boomer parents had to theirs. Most have been raised by dual-career moms and dads. In a 1997 survey, *American Demographics* magazine found that they think their parents are cool. Nearly half said they think their parents' musical tastes are up-to-date, and most said they value their parents' opinions about drinking, spending and sex. While teens will always rebel at least mildly, the Millennials apparently do not feel the sense of alienation and generation gap that the Boomers felt towards their Veteran and Traditionalist parents. There is no anti-war movement today to crystallize the rebellion. Millennials do not espouse free love—unfazed by the pill, which was a novelty for Boomer teens—and they are relatively cautious and concerned about sexually transmitted diseases.

Today's teens have tremendous economic clout. Like their parents, they represent a demographic tidal wave, especially in the U.S., that will help shape trends, attitudes and commerce for much of the first half of the twenty-first century.

The U.S. has the highest ratio of youth under the age of eighteen relative to elders over the age of sixty-five in the G7. This suggests that the U.S. will continue to have the strongest, most vibrant consumer market in the industrial world. The demand for consumer goods will be more robust than in the rest of the G7, and the labour force will enjoy new, technically well-trained entrants in the first twenty years of the new millennium.

Canada, as neighbour and trading partner of the United States, will gain the most by selling into the U.S. consumer market. Moreover, we have quite a sizable youth market of our own, second largest in the G7 as a percentage of the population, and it too will be augmented by increasing immigration. What we want to make certain is that we create an economic environment that will keep our most talented youth. We have more to do on that score.

Life Cycles

Most people's lives follow a broadly predictable pattern: birth, education, job, pairing, kids, empty nest, retirement, death. Some of us skip steps along the way, and the range of alternative lifestyles is broadening, but the general pattern for the majority of the population remains the same. That is why the study of demographics to predict the economic and financial horizon has become so popular. Where the caveats arise, however, is in the timing and specific choices that each generation will make. These will differ from generation to generation because each is motivated and driven by very different underlying values and attitudes, as we have seen in the last chapter. This does not, however, invalidate the analysis of life-cycle behaviour. All of us will eventually grow old and retire; the question is when and how.

Let's look first at the general life-cycle pattern and then at the implications of this for countries with very different demographic characteristics—"young" countries like much (but not all) of the emerging world, and "old" countries like Japan, Germany and Italy. We will see that the United States and—to an only slightly lesser degree—Canada have a huge demographic advantage. We have a very strong contingent of highly educated people in their forties, nearing their peak earning, spending and productivity years; and we have a large youth contingent as well, providing the fuel for today's consumer market and tomorrow's highly skilled labour force. This is another important factor that will contribute to our leadership in the upwave of the technology revolution.

The Spending Cycle

Two U.S. economists, Franco Modigliani and Milton Friedman, both of whom were later awarded the Nobel Prize in economics, looked at household spending behaviour and saw that it was determined not just by today's level of disposable (after-tax) income, but also by our notion of our income in the future. We spend based on today's income level and our expectation of what Friedman called our "permanent" income level—the average level of income we expect to earn over the longer term—which might be higher or lower than today's income, depending on your age. Modigliani's life-cycle theory of household spending was similar; we spend and save over our lifetimes in an effort to smooth out our living standards. We go into debt as students or young marrieds, expecting that our incomes will rise in the future. We accumulate wealth in mid-life when incomes are peaking, expecting our incomes to fall as we age.

Today's Boomers are thirty-four to fifty-three years old. The bulk of them have not yet hit their peak spending years, generally around age forty-five to forty-eight, depending on how late they had children. Income usually peaks about eight to ten years later, again depending on how long you work and what work you do. The average Boomer is just about forty. Over the next ten years, we will see continued strong household consumption coming from this most powerful generation. Over the next twenty years, wealth accumulation will mount as Boomers save for retirement. They will never save as much as their parents, however, or as much as they should, because Boomers live for today. Already, the savings rate in Canada and the U.S. has fallen to record lows.

Spending patterns follow the life cycle of individuals and families. People typically take their first full-time jobs right after graduation, generally in their late teens or early twenties. This age has been rising over time as more are going on for advanced degrees. They begin to purchase a wide array of consumer durable goods and clothing: their first car, a sound system, work wardrobe, TV, computer.

The costs of setting up house can be daunting, particularly on entry-level salaries, and good jobs are often hard to get, so many are delaying the move from home or returning there after graduation, at least for an interim period. High tuition fees and a tendency for young people to delay marriage have also provided impetus for this trend. A recent report from Statistics Canada shows that a higher percentage of adults between the ages of twenty and thirty-four—more than half— were living with parents in 1996 than at any time in the past fifteen years. This boomerang effect is more common for young men than women. Roughly 56 percent of unmarried young men, compared with only 47 percent of unmarried young women, lived in their parents' home. Guys apparently appreciate the comforts of Mom's cooking and laundry service, while young women are more keen to try their wings. It used to be that a young woman had to marry to leave home, but that has changed now as the average age of first-time marriages continues to rise. Many, however, will take roommates to help make ends meet. Once young adults do leave the nest, their spending increases rapidly with income. Indeed, new entrants to the consumer world often quickly become net debtors—car loans, credit card loans and, some years later, mortgage loans.

Roughly 70 percent of households in Canada are considered by Statistics Canada to be families. The proportion of those that have dual earners has surged over the past twenty years and now stands at 56 percent of all families, compared with 34 percent in 1976. The proportion of single-parent families has doubled, from 5 percent to 10 percent. The prevalence of the 1950s-style family—Mom stays home while Dad goes to work—has fallen markedly, from more than 3.2 million, or 54 percent of all families, in 1976 to less than 1.5 million, or a mere 23 percent, today. It is still relatively rare for Dad to be at home while Mom is at work—5 percent of families today—but it is up from 2 percent ten years ago. However, while most stay-at-home moms say it is by choice, stay-at-home dads generally attribute it to involuntary unemployment. The remaining 30 percent of households are non-family, most of which— more than 80 percent—are one-person households.

People marry for the first time usually by their mid- to late twenties, although the average age of first-time marriages is rising, and it is higher the greater the level of education and, to some extent, income. The Xers have been called the earliest copulating and latest marrying generation in history. It is now quite common for couples to live together for a few years before marriage.

Several years later, young marrieds typically begin to have children. The average age of first-time mothers, however, is rising too, as many women choose to cement their careers before having kids and couples enjoy the freedom and relative affluence of two incomes with no children. The early Boomer women pushed the envelope here, as we were often gender pioneers in our fields and felt a serious risk of career penalty if we had children too early.

While the mix of households has changed and alternative lifestyles are more common, the bulk of the adult population still has kids, and when they arrive, spending surges—as does debt, particularly mortgage debt. Most households continue to be net borrowers well into their forties, and often into their fifties. The Boomers hold the record on debt. Household income growth slowed dramatically in both Canada and the U.S. beginning in the mid-seventies, despite the dramatic rise in two-income families. Boomers responded, not by denying themselves, of course, but by going increasingly into debt. Boomer debt levels relative to income levels are the highest in history. It's a good thing that interest rates have plunged with the decline in inflation since 1982, or we would have an even more difficult time servicing all this debt.

For most of us, income peaks at about age fifty-five, give or take a few years, although the peak-income age will likely rise in the future as people live and work longer. Of course, all the corporate downsizing in recent years has caused some to retire early, but many of those are taking on new careers. Spending typically peaks at about age forty-five to forty-eight, when the last tuition bills are paid—later if children were postponed.

In the past, households began to pay down their debts in their late forties. Historically, Canadians were very good at paying down debt, including mortgages. Indeed, half of Canadian households age forty-five to fifty-four were mortgage-free in 1996. In the United States there is less incentive to pay down the mortgage because mortgage interest is tax-deductible.

Earlier generations began to accumulate wealth in their mid-forties. They may still have had large debts outstanding, but their after-tax cash flow allowed for some net saving after expenditures and debt servicing. From the mid-forties until retirement, wealth accumulation continues (figure 7.1). This has become increasingly difficult for Boomers—particularly in Canada, with large debt burdens, the non-preferential tax treatment of mortgage interest, slow income growth, a falling Canadian dollar, an inordinate tax burden and high unemployment. Furthermore, the Canadian stock market has dramatically underperformed in comparison to the U.S. since 1980, so even if we did accumulate wealth in Canadian stocks, they haven't done nearly as well. Canadian family living standards have fallen meaningfully in relation to the U.S.

FIGURE 7.1

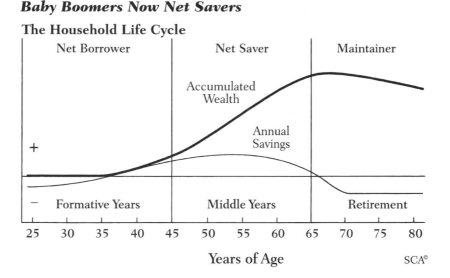

Baby Boomers Now Net Savers

This savings shortfall is particularly troublesome because of the shift away from guaranteed pension support from the corporate world and from government. We talked earlier about the declining role played by the big defined-benefit pension plans that guarantee about 60 to

70 percent of your top income in retirement after about thirty years of service. Boomers don't typically work thirty years for a single employer any more, and Xers certainly won't. We are left increasingly to save for ourselves in our RRSPs. Many, if not most, Boomers will have insufficient savings to retire at sixty-five. They are likely to postpone retirement for as long as possible. Life expectancies are rising and will increase further with coming biotechnology and pharmaceutical breakthroughs. Who wants to play golf or putter about in the garden for thirty years, anyway? Certainly, most Boomers won't.

The general life-cycle pattern suggests that for twenty years or more, households shift increasingly from a net-debtor to a net-saver position as incomes peak and spending slows. Children leave for university, and once those bills are paid—in the U.S. they are multiples of their level in Canada—spending generally falls appreciably.

The Dire Forecasts of Boomer House Sales

A common misconception is that empty-nesters downsize immediately. Only about 20 percent of people move out of their family homes when they first retire, which is usually many years after becoming empty-nesters. Most downsize much later, well into their seventies, and only reluctantly, when they are too old to care for their homes. This is unlikely to change. First there is the boomerang effect—grown kids staying longer or returning home. No sooner do you send the youngest off to university than the oldest is back at home for a few years. Boomers rarely did this, but we got married a lot younger than they do today. Also, we believed in the "generation gap."

A huge question for the future of house prices is: will the Boomers downsize en masse, as many predict? I'd guess not. And by the time they do, the Millennials will be there to buy attractive properties or even fix-ups. I'm not suggesting that residential real estate will boom; I just don't believe it will crash. House-price movements are likely to be quite muted.

Some of the early Boomers are already becoming empty-nesters, and the more well-to-do among them are asking for something new: luxurious, maintenance-free living in a house of comparable size to their family homes. Big kitchens, glitzy bathrooms, floor-to-ceiling windows, with community amenities like tennis courts and bike trails. Even the less privileged among them generally prefer to keep the extra bedrooms.

As Boomers' family responsibilities wane, as their hectic two-career family lives decelerate, they will—true to form—focus more on themselves. More time for self-actualization, a second career, a new business, new hobbies; life does not become more insular, it becomes more expansive. Vast new horizons open up. Their seemingly large homes—too large for just a couple—will give them room to breathe, to think, to plan, to recharge their batteries for the next mountain that needs climbing. Homes will increasingly have to accommodate workspaces, as many Boomers will work part-time or full-time out of their residences. Houses will need to be wired for the Internet and include technological command centres.

Once again, Boomers will break with conventional wisdom. They may sell their family homes, but they will not necessarily downsize. With the kids gone, they will have more money. Although they should save most of it, many won't; they will provide the support for the high end of the real estate market for many years to come. Trade-up buyers have been driving this end of the housing market since 1996, and much more is in store.

After all, Boomers have always associated security with home. Mom was in the kitchen when they got home from school. The good life that home provided was no remote dream in the suburbs of the fifties and sixties, with their dens, barbecues, patios, televisions, rec rooms, swing sets. When Boomers got their own homes, they became showplaces, trophies. The size increased dramatically. They grew up with one bathroom for four people and moved into houses with one bathroom per person. Kitchens exploded in size, even in houses without gourmet chefs. They did this, of course, with two incomes, not one, and with huge mortgages.

The late eighties proved that houses were no longer an investment, tied to a profit and loss statement. We saw, with the plunge in house prices, that these would no longer be the key to a secure financial future. As the world became more hostile and uncertain, our houses became a refuge, a peaceful haven in a stressful life. More and more now, Boomers buy and build to create a house with soul, a place of peace and tranquillity, a safe, stress-free haven from the outside world of mergers and downsizing. The renovation and landscaping businesses are booming. We are spending more on our houses than ever before. Retailers like Home Depot are benefiting. So are those that sell home entertainment systems, wine cellars, household gym equipment, and every manner of kitchen and bathroom upgrade. People are entertaining at home again.

Boomers who can afford it will buy second homes, in the country or at the beach or the ski hill. With the oldest Boomers in their fifties, this craze is just beginning. Many big-city Boomers will want to stay where the action is, for at least part of the year, but others will not. With telecommuting gaining favour, many will choose to live in more remote, less expensive locales. University towns and small towns in pleasant climates are growing in popularity. Canadians, as always, will look south for winter homes, returning for at least six months each year so they can continue to use the Canadian health care system. Florida, the Carolinas, Arizona, Nevada, New Mexico and California will remain popular destinations for Canadian Boomers. However, the migration south will be limited by the weak Canadian dollar.

In the U.S. especially, the safety issue and the quality of health care services are essential considerations for retirees. In Canada, places like Victoria and Kelowna in British Columbia will continue to attract retirees for their mild climates; but Boomers won't want traditional retirement-community living. Keep in mind that Boomers will never admit to growing old; they will always want a "youthful" environment, even in old age.

Xers too dream of home ownership, but for many it is one of their biggest worries. Housing is very expensive in most big cities, and Xers, unlike Boomers, feel they cannot presume success. Nevertheless, many are making and will make the plunge. Xers will not be as nostalgic about their homes as the Boomers are. They do not have the happy childhood memories of Mom and Dad in the suburbs that most Boomers have. They will create new memories, a new notion of home for themselves. A bit retro, a lot new wave, the Xer dream house will no doubt be as unique as their generation. Xers may well love the "vintage" homes that the Matures will be selling; Xers find retro-eclectic chic and will enjoy renovating, doing the work themselves.

The Matures will look for retirement living that affords them the best in technological long-distance health care monitoring systems. They will want to enjoy the fruits of their labours, have some fun and enjoy life. Casinos, theatres and shopping centres will thrive in this market.

The bottom line: the talk of the demise of the residential real estate market, and of family homes in particular, when Boomers' children leave home is greatly exaggerated.

Retirement Spending

Eventually, even the Boomers will retire. Healthy Boomers today can expect to live well into our eighties, and even if we postpone full retirement as long as possible, chances are we will spend many years with relatively little earned income coming in. About half the Boomer population in Canada, less in the U.S., will have some form of defined-benefit pension plan income. We will all have government support from the Canada Pension Plan, although it will be far less than many of us need to live comfortably. And we will have our savings—what we have accumulated in RRSPs and non-tax-deferred investments.

If this sounds frightening to you, you are not alone. Most Boomers have not yet saved enough to ensure financial security in old age. There is still time—more than twenty years for most—but it will be very difficult, both psychologically and financially, for many. Because of this, even the Boomers will tighten their belts a bit in retirement.

One mitigating factor is the massive intergenerational transfer of wealth that will occur between the Matures and the Boomers. Estimates of the amount of money that Boomers stand to inherit vary, but the numbers are huge—in the trillions of dollars in Canada and the United States. While this factor will be meaningful, it is unlikely to be the answer to all our financial worries. Firstly, Matures too will be living longer than ever before, and many sixty-something Boomer retirees will have parents to care for. Secondly, long-term elder care is getting more and more expensive, even in Canada—particularly high-quality, round-the-clock, at-home care. Thirdly, Matures will divvy up their estates between a number of children, grandchildren and favourite charities. Finally, many will enjoy life in their final years and spend at least some of the money. I certainly hope so. They are packing the cruise ships, the resorts around the world, the beaches, the golf clubs and the casinos. It looks to me like they are not going to be held responsible for bailing out their profligate Boomer children, nor should they be. For most of us, then, we will be essentially on our own.

Inevitably, the growth in Boomer spending will slow in full retirement. This will occur for the bulk of Boomers around 2025 and will coincide with the peak in the long-cycle upwave. The good news is that, at that time, the Millennials will be approaching their peak spending years, and they will outnumber the Boomers, at least in the United States. This will provide a huge cushion for the U.S. economy. Millennials, however, do not outnumber Boomers in Canada, so we have to either step up the immigration of young people soon or risk a significant demographically induced slowdown around 2025. Significant tax cuts in this country would encourage such a net in-migration of people, just as we have seen in Ireland in recent years.

Even in retirement, at least in the early years, Boomers will be reluctant to dip into their capital, not knowing how long they will live. We will be reluctant to exit the stock market as well, because we will still want to maximize the return on our savings. New investment vehicles will continue to surface—tying insurance products to stocks—giving us a guaranteed principle and upside possibilities. We will discuss these and other investment strategies in a later section.

The fact is, like in the housing market, Boomers will remain invested in stocks a lot longer than people expect. Many have predicted a crash in stocks when the oldest Boomers begin to retire in 2011 or so. I disagree. Firstly, people will not magically retire fully at age sixty-five any longer. Secondly, even when we do retire, we will still hold stocks. Thirdly, the bulk of the Boomers won't retire until much later, around 2025. Fourthly, the Xers and the Millennials, who will be much better savers than the Boomers, will pick up the slack. Most of them will have only defined-contribution pension plans and will have to begin saving for their own retirement at a very early age. Finally, foreign investors will plow into stocks as the relatively young emerging-market middle-class populations burgeon. If I am right that we are embarking on the upwave in the long cycle, the stock market will do very well over the next twenty to twenty-five years. This will be especially true in the United States—the global leader in the technology revolution—even though the U.S. market has already boomed for many years. To the extent that we catch this wave, and I believe we will, the Canadian stock market will surge as well.

Xers and Millennials will want to ride this wave too, so funds available to flow into the stock market will remain sizable. Indeed, liquidity will continue to be a powerful force rocketing stocks higher for decades to come. This means that stocks could remain overvalued by traditional standards for extended periods. The U.S. stock market has been seen by many to be substantially overvalued; prices have risen to levels much higher than prospective corporate earnings or the level of interest rates would warrant. Markets will correct. Sometimes the corrections will be huge; 20 percent or 30 percent corrections are possible, even likely. Expect volatility, invest for the long run and see these corrections as a buying opportunity. Don't panic and sell into them.

Those that see these trends today and act on them will benefit. That is why I am urging everyone to save as much as possible and invest regularly in a diversified portfolio of stocks. If I am right that the general trend will continue to be up for the next twenty-five years or more, buying stocks regularly is key to your financial security in the future. Paying down debt—all debt—is also critical. And, as this chapter suggests, there is no need to bail out of your family house if you don't want to. There will be plenty of support for the real estate market in times to come. The best support will be continued relatively low interest rates and economic prosperity.

Spending during retirement is, for most, relatively cautious and frugal. People try to live on the income generated by their savings portfolios and are reluctant to dip into the principal for fear of running out of money. It is often not until well into retirement that households once again begin to spend more than they earn, dipping into their principal to help maintain lifestyles. At this stage of life, demand for services is greater than demand for consumer durable goods and housing.

Demographics—
A Global View

C anada and the United States have a huge demographic advantage. For industrialized countries, we have a relatively young, highly educated population. The bulk of the population is approaching its peak productivity years, years during which income and spending will continue to rise. In addition, and equally important, there is a large youth contingency coming up behind, especially in the United States.

The demographic situation is very different in other countries. While most of the emerging world's population is generally much younger and is growing more rapidly, they are not as highly educated and lack the Boomer anchor so evident in Canada and the U.S. In countries like Japan, Germany, France and Italy, the population is much older than in North America. They did not experience a postwar baby boom and will suffer the effects of a demographically induced slowdown in the years ahead. Australia did experience a postwar baby boom, but more tightly linked to Asia, Australia is overcoming its reliance on the region.

The world's population is rapidly approaching 6 billion people. There is, of course, great diversity of political, cultural and societal experience from country to country. Nevertheless, the life cycle of the population has a strong bearing on longer-term economic trends. The younger a population, the greater the demand for consumer durable goods and housing, particularly if the economy is advanced enough to have a sizable and growing middle class. This is the case for many of the emerging economies around the world, particularly those in Asia and some in Latin America. It is much less the case in Africa, where education levels for many have not been sufficient to create a sizable middle class. Instead, the distribution of income remains highly uneven; the masses are barely above subsistence level and a small minority are extremely rich.

Conversely, older populations have slower-growing demand for goods and many services. Populations with most people in their fifties and sixties—like Japan, the oldest population on the planet, or Germany, Italy and France—will be characterized by high savings rates and low spending rates. In an aging population, household formations slow as there are proportionately fewer and fewer twenty-five-year-olds to set up house. Fewer babies are born and the demand for housing-related goods and services diminishes. Not as many schools are built, and the overall youth market, so important for economic buoyancy, remains modest. On the other hand, older people do demand some key services, and they do have a lot of capital to invest. Sectors like financial services, leisure services and health care grow rapidly. The investment business booms and capital is available to flow to regions of the world that are growing rapidly.

In the next several decades, Canada and the United States will benefit from an explosive growth in exports to the young emerging countries—exports of technology products, expertise and capital. Natural resource exports will be much less important than in earlier eras because of the demise of the heavy-metal manufacturing sector, the growth of the knowledge-based information economy, competitive pressures, biotechnology and the substitution of synthetic for traditional commodities. In a world of intense price competition, if you are not the low-cost producer of a commodity, you will be out of business. There are only a few commodity sectors today where we are the low-cost producer.

The characteristics of national populations are but one factor in the global economic mélange. Overriding events—wars, weather and political upheaval—often blur demographic forces. Furthermore, the freeing of trade and enhanced global communication undoubtedly decrease the isolation of each individual national economy. Markets all over the world are interconnected as never before. Youth activists in China use fax machines and the Internet to communicate with those in the U.S. Software programmers in India, Romania and Bulgaria work online for American companies in Seattle. CNN and the Internet have opened communication and the dissemination of information to all but the most remote places on the planet. Even so, the demographics of the domestic population base set the stage.

We turn now to a review of some of the most salient national demographic characteristics of a selection of the countries in the world that did not experience a postwar baby boom.

Emerging World

Most of the emerging world is quite young, with rapidly growing populations. The exception is the former Soviet bloc countries. Their populations are relatively old—averaging close to age forty, compared to thirty-one in the U.S.—which will be a big disadvantage in the future. For the rest, the key to future economic prosperity will be education, labour market flexibility and a strong work ethic. Most of developing Asia has all of this, and despite the late-1990s crisis in Asia, this area of the world has tremendous potential. Some of Latin America might too, but an unequal income distribution and a sub-par education system will continue to be a problem.

The real laggards will be most of Africa. South Africa has enormous potential if it can educate the black population quickly enough and deal with the enormous housing and unemployment challenges; today, the very unequal income distribution remains a large and growing problem. The countries of the Middle East and northern Africa, characterized by dictatorships, also have young populations, but they will be held back by the extremist positions of their governments, which subjugate much of the population, discourage innovation and restrict education for all, especially women. This is certainly evident in countries like Iran, Iraq and Libya, and will show up in others if extremist forces come to dominate.

The Americas

The countries of Latin America have relatively young populations, but they are undereducated and have comparatively low incomes. Population growth is rapid, and as the working-age population rises in the future, income growth will accelerate, driving up demand for housing and consumer goods. The more underdeveloped countries are the youngest; these include Argentina, Bolivia, Paraguay and Guatemala. For most of the countries with larger economies—Brazil, Mexico, Venezuela, Colombia and Uruguay—thirty- and forty-year-olds dominate the population, only slightly younger than in Canada and the U.S.

The educational systems in all of these countries are substandard, and therefore it is unlikely that they will play an important role in the technology revolution. Income distribution is unequal, and there remains too much reliance on natural resource and agricultural production.

Emerging Asia

Asia, including Japan, was once the fastest-growing third of the global economy. That, of course, came to a screeching temporary halt when Thailand devalued the baht in July 1997, triggering the start of what became known as the Asian crisis or Asian flu. The seeds of the crisis were planted much earlier, however, with the rise of crony capitalism in so many of these countries. Unlike market capitalism, where the invisible hand of supply and demand makes allocation and spending decisions, crony capitalism allows the government, in cahoots with their colleagues in business and banking, to make the allocation decisions. It is not nearly as efficient, as we have discovered. What happened was massive overbuilding in countries like Thailand, Indonesia, Malaysia and Hong Kong, financed by cheap credit. When the system began to collapse, the stock markets in the region nose-dived, taking the banks with them. Real estate values plunged, exacerbating the stock market decline. Most of the stock market capitalization in emerging Asia and Japan was originally in bank and real estate–related stocks, so the crisis triggered the collapse of a house of cards. It began in Japan in 1989 and continued through most of the decade. The stock markets of these countries started to rebound in 1999, reflecting the widening evidence of a nascent economic resurgence.

Emerging Asia—at least the wealthier countries—remains one of the most compelling regions of the world owing to a large, young, well-educated, technically trained and very hard-working population base. Almost half of the twenty-three countries in emerging Asia have young and rapidly growing populations. Many will industrialize speedily, following the lead of Hong Kong, Taiwan, Singapore and South Korea.

China, with its 1.2 billion people, is moving quickly towards a market economy. Although serious problems remain—huge losses at state-owned enterprises, a very large uneducated peasant population, political unrest, enormous governmental inefficiencies, a banking crisis similar to that in Japan, red tape and graft—the potential is enormous. A significant proportion of the population is highly educated, technically sophisticated and highly entrepreneurial. The middle class is burgeoning. China is now the third largest economy on earth, behind the U.S. and Japan, and will likely surpass Japan in the next few years. China has the ingredients to become the economic leader of Asia. China and emerging Asia will provide important markets for American and Canadian products and services.

Today, however, the majority of the populations in the region are agrarian, rural, undereducated and poor. The youngest populations of Asia are the most underdeveloped: Afghanistan, Laos, Malaysia, Nepal and the Philippines. Other Asian countries—Australia, China, Hong Kong, India, Indonesia—are dominated by people in their forties and fifties, similar to Canada and the United States.

Eastern Europe

Eastern Europe has serious demographic problems. Unlike most other emerging nations, the population is decidedly middle-aged. The region benefits from a technically well-trained and cheap labour force, but it is now challenged by the political and economic meltdown in

Russia. Russia's long tenure under totalitarian rule, Communism and, before that, the czars and serf-based agriculture has markedly reduced the work ethic and entrepreneurial spirit. This is in contrast to China, where Communism began much later and, even under Mao, maintained a bit of an entrepreneurial culture.

The tax and legal systems in Russia have been insufficient to cope with the attempted move to capitalism. The insufficiencies in this area have led to a Mafia-like criminal dominance of economic power. The government lacks the ability to collect taxes and is, in essence, bankrupt. The de facto currency has for some time been the U.S. dollar, and the economy has shifted increasingly to a barter system.

The only legitimate means to raise foreign exchange has been through commodity markets. The Russians, therefore, dumped commodities on the marketplace, putting further downward pressure on the price of gold, oil, aluminum, copper and nickel in 1998. Economic tensions eased in 1999, Russian stocks took off and commodity dumping ceased, helping to contribute to the 1999 rise in oil and base metals prices. With rampant political instability in the country, and economic and social unrest, the frightening possibility of Russia selling some of its nuclear arsenal cannot be ruled out; there are, alas, plenty of willing buyers. Its relatively old population only exacerbates Russia's problems. The NATO military attack on Yugoslavia highlights the instability in the region.

The more underdeveloped countries of Eastern Europe have the highest concentration of their population among the young. These countries include Turkmenistan, Uzbekistan, Turkey, Albania and Moldova. The bulk of the larger countries have an increasing number of fifty- and sixty-year-olds: Russia, Poland, the Czech Republic, Hungary and Slovakia. This means relatively slow growth ahead for these countries, exacerbated by military tensions.

The Industrialized World

The growth leaders in the G7 in the nineties were the United States, Britain and Canada—the Anglo-Saxon economies—boosted by low inflation, low interest rates and a move to budgetary surpluses. The debt ratios in these countries is falling, with Canada still having the highest in the group. Technology and globalization were also important catalysts for growth. Both Britain and the U.S. have been reaping the benefits of the policies introduced in the early eighties by Thatcher and Reagan: tax cuts, privatization, enhanced labour market flexibility and a pro-business environment.

Core Europe—France, Italy and Germany—have languished under the weight of large budget deficits, highly inflexible labour markets and high unemployment. Continental Europe, however, had been preparing for the European Monetary Union, and the EMU will be a very positive development for the region. Gone are the inefficiencies of converting eleven currencies across eleven different countries. Today, they are replaced with one currency, the euro, and all will benefit. The union of eleven very different economies under one monetary policy umbrella is difficult, but potentially beneficial. The younger countries like Spain, some of the soon-to-join members in Scandinavia, as well as Britain, will help to infuse some economic strength into the older countries like Germany, France and Italy. Labour market rigidities, while still far worse than in the U.S., will begin to diminish over time, although true labour mobility is never likely to become as widespread as in countries like the United States and Canada, due to continued language and cultural barriers.

Western Europe

The long-term problem for Europe's economic growth is a rapidly aging population that is not replacing itself. This is compounded by highly inflexible labour markets in countries like Germany, France and Italy, where unions are very powerful and restructuring is extremely difficult. Most populations of Europe are literate and well educated, but not well trained technically; this limits the ability of the workforce to advance in the twenty-first-century economy. Although per capita income is relatively high, personal tax rates are quite burdensome and unemployment is very high. Labour market restrictions and militant unions have contributed to high levels of long-term structural unemployment, especially for the young—unemployment caused by a mismatch of skills, occupations and locations, rather than by cyclical moves in the economy.

Europe's aging population and diminishing workforce is a problem. The dependency ratio is the name given to the number of elderly people relative to the number of workers. Sometimes we include children with elderly people to determine the overall number that are dependent on the working-age population. The elderly dependency ratio in Europe was 22.7 percent in 1995 and will rise to 36 percent by 2025—much higher than in the U.S. or Canada. Italy has the worst demographic situation, followed by Germany and France. The United Kingdom is in considerably better shape. Looking at the total dependency ratio—children and elderly as a percentage of workers—the ratio in the U.S. and Canada in 2030 will be lower than the level in 1960, but it will rise sharply in Japan and Germany. The elderly will be a huge drain on the government pension systems of Europe, many of which are overgenerous and underfunded. The aging population poses a meaningful budgetary risk in Europe. The situation may seem dire in Canada and the U.S., but it is much worse in European countries.

While the data imply very slow labour-force growth in the United States and Canada, there will be actual declines within the EMU. This has profound implications for the relative growth rates of real GDP. Continued growth is almost certain in North America. In the EMU, growth will only remain positive with significant increases in productivity, helped along by the so-called peripheral high-growth EMU countries like Ireland, Finland, Spain and Portugal. Economic growth in core Europe will depend on technological innovation and investment. Barriers to productivity growth there—labour market rigidities, excessive regulation and high taxes—will have to be eliminated if they are to come close to matching the growth pace of the U.S.

The younger populations of Europe are found in the Nordic countries—Sweden, Denmark, Norway—as well as the United Kingdom and Spain. These countries have a relative economic advantage over the remainder, which are dominated by fifty-year-olds and older: Switzerland, France, Italy, the Netherlands, Germany and Finland.

Japan

Japan has the oldest population in the world—one of its many current problems. It also has the highest life expectancy, and birth rates are very low. Japanese birth rates are only 10 children per 1,000 population, compared with 14.6 in the United States and 12.4 in Canada. In the year 2000, 16.5 percent of the Japanese population will be over the age of sixty-five, compared with 12.4 percent in the U.S., 12.6 percent in Canada and 14.6 percent in Europe. By the year 2050, almost one-third of the Japanese population will be over sixty-five. There are now fewer people in Japan under the age of eighteen than there are over the age of sixty-five. In the United States, the ratio is two to one, and in Canada it is just under two to one.

The Japanese economy began to turn down in 1989, when the stock market bubble burst. The Japanese stock market, which had been fuelled by very cheap credit and raging real estate prices, peaked in 1989 at 39,000. It subsequently fell by almost 60 percent, and remained mired at the near bottom until early 1999. The economy moved into a deep deflationary recession in 1998 and only now looks like it is coming out of it. Significant policy mistakes have exacerbated the situation, a consumption tax hike in 1997. So have the rapidly aging population, low consumer and business confidence that leads to an excessive rate of saving, an insolvent banking system and an overbearing government bureaucracy that overregulates and interferes with market forces. Once an economic powerhouse and competitive giant, Japan fell to the weakest position in the G7. Bankruptcies surged and unemployment rose, obliterating their system of lifetime employment despite repeated efforts by the fiscal and monetary authorities to stimulate the economy. The jobless rate in Japan today is well above that in the United States for the first time in the modern era.

The Japanese banks, once the largest in the world, have long been overextended, with bad loans and bad stock investments. Many were insolvent. The government is in the process of a major bailout and restructuring plan. These banks were formerly the primary source of funding for emerging Asia and Russia. Now they have pulled in their horns, leading to a credit crunch. Evidence suggests that the rest of the region is making a comeback; Korea has already rebounded, and while the Japanese economy will also rebound, Japan faces unique demographic problems.

The Demographic Advantage of the U.S. and Canada

Japan, Germany, France and Italy have rapidly aging populations that are not replacing themselves. This will be a drain on fiscal resources and will slow economic activity. They will experience a contraction in the labour force—not just a slowing in the growth of the labour force, as in the U.S. and Canada—which means that only increased productivity and/or net in-migration of workers will allow growth to continue. Germany, France and Italy, in a misguided policy, discourage the in-migration of workers, thinking that immigrants increase the domestic jobless rate. The European Monetary Union will help spur capital flow and human capital shifts from the younger European countries to the older ones; however, language and other barriers will make this a slow and difficult process.

Japan, on the other hand, has an old and aging population with no immediate solution on the horizon. This helps to explain why private-sector economic activity has been so weak, even in the face of extraordinary fiscal stimulus and record-low interest rates. A major influx of young immigrants would help, but Japan has long been a very insular society, discriminating against and discouraging outsiders. This may well be the key to their downfall: the homogeneity of the population has discouraged out-of-the-box thinking. A substantial change in immigration policy, both politically and socially, is needed to infuse the society with young, aggressive new blood. This is not likely in the near future.

Among the developed nations, the United States and Canada have a huge competitive advantage. Our population is aging but not aged, education levels are high and the work ethic is strong. For example, the average hours worked in manufacturing is forty-two hours per week in the United States and thirty-eight hours in Canada, compared with thirty-five in France and Italy. In addition, there are a large number of youth under the age of eighteen coming up behind the Boomers, particularly in the United States. Moreover, the U.S. birth rate is forecasted to remain high and even to rise.

As the Boomers move through their peak spending and earning years, they will drive economic growth. The growth of the labour force, however, peaked in the early eighties and will continue to edge downward through 2020 in both the U.S. and Canada. This will continue to mitigate inflation pressure and ensure that interest rates ultimately fall even further, to levels not seen since the fifties and sixties. The Boomers will save somewhat more, as the bulk move into their forties and beyond. Net wealth accumulation will likely continue well after their mid-sixties, as retirement age and life expectancy rises. This is a positive harbinger for financial asset values—stocks and bonds.

The U.S. and Canada will be net exporters of capital to the developing world. We will also be net exporters of the goods and services demanded by these rapidly growing consumer markets. The real opportunity for the U.S. and Canada will be to provide the infrastructure, consumer durable goods and technology for the rapidly growing countries of Europe and the emerging world.

Part 4

A New Economic Paradigm

The Great Savings Shortfall

Today's Boomers have the lowest savings rates on record. This is true in both Canada and the United States. In many ways, we have not saved for a rainy day because we have not felt we needed to. Access to credit is easier than ever before. Just as the fifties boom in car sales was fuelled when car companies lengthened the credit period on financing new cars from twenty-four to thirty-six months, so the decline in personal savings in recent years might in part be a reflection of the ease of borrowing. Fifteen years ago, for example, it was not easy to get a second mortgage on your home; today, home-equity loans can be arranged in a matter of hours. Some are even recommending that you mortgage your house to buy stocks. Credit cards too are a lot easier to get than they used to be. In the past decade there has been ferocious competition among financial institutions to lend to lower-tier borrowers, particularly in the United States. Virtually anyone can get a credit card today. Personal bankruptcies have become more common, are easier to declare and are tarred with less social stigma than in the past.

Are these low savings rates reflective of a generation of profligate spendthrifts, hell-bent on living for today and forgetting about tomorrow? I don't think so. Yes, it is true that Boomers will never have the frugal mind-set of their parents, but they are not irresponsible either. The fact is, it is a lot harder to save money today than it was for the Matures.

The Great Economic Slowdown— An Income Problem

Family income swelled in the fifties and sixties, the last upwave in the long economic cycle. The real purchasing power of households surged, up about 4 percent annually in the U.S. and a whopping 5 percent in Canada. This was typically with only one income in the family. Canada was a global growth leader, and living standards improved to show it. Boomers grew up in these good times. Personal savings rates in Canada averaged 5 percent in the 1960s, compared to 7.5 percent in the U.S.

Fast-forward forty years. Savings rates in Canada today are a mere 1 percent, and they have touched negative territory in the U.S. What happened? The downwave happened. Beginning in the mid-seventies, the average annual growth in real after-tax family income ratcheted downward. Compared with 5 percent in Canada and 4 percent in the U.S. before 1974, it has fallen to only 2.6 percent ever since. In the U.S., family purchasing power is on an up-trend once again as we begin the new upwave; but in Canada there is no sign of a turnaround yet. Any gain in household income in Canada in the nineties has been eaten up by an ever-increasing tax bite. Compound this with the long-term decline in our currency and you see why Canadian living standards are falling.

What is particularly disturbing and surprising about this slowdown in the growth of family purchasing power is that it has occurred despite the tidal wave of women entering the labour force. Almost half the labour force today are women. By 1985 the majority of households had two incomes and still the growth of after-tax real family income slowed. This very slowdown helps to explain why so many mothers with young children continued working over the past twenty-plus years. A 1994 Angus Reid Group national survey found that almost half of all working mothers agreed that, if they could afford to, they would stay home with their children. The same survey found that two-thirds of all Canadian adults believed that it is not possible to support a family on one income.

What Changed?

The fifties and sixties was a period of rapid growth. Most importantly, it was a period of mass consumerism, fuelled by the baby boom. Global demand for Canadian agricultural and natural resource products was strong. Inflation was low, productivity was high and real wages continued to rise. The tide began to turn in the mid-sixties when President Lyndon Johnson cut taxes, but still attempted to finance the Vietnam War and the Great Society social programs. He believed he could fight a land war in Asia and, at the same time, pursue the domestic spending programs of the Great Society war on poverty. This "guns and butter" deficit spending led to the first serious inflation threat in the post-1951 period. Vietnam continued to drain American resources until Nixon ended U.S. military participation in the war in 1973. The downwave in the long cycle is often preceded by an unpopular war, and this time was no different.

Despite the winding-down of the military commitment in Vietnam, inflation continued to mount. The OPEC-induced oil price shock of October 1973 caused the deep 1973–75 recession, touching off a prolonged period of stagnation and inflation, known at the time as stagflation. In 1979 the gasoline lines were back in the U.S. with the second oil crisis, and inflation surged to double-digit levels. The Federal Reserve responded by raising interest rates. From late 1979 to 1982, Paul Volcker, the Fed Chairman, moved the overnight federal funds rate—the rate of interest banks pay each other to borrow money overnight—up from 12 percent to an unprecedented 19 percent. All interest rates ratcheted higher. Mortgage rates in Canada peaked at a whopping 22 percent in 1981. The economy moved into the 1981–82 recession.

Household income did not keep pace with the inflation of the seventies and early eighties. Furthermore, over this same period, job growth in both Canada and the U.S. shifted away from the higher-paying industrial sectors like mining, construction, transportation, manufacturing and wholesale trade to lower-paying service sectors. Economic restructuring, especially after the 1981–82 recession, eliminated many high-paying, low-skill jobs. Restructuring also spelled the end of many middle-management jobs and meant early retirement for more expensive workers aged fifty and over. The shift to outsourcing also began, eliminating whole departments in big businesses in favour of purchasing goods and services from cheaper sources outside. Businesses relied increasingly on part-time and temporary workers, giving them more flexibility to adjust payrolls quickly, thus significantly reducing the costs of providing employee benefits.

Wanted: Incentives to Invest

This economic restructuring—economizing on labour costs—continues today. As businesses face mounting global competitive pressures, increased by Internet commerce, their profit margins are squeezed. Most cannot raise prices without losing market share, so they must reduce costs. For most businesses, labour is two-thirds of the cost of production, so that is where cuts are made. Savings are achieved by automating, investing in technology that can replace people: automatic teller machines, computer-voice telephone "operators," self-serve gas stations and the like. They also reduce labour costs by shipping low-skill jobs to places where labour is cheap—such as Mexico, China and India.

With low profit margins, firms look for larger and larger markets to increase revenues. They go global. Many are merging to take advantage of synergies, tap global capabilities, increase capital and spread their costs over a much larger revenue base. This inevitably means layoffs—redundant labour is hived off.

High-paying muscle jobs are a dying breed in the U.S. and Canada. If your job can be done by computer, watch out: you are on the endangered species list. Over the past twenty years, high-paying, low-skill muscle jobs have been either automated out of existence or shipped off to cheaper foreign locales. The only sector of the labour force that has enjoyed substantial real-income growth in the past twenty years has been knowledge workers—those highly skilled technical and professional people who are in the highest quintile of real average household income.

In Canada, even this group has not gained meaningfully because it has been disproportionately burdened by the dramatic rise in tax rates since 1980. While this means that income distribution in Canada is more equal, and some would say more fair, it has cost us dearly. It means that there is less incentive in Canada for excellence, for entrepreneurial spirit, for risk taking, for innovation. It means that many of our best and brightest leave for the rosier pastures south of the border, where if you win, you can keep more of your winnings; if you succeed, you can bear more of the fruits of your success. Like it or not, it is human nature to want to hold on to what you have worked for. The Communist systems discovered this truth by denying it. No incentives meant no innovation, no entrepreneurial spirit and ultimately the collapse of the system. While Canadians are willing to pay somewhat higher taxes for health care, safe cities and good schools, we have gone too far. The tax burden has become too great— both in absolute terms and relative to the U.S.—and the currency has fallen too far. Our most talented labour is our most mobile labour. Our capital is mobile too. Canadians are sending record amounts of capital outside the country, and for good reason: to maximize their rate of return.

Debt Binge

Boomer households did what they could to maintain living standards. Women stayed in jobs even after their babies were born. The average family size declined; gone were the booming fifties-style birth rates, peaking at 3.7 children per household in Canada in 1957. But that wasn't enough. Households went increasingly into debt.

The surge in house prices and interest rates in the late seventies and early eighties made it more difficult to make ends meet. So did rising inflation. Borrowing surged, hitting record levels by the late eighties. In the U.S., household debt ratios—debt as a percentage of financial assets—peaked at 31 percent in 1980 and have edged down ever since. In Canada, on the other hand, debt ratios remain high, currently standing at 57 percent. No wonder Canadian households have trouble saving money. The good news is that interest rates have declined dramatically since 1982, making it easier to service all of this debt.

Canadian families have been especially hard hit because of rising taxes and a falling dollar. All measures of economic well-being have deteriorated since the mid-seventies. We have underperformed in the jobs market and in overall economic growth, as well as in the currency and stock markets relative to the U.S.

Savings Rates Plunge

In both countries we have seen a significant decline in household savings rates. The standard-measure—which subtracts consumer spending from personal income after tax—has fallen to only 1 percent in Canada and has dipped into negative territory in the U.S. These figures are distorted on the low side, however, because of huge gains in the stock market, especially in the U.S. The capital gains tax payments are subtracted from income when calculating the savings rate, while the gains themselves are not included. An alternative measure of the savings rate—the flow-of-funds measure—looks at the net change in household wealth. Thanks to the surge in U.S. stock prices, the flow-of-funds savings rate in the U.S. is a whopping 41 percent, compared with only 5 percent in Canada.

Savings rates are likely to rise as Boomers move through their peak earning years. Typically, after about the age of forty-five or so, income begins to rise faster than expenses. When that happens, families begin to pay down debt and accumulate wealth. This generally continues for twenty years or more.

The awareness level is rising for many. The great wake-up call that it is time to start saving will soon be heard loud and clear. We recognize that government cannot take care of us in our old age. Job security is a thing of the past. Therefore, more and more people will need to save for their own retirement. We will discuss how to do this in greater detail in the final section of this book.

Good News—The Upwave

Good news is coming. We are in the early days of a long-cycle upwave, already evident in the United States. Family income growth will start to rise and remain on an up-trend for years to come. This will be the result of the technology revolution, the end of the Cold War, a productivity-induced continued moderate level of inflation, and positive further appreciation in stock prices. Many will share in the prosperity as we take advantage of the plethora of training and educational opportunities out there to prepare us for the high-skilled jobs of the twenty-first century. Fasten your seat belts, there will be a good deal of volatility—and come along for a spectacular ride.

The End of the Millennium— A New Economic Paradigm

The 1990s has been a period of massive economic transition and contradiction in Canada. We opened the decade with the strongest Canadian dollar in years, thanks to the high-interest-rate policies of John Crow, the former Governor of the Bank of Canada, only to close the decade at near record-low levels. We moved from inflation to deflation, as did most of the global economy—taking our inflation rates down to levels well below the U.S. for much of the decade. We recovered from the worst postwar recession in history, yet the unemployment rate remained disturbingly high. We freed trade and eliminated some of the more interventionist anti-business policies of the Trudeau era, only to languish in economic malaise in our resource sector and to become ever more uncompetitive in our manufacturing base. We emerged victorious in our battle against budgetary deficits and inflation, yet the world granted us no kudos. Our dollar still declined, taking living standards with it.

The price for budget surpluses was ever higher taxes, a health care system that seemed to be fraying at the edges, and continued unrest in the schools and universities. Increasing numbers of our best and brightest were leaving the country. Those who stayed felt they might soon be out of work. Our stock market failed to share in the American and European equity boom. We watched CNN and CNBC, telling us daily about the exuberance in stocks, the creation of household wealth, and wondered why we hadn't been invited to this party. In mid-decade

Quebeckers again voted no to sovereignty, yet the PQ government reigned victorious at the end of the decade. While we know things are better than they were during the recession, we sense that things are still not as they should be. We are right.

In dramatic contrast, the United States is booming. The U.S. is in its ninth year of economic expansion. The unemployment rate is at its lowest level in thirty years; so is the crime rate; so are the welfare rolls. Many indications point to a return to more traditional family values. Divorce rates are down and the labour force participation rate of women has peaked. The number of two-parent families began to stabilize in the nineties, according to the U.S. Census Bureau. The percentage of children living in single-parent families doubled from 1970 to 1990, but in the nineties it rose only slightly. In part, the slowdown occurred because the divorce rate dropped to 4.3 per 1,000 people in 1997 from 4.7 in 1990 and 5.0 in 1985.

The epidemic of out-of-wedlock births has slowed. After rising steadily through the eighties, the birth rate for unmarried women in the United States has stabilized. From 1994 to 1996, the rate fell 4 percent to 44.8 births per 1,000 unmarried women. For white women, the rate edged up in 1996; for Hispanics, it edged down. The real change has come in the black community. The rate of births for unmarried black women has dropped significantly and has now reached its lowest level since the government began recording the data in 1969.

Teen pregnancies are down as well. Since 1990, the overall teen birth rate in the United States has dropped almost 9 percent. Among black teenage girls, the drop has been far more dramatic, almost 19 percent. At the same time, the abortion rate has fallen to its lowest level since 1975.

Outside the family, there are other good signs that the magic of economic prosperity is doing its job in the United States. The murder rate fell 9 percent in 1997. The violent-crime rate fell 5 percent. Some of this improvement might be demographic, reflecting the aging of the population and the fact that younger people commit most of the crimes. Crime rates in Canada are down as well. The national homicide rate in this country fell in 1997 to its lowest level since 1969. The incidents of violent crime declined as well, for the fifth consecutive year.

Many would be surprised to know that New York City is now considered the safest large city (population over 1 million) in the United States. Over the past four years, as the city's economy has boomed, it has boasted the biggest sustained decrease in crime of any city in the United States. The murder rate was down 22 percent, compared with 9 percent for the U.S. and Canada nationwide, and the violent-crime rate was down 6 percent, compared with a 5 percent dip for the U.S. and 1 percent in Canada. Mayor Rudolph Giuliani, of course, takes full credit for this, while the demographics might explain much of it; but statistics for teenagers and young adults suggest that the buoyancy of the U.S. economy had a meaningful role to play as well.

The decline in the teen and unmarried women birth rates, especially in the black community, helped to reduce the numbers on welfare. Teen crime rates are down and the U.S. high school dropout rate also fell in the nineties: it stood at 12.8 percent of the eighteen- to-twenty-four-year-old population in 1996, down from 13.6 percent in 1990.

The long U.S. economic expansion has taken the unemployment rate down precipitously, and major state-by-state tax and training incentives have been created to move people off welfare and into the labour force. The proportion of people on welfare has fallen to a near thirty-year low. The unemployment rate for high school dropouts over the age of twenty-five has declined sharply, from 11.6 percent at the end of 1992 to 6.6 percent in mid-1999, adding to the downturn in the crime rates.

The shift to family values in the nineties may well be a reflection of the maturing Boomers. They have shifted from their wanton ways; stable middle age has set in. But the economic buoyancy in the U.S. has certainly helped. Jobs are easy to get. The unemployment rate for university graduates is around 2 percent, and just over 4 percent for the labour force as a whole. Even with record layoffs and restructuring, labour shortages are evident everywhere and wage rates are rising. Surprisingly to many, consumer price inflation has remained muted, even with the springtime commodity-induced rise, and prices continue to fall in many sectors. Consumer confidence is near record highs, household wealth has been surging, the housing market is booming and debt servicing costs are very low, even with the 1999 rise in interest rates.

Business confidence, though off its peak, is still very strong. The American economy has been ranked, once again, as the most competitive in the world by a prestigious independent think-tank in Switzerland. Without doubt, the U.S. is the global leader in the technology revolution, and it leads in other areas as well: financial services, retailing, entertainment and advertising, to name a few. Capital is cheap and reasonably easy to get. Mammoth investments in technology have dramatically increased industrial capacity, mitigating the potential for supply bottlenecks despite continued strong growth. Price competition is intense, labour costs are rising moderately, yet corporate earnings continue to surprise on the upside.

Why is the U.S. doing so well in comparison with Canada? Why are labour markets so much tighter, jobs so much easier to get, the currency so much stronger, the rise in the stock market and wealth accumulation so much greater? Does it have to be this way? I think not. Canada too could be a growth leader in the global economy. After all, we once were—for the thirty years following World War II. The resource industry will not pave the way to prosperity as it did then, at least not in the traditional way; but technology-driven resources might help. As we discussed earlier, bioengineered resources, high-tech mining and forestry, genetically engineered agricultural, fish and livestock production, biofuels—all could be areas of strong competitive advantage.

Today, however, the Canadian government continues too often to prop up declining industries, standing in the way of creative destruction—subsidizing depleted fisheries and decrepit mines and pulp mills. Instead, precious government money should go to education and training in the global growth areas of the future—information and communications technology, biotech, pharmaceuticals and knowledge-based services—encouraging business to get more involved in the education process. Some of this is happening, and we will devote a chapter to these good-news stories, but more can and should be done. We have underperformed in the technology sectors, particularly given the resources we already devote to education; only 14 percent of our manufacturing sector is high-tech, compared with 35 percent in the U.S. In *Business Week*'s 1998 list of the top one hundred technology companies in the world, only two were Canadian. We are making strides in this area, but much more must be done.

The incentive structure is all wrong in this country. We have been burdened by excessive taxes. Profit is seen as a dirty word. This sentiment is inculcated into the population by the schools, the media and the government. It is a part of the Canadian psyche, which seeks to dramatically differentiate itself from the American mind-set. It is as if companies that are profitable are suspect, as if they have ripped someone off, as if unprofitable companies could create jobs. Nowhere was this more evident than during the bank-merger debate.

Canadians are not sufficiently encouraged to take risks—risks that create businesses, risks that provide capital for start-up operations and economic innovation. In the U.S. today, the capital gains tax rate is 20 percent, and there is talk of reducing it. In Canada, the top rate is nearly double that, about 38 percent, and it is anathema even to discuss a reduction; a cut is seen as a boon to the rich. Since 1980, the tax gap between Canada and the U.S. has widened sharply. Canadians' tax burden is a disincentive to entrepreneurial spirit, but more than that, it has markedly reduced our standard of living, our economic well-being, in absolute terms and relative to our American neighbours.

While the U.S. is ranked number one in competitiveness, we are ranked number ten. Productivity growth has lagged since 1979, as Canadian companies rely on an ever-declining dollar to make their products appear competitive outside the country. We have not, however, invested sufficiently in the information economy. Despite recent improvements, our labour markets are still more rigid, our labour still less mobile, our government still too interventionist.

I am optimistic, however. I do believe there is growing grassroots support for change. There are actions we could take, should take, to alleviate the roadblocks to progress. I will delineate these in a later chapter, but first let's look at where we are today.

The Great Divide: Taxes

As we have seen, the great divide between Canadian and U.S.–U.K. policy widened dramatically in the early eighties with the left-wing government of Pierre Trudeau and the right-wing governments of Ronald Reagan and Margaret Thatcher. While they were busy cutting taxes, privatizing, deregulating, limiting union power and creating a pro-business environment, we were busy doing the opposite. The Mulroney government attempted to improve the business environment by eliminating FIRA and the NEP, as well as by signing the free trade agreement with the U.S. and then NAFTA, but there was still one gigantic difference: taxes.

While they cut taxes, we increased them, not just federally but provincially too. "Temporary" income surtaxes were introduced in 1985 and increased repeatedly. The government eliminated the indexation of tax brackets and personal exemptions for levels of inflation less than 3 percent in 1986; this led to so-called "bracket creep," insidiously increasing taxes by bumping people into higher tax brackets as incomes rise owing to moderate inflation. A C.D. Howe Institute report concludes that the average Canadian family is paying $1,000 more each year in income taxes than they did a decade ago on the basis of this hidden tax grab alone. As taxes increased, personal debt levels in Canada grew faster than in any other G7 country.

Even with Finance Minister Paul Martin's 1998 increase in the personal exemption, Canada still has one of the lowest tax starts in the industrial world. The income level at which citizens begin to be taxed is $6,956 for low-income Canadians. The figure is about $10,500 in the U.S. and $10,200 in the U.K., and even higher in most other countries.

Many personal deductions were systematically removed. Capital gains tax rates were hiked by raising the proportion of the gain that was taxable at ordinary-income rates from 50 percent to 66.7 percent in 1987, and then to 75 percent in 1990. Furthermore, the lifetime exemption on the first $100,000 in capital gains was expunged in 1994. According to the Canadian Taxpayers Federation, this has hurt far more than the rich: nearly 60 percent of the 800,000 Canadians who reported a capital gain on their 1997 tax returns earned less than $50,000 that year.

Payroll taxes have been bumped up considerably as well. Over the years, CPP contributions and Employment Insurance (EI, formerly Unemployment Insurance) premiums have risen steadily. Mr. Martin's recent reduction in EI premiums is minor in comparison with the hike in CPP contributions in 1999. Indeed, the single largest tax hike in history is the CPP contribution rise, slated to leap to 9.9 percent of contributory earnings by the year 2003, up 90 percent from 1994.

Sales taxes and excise taxes were hiked repeatedly, and in 1991 the GST was introduced, applying sales taxes to services for the first time. So, for example, sales taxes (GST plus provincial tax) are 15 percent in Ontario and only 8 percent in New York State, where they apply only to some goods and no services.

Adding further to the tax burden was the dramatic rise in most provincial tax rates. For example, residents of Ontario were hit with sixty-five different tax increases between 1985 and 1995. Over the same period, the ratio of tax revenues to GDP in Ontario alone jumped from under 14 percent to 16 percent, and the province's personal tax rate went from 48 percent to 58 percent of the federal rate. Tax rates increased sharply in Quebec and British Columbia as well.

Corporate tax rates are also very high. Our top corporate tax rate of 44.6 percent was, at the end of 1998, second only to Japan's 48 percent, the highest in the world until Japan cut rates in 1999. Now ours is the highest, well above the top rate of 40 percent in the U.S. and 30 percent in the U.K. While business tax credits reduce our effective tax rates, Canadian corporate tax revenue as a percentage of corporate profits is meaningfully higher than in the U.S. Moreover, many of the tax credits are biased towards resource and old-line manufacturing companies.

For the country as a whole, the tax-to-GDP ratio has risen from 36 percent in 1980 to 44 percent today. This compares with 32 percent in the United States. Canada has some of the highest rates of income tax and profit tax in the industrialized world as a percentage of GDP. We also top the list in paying the steepest property taxes. A 1999 article in the *Financial Post Magazine*, called *Taxed to Death*, found that "when you take into account all of the increases in personal income tax, goods and services, and property and hidden taxes, Canadians now work six months of the year to fill the government's coffers, a 55-day jump since 1961."

Canada in the Nineties—Disappointing Underperformance

We entered the nineties with extremely high interest rates as John Crow, then Governor of the Bank of Canada, attempted to eliminate inflationary pressure. At one point, our short-term interest rates were six hundred basis points—six full percentage points—above those in the United States. The Canadian dollar, temporarily reversing its long-term decline, surged to above 85 cents U.S. and our trade surplus plummeted. This was the period of extensive cross-border shopping—north to south. The economy slowed under the weight of this and inflation plunged.

Around the world, the Cold War was ending. Between 1985 and 1991, Soviet president Mikhail Gorbachev implemented a program of political and economic reform called *perestroika*—meaning "restructuring" in Russian. This was closely linked to his concept of *glasnost*, or openness and democratization. The forces of change led to the breakdown of the Communist system and the dissolution of the USSR in 1991. The Soviet satellite system in Eastern Europe underwent a collapse, the highlight of which was the opening of the Berlin Wall in late 1989. East and West Germany were united in 1990. Communism was on the decline everywhere. Even the murder of democracy protestors in Tiananmen Square in June 1989 did not stop the move to a market-oriented economy in China. These developments had a profound effect on the global economy, increasing competitive pressures worldwide and adding 1.7 billion people to the free marketplace—potential customers, low-cost labourers and producers.

Iraq invaded Kuwait in August 1990, precipitating the Gulf War, which was an amazing show of unity among Middle Eastern and Western nations. Oil prices temporarily surged. In a momentous political error, riding on the heels of his Gulf War popularity, U.S. president George Bush cut government spending and raised taxes, despite his "read my lips" election promise never to do so. These actions ultimately contributed to the budget surplus in 1998, but they rang the death knell for his political future. The economy slowed sharply, contributing to the 1990–91 recession in the U.S.

The slowdown in the U.S. took a weakened Canada with it. As the U.S. sneezed, Canada caught a major bout of flu. The 1990 recession was very mild by historical standards for the United States, but for Canada it was virulent, deep and long. Already weakened by sky-high interest rates and a very strong dollar—stronger than our level of productivity growth would warrant—our economy nose-dived in April 1990 and remained in recession until November 1992, one year after the start of the U.S. recovery. The unemployment rate surged to a high of 11.9 percent and Tory leader Kim Campbell, in her ill-fated 1993 election campaign, suggested that double-digit unemployment was our fate for the indefinite future. Not surprisingly, the Liberals, under the leadership of Jean Chrétien, won in a landslide defeat of the Tories.

The economy recovered over the next few years, but the pace of progress was frustratingly slow. The real success of the Chrétien government was the commitment of Finance Minister Paul Martin to eliminate the federal budget deficit. Through a combination of tax increases (many of which were introduced earlier by the Mulroney government), program spending cuts and reduced transfers to the provinces, they turned budgetary red ink black. They started the process of paying down the debt. This tightening of fiscal policy took its toll on the economy, but the price, in large measure, was worth paying.

The Bank of Canada was able to offset some of the pain by easing monetary policy—reducing interest rates. Indeed, for a stretch of time ending with the mid-1998 dive of our dollar, Canadian interest rates were meaningfully below those in the U.S. This reduced public interest charges on the debt, augmenting the move to a budgetary surplus. Canadian inflation had fallen well below U.S. levels, and for a while we were making more progress than the Americans on the budget front. That changed in 1998 as U.S. inflation fell to rates approaching ours and—thanks to strong growth, a booming stock market and the Bush initiatives to balance the budget—they posted a very large budgetary surplus.

Our economy gradually began to pick up steam. We were boosted at first solely by the strength in the U.S., which created a huge demand for our exports. Our trade surplus surged through most of the mid-nineties, as auto, lumber, oil and gas, and other resource exports to the

United States hit record highs. However, our domestic economy remained weak at first, keeping the lid on imports. The financial markets breathed a sigh of relief in October 1995 when Quebeckers narrowly defeated the referendum on sovereignty, and by the second half of 1996 the domestic economy was coming back. We were well on our way to outpacing American growth in 1997 when the Asian crisis caused a dramatic slide in commodity prices as Asian economic activity crashed. Canadian commodity producers were hit hard, especially those in British Columbia, where trade with the Pacific Rim represented 35 percent of exports. The return of Hong Kong to Chinese rule and the wealth losses of many Asians living in Vancouver compounded B.C.'s problems. The housing market and retail sales slowed. British Columbia moved into recession, or close to it.

The fall in commodity prices, which accelerated in 1998, helped to take the Canadian dollar down further. But other factors added to the weakness, most notably the ill-timed comments by the Bank of Canada that they would not raise interest rates. At the time, Canadian interest rates were below those in the U.S. International investors, concerned about Bank of Canada credibility and continued political uncertainty in Quebec, decided it was too risky to hold Canadian dollars. This trend was exacerbated by the extension of the Asian crisis to Russia. When Russia defaulted on its debt in August 1998, investors everywhere fled to the safe haven of U.S. government Treasury bills and bonds, leaving the Canadian market in the lurch. Our currency nosedived, not just with respect to the greenback but relative to literally all of the world's major currencies.

This took an enormous toll on Canadian living standards, a toll that was compounded by our inordinate tax burden and relative weakness in economic growth. We can see vivid evidence of our decline around the country. Canadians are unable to contribute fully to their RRSPs. The most popular car in Canada is the Honda Accord, 25 percent cheaper than the Toyota Camry, the best-selling car in the U.S. Income per capita after tax is so much lower in Canada than in the U.S. that we can only attract the budget U.S. retailers like Wal-Mart and Home Depot, not the upscale merchandisers like Neiman Marcus, Nordstrom or Bloomingdale's, even though they could buy Eaton's for a song. We have become a polyester nation, unable to afford cashmere and pearls. People don't like to hear this. Some might want to shoot the messenger, but it doesn't have to be this way.

The Canadian dollar retraced some of its loss with the signs in 1999 of a rebound in Asia and the resulting rise in some commodity prices. Oil, copper, nickel, lumber and aluminum prices rose in the first half of 1999, taking oil, forest products and metals stocks up with them. Gold prices continued weak as the U.K. announced huge gold sales, to be followed by the IMF and maybe Switzerland. The Bank of Canada cut interest rates twice in the first half of 1999 to offset the dampening effects on economic activity of the rising currency. Intermittent U.S. inflation fear limits the degree of further rate cuts over the near term. Canadian interest rates, once again, fell below those in the U.S.

The U.S. in the Nineties—Tremendous Outperformance

The 1990s was a period of economic dominance for the United States. The growth leader in the industrialized world, the U.S. has enjoyed its longest economic expansion in the postwar period. This goes a long way towards explaining why President Bill Clinton, elected in 1992, enjoyed such a high approval rating despite his many travails; his campaign mantra was correct—"it is the economy, stupid."

Remarkably, despite the late stage of this U.S. expansion and the surprising strength of the economy, any sign of a rise in the general level of inflation didn't surface until the April 1999 CPI report. The bond market was already spooked by the earlier rise in some commodity prices. But none of the typical supply-side constraints of the past were evident. The bottlenecking, vendor delivery delays and unfilled orders that previously caused inflation pressure to rise were hardly visible. Instead, businesses had invested extensively in technology, increasing industrial capacity by an average of 4.0 percent per year since the end of the recession in 1991. Contrary to historical experience at the late stage of a business cycle, capacity utilization rates were much lower than normal and so was inflation. Indeed, around the world, the prevailing concern was excess supply, not excess demand. For example, there is roughly 35 percent overcapacity in auto production worldwide. The globe is awash in oil reserves (the early 1999 price gains notwithstanding) and gold and copper supply continues to exceed demand.

Even with the mid-1999 uptick, inflation in the U.S. remained relatively moderate and it has trended downward virtually everywhere else in the industrialized world. Canadian inflation in its broadest measure, the GDP deflator, has been running at less than a 1 percent annual rate. Non-oil import prices in the U.S. are down roughly 2 percent in the past year owing to 1998 currency devaluation in Asia and elsewhere; this increased competitive pressures for domestic producers of import-competing products. Many businesses continue to report they have little pricing power. If they were to raise prices, they would lose market share and subsequently be forced to roll them back. As an example, prices in the U.S. for domestically produced cars were reduced 1 percent for the 1999 model year from the 1998 listings, and financing incentives were offered to boot. This is not an isolated phenomenon, as the price of U.S. durable goods fell 0.5 percent in 1998. Wholesale prices are edging moderately higher, having fallen precipitously in recent years, and there is little underlying price pressure in the pipeline. The rise in oil and base metals prices has raised the headline consumer price index (CPI) figures, at least temporarily. U.S. core inflation—the CPI excluding the volatile food and energy sector—has remained stable at just over 2 percent. The Federal Reserve raised interest rates in the summer as early signs of rising inflation continued to mount. Immense global competitive pressure is likely to keep any 1970s-style inflationary process at bay, especially given the intense price cutting on the Internet.

A New Economic Paradigm

The real surprise on the inflation front has been the breakdown in the traditional relationship between tight labour markets and rising inflation. The unemployment rate in the U.S. long ago fell below levels formerly thought by economists to cause inflation pressure to grow.

Economists believed that as labour became scarce and job vacancies mounted, companies would increase wages to keep workers and to bid them away from other companies. This, in turn, would reduce corporate profits unless they passed the cost along to the consumer in the form of higher prices. In this way, low unemployment led to inflation.

Instead, the nineties expansion was very different. Almost no one believed that the 4 percent real GDP growth of the last three years would go hand in hand with lower inflation. Unemployment rates in the U.S. fell to very low levels, and there are labour shortages in many regions and many industries and sectors. Not only is the jobless rate low, but the participation rate—the percentage of the population in the labour force—is at a record high. Never before has such a large proportion of the adult population been working. Many who exited the labour market—such as retirees—are returning to work because jobs are so easy to get. It is a seller's market. Companies are so desperate for help that they are willing to negotiate such things as hours, benefits, signing bonuses, job location (telecommuting from homc) and job sharing.

Wages are rising, but not excessively. They are up about 3.6 percent over the year ending mid-1999, and their gain actually started to slow in late 1998. These wage trends flatly contradict the concerns and predictions of traditional economists. How could anyone argue that the unemployment rate was so low that it was threatening inflation at the same time that wage increases were slowing? Workers don't demand excessive wage increases when they feel little job security. Ironically, even with the tightest labour markets in years and strong economic growth, layoffs are still high. Why? Because business continues to restructure and downsize in a rapidly changing world. Merger activity remains strong, and churning in the labour market is a reflection of the powerful forces of creative destruction in a buoyant and innovating economy. Furthermore, even these modest wage gains have in large measure not been passed on to the consumer. Many American businesses would lose customers to the competition, both domestic and foreign, if they were to increase prices.

The other very positive development on the inflation front has been the surge in U.S. productivity—output per worker. Economy-wide productivity growth at the end of 1998 was the strongest in six years and it was strong in early 1999. Rather than a flash in the pan, the data suggest that trend productivity growth is rising, as the three-year gain is also on an upward trend. The rising course of productivity is largely a reflection of the substantial improvements in technology; rote, repetitive, left-brain tasks can be done by computer. Efficiency improves. People and businesses can purchase, communicate and research on the Internet in a fraction of the time and cost. Biotechnology is increasing food and resource supplies and reducing the costs of production there too. It takes fewer people to produce the traditional goods and services, freeing knowledge workers to broadly increase the volume and array of economic product.

Unit labour costs in the U.S.—wages per unit of output produced—actually fell in the fourth quarter of 1998, at a 0.4 percent annualized rate. This lowered the 1998 rise in unit labour costs to a two-year low of only 2.0 percent. With productivity rising, businesses can afford to raise wages without passing the cost on to anyone. As labour becomes more productive—as it produces more for the same hours worked—there are greater profits to pass around. Real wages—wages after inflation—are rising in the U.S., increasing family living standards for all segments of society. Some people question how long this will last, particularly as those left unemployed today are generally relatively low-skilled, with relatively low productive potential. The surge in productivity at the end of 1998 and early in 1999 is unlikely to be repeated, but the trend growth for the next decade or more is likely to far surpass the weak productivity performance in the seventies and eighties downwave. Alan Greenspan has warned that the rate of growth of productivity cannot accelerate forever. Caution is warranted. Inflation pressures will mount intermittently; but the general pace of inflation will remain muted, in large measure thanks to the gains from computerization.

Canada—A Laggard

In direct contrast, Canadian productivity growth has significantly underperformed the U.S. and many other major industrialized countries. The record weakness in the Canadian dollar caused a sharp rise in import prices, up 4.6 percent in 1998. Canadian companies, therefore, have not felt the competitive pressure to restructure, reduce costs, increase productivity. Our manufacturers are not investing in technology and restructuring to the degree necessary to win in the global competitive race. Neither are our resource producers. All are hiding behind the relatively weak loonie.

The real loser is the Canadian consumer, forced to pay higher prices for imports, to cancel international travel plans, to tighten our belts ever further to make ends meet. We can't easily buy only Canadian-made products; orange juice, pineapple, bananas or most fresh fruits and vegetables in the winter are not produced in Canada. There is no Canadian substitute for Windows 98. If we were forced to stop buying these products, our standard of living would fall even further.

Also hurting Canadian household balance sheets is the underperformance of uncompetitive companies in our stock market, exacerbated by foreign fear of Canadian-dollar investments. Foreign investors have been burned before, buying Canadian stocks only to see the currency decline. Canadians themselves are sending huge volumes of capital outside the country; but no one can escape the damage that our underperformance inflicts on us. The government requires that we keep 80 percent of our pension money in Canadian investments—a major drag on our wealth as our stock market has provided relatively disappointing returns for almost twenty years.

Low Inflation is Likely

While actual declines in prices—deflation—may seem strange to Boomers and Xers, who lived through the inflationary periods of the seventies and eighties, figure 10.1 shows that periods of wholesale price deflation were not uncommon in the past, especially during periods of rapid technological innovation. We are certainly in such a period today.

Deflation does not have to be the scary thing it was in the 1930s, when demand plunged because of the government policy errors we discussed earlier. In the thirties, prices fell because of insufficient demand, as the unemployment rate surged to record highs. Look back instead to the deflation in the period following the U.S. Civil War—the industrial revolution in the U.S.—a deflation caused by technological advancements that dramatically increased productivity and lowered prices. As industry and transcontinental railways flourished, real GDP grew at a 4.3 percent annual rate in the U.S. between 1869 and 1898. Wholesale prices fell by roughly 50 percent over this period. Increased output and falling prices propelled demand, which was outrun by supply. Living standards surged, as real household income growth increased. That is the kind of deflation we see in many sectors today, driven by global excess supply, increasing competition and the declining cost of technology and production.

FIGURE 10.1

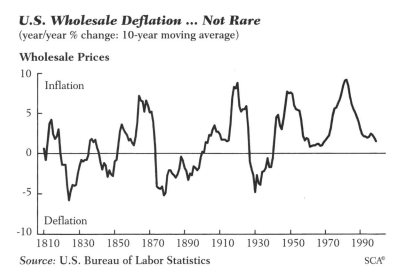

U.S. Wholesale Deflation ... Not Rare
(year/year % change: 10-year moving average)

Wholesale Prices

Source: U.S. Bureau of Labor Statistics   SCA©

Many sectors have long lived with deflation. Knowledge sectors are always prone to deflation because of the increasing returns to knowledge: the more you learn, the easier it is to learn and the greater the rate of return on learning. Since their inception, computers and the high-tech industry have experienced ongoing deflation. The product life cycle is very short, innovation is constant, obsolescence rapid. To be profitable, technology companies have to stay at the leading edge and garner sufficient sales of each new product to warrant the initial investment in research and development. These global competitive pressures mean that, if you are in a commodity business, you had better be the low-cost producer or figure out how you can add value to the product to differentiate it from your competitors'.

Even the prices of many basic retail products are falling because of new distribution channels through the Internet. Amazon.com has reduced the price of books and CDs. Sears has announced the formation of a new Web site to sell appliances at cut-rate prices and Safeway, a major U.S. supermarket chain, has done the same. Brokerage fees are falling, insurance commissions have been slashed; no business is immune.

The plunge in inflation was evident throughout the world. Central banks have become vigilant inflation fighters. The bond markets themselves built in huge inflation premiums in the form of high interest rates, much higher than current inflation rates would warrant. The traders in these markets remember having been burned in the past by unexpected surges in prices. These high real interest rates slowed economic growth and reduced inherent inflation pressure. Governments around the world are working hard to reduce budget deficits, and in some cases, like Canada, the U.S., the U.K., Ireland and Finland, they have succeeded. The end of the Cold War accelerated this deflationary process by reducing defence expenditures and opening the world to enhanced competition, in terms of both cheaper sources of abundant labour and materials, and broader consumer markets. The war in Kosovo, if it had lasted long enough, would have eliminated some of this peace dividend—a factor that made the markets very nervous in the spring of 1999.

Commodity prices plunged with the Asian crisis in 1997 and 1998. The demand for commodities fell sharply while the supply continued to grow. The Japanese economy—the second largest on the planet—moved into a deep recession, taking the rest of Asia with it. Japan is the largest single net importer of commodities, but non-Japan Asia, in total, is even more important. Moreover, commodity-producing nations like Indonesia, Russia, South Africa, Brazil and Venezuela were hit hard by the plunge in prices, and increased production in an attempt to earn foreign exchange. This exacerbated the commodity price decline. Some commodity prices are rising once again, as we mentioned earlier. Judging from the experience of the past two hundred years, these gains are likely to be short-lived. Real commodity prices have been in long-term decline since the War of 1812. Meaningful price spikes occurred during wars and the OPEC oil crises of 1973 and 1979, but that is it.

The traditional commodity sector is not where the future lies. The demand for commodity inputs in the production process is waning. As an example, look at the automobile, the new technology at the turn of the last century. Almost two-thirds of the value of a car was made up of commodities like steel, rubber, copper, lead and plastic. In contrast, only about 2 percent of the value of the personal computer comes from raw materials. The same is true today even in basic activities like construction and communication: proportionately, far less of the value added is in commodities. A shift in economic output from heavy-metal bashing industries to services and information technology means that any given increase in GDP produces a smaller increase in the demand for raw materials. Alan Greenspan recently commented that only "a small fraction" of global economic growth in the past several decades "represents growth in the tonnage of physical materials—oil, coal, ores, wood, and raw chemicals. The remainder represents new insights into how to rearrange those physical materials to better serve human needs."

As we discussed earlier, biotechnology is making enormous strides in re-engineering much of the agricultural and natural resource base in the world. In many instances, genetically altered or synthetic products will replace raw materials. In other cases, the technology break-throughs in the life sciences will reduce the cost of production and increase the global supply of many of these products. Technological advances have both increased the supply of commodities, through higher rates of mineral extraction and crop yield, and reduced demand, as plastic has replaced metal or fibre optics have replaced copper wire.

In either case, the growth leaders in the sector will be those with the best technology, the most applied knowledge. Canada can and should be a leader here, but not without adjusting our focus in the sector. All of these technology-related developments in the information and life sciences dramatically increase productivity and reduce prices. They are highly deflationary.

This does not mean that prices will never rise. For goods and services that are traded only in local markets, price increases might periodically be evident. Commodity prices will rise and fall based on supply and demand conditions, taking other prices with them. For example, jet fuel prices increased 30 percent with the war in Kosovo, leading to a temporary surge in airfares. Growth in many sectors might lead to temporary upward pressure on prices. On the whole, however, the overall price index will experience only moderate inflation pressure for the next twenty years or more. Price increases in some sectors will largely be offset by price decreases in others. Competition will cause business to continue to reduce costs, invest in technology and become ever more productive. The technology revolution, the freeing of trade, the end of the Cold War and the demographics all point this way. So does the immediate sensitivity of the bond market to real or imagined inflation pressure. Bonds sell off and interest rates rise even before the ever-vigilant central banks can respond. We saw this vividly in 1999. Moreover, the central banks do respond, as the Fed has once again proven.

Low Inflation = Low Interest Rates

Interest rates peaked in 1982. That was the year that Paul Volcker, Chairman of the Federal Reserve Board, began to ease monetary policy. He did so not because he had broken the back of inflation (although fortuitously he had); he did so because of the Latin American debt crisis and its potentially negative impact on the U.S. and global banking system. This is similar to what Chairman Alan Greenspan did in 1998 in the face of the Asian crisis. But long-term interest rates have not declined for seventeen years simply because Paul Volcker cut overnight rates in 1982. Interest rates have been on a long-term downtrend ever since, and it isn't over yet (figure 10.2). Canadian interest rates have for the most part followed U.S. rates down.

FIGURE 10.2

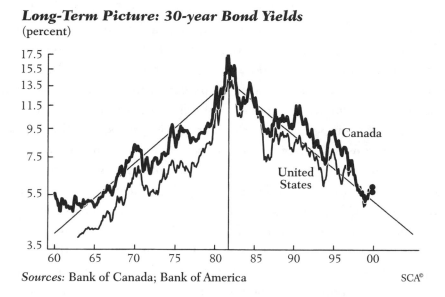

Long-Term Picture: 30-year Bond Yields
(percent)

Sources: Bank of Canada; Bank of America   SCA©

Demographic forces have been a major factor. Not coincidentally, 1982 was the year that labour-force growth peaked in both Canada and the United States (figure 10.3). By 1982, the youngest Boomers were finally taking their first full-time jobs. Labour-force growth has slowed consistently ever since. The slowdown in labour-force growth will continue through the year 2020, according to the U.S. Census Bureau and Statistics Canada. This will lead to a further slowdown in the growth of nominal GDP—the broadest measure of overall economic activity and price changes—as seen in the chart. This is because labour produces GDP and labour buys GDP.

FIGURE 10.3

Fewer Workers Means Slower Growth
(annualized % change from ten years ago)

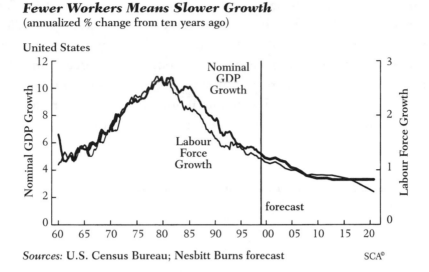

Sources: U.S. Census Bureau; Nesbitt Burns forecast   SCA©

Real GDP is nominal GDP excluding inflation. The great news for the U.S. has been that all of the slowdown in nominal GDP growth since 1982 has been the result of a slowdown in inflation. In other words, real GDP growth—the expansion of economic activity excluding inflation—has remained relatively stable, averaging 2.8 percent over the period (figure 10.4). While the Canadian inflation decline has been similar to that in the U.S., our relative real GDP growth has deteriorated.

FIGURE 10.4

GDP Growth and Inflation
(annualized % change from ten years ago)

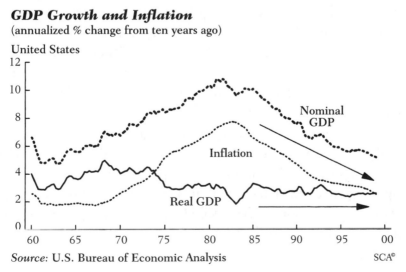

Source: U.S. Bureau of Economic Analysis   SCA©

Over long periods of time, the level of long-term interest rates—bond yields—trends to the growth of nominal GDP (figure 10.5). The process is already well in train. Long-term interest rates have fallen from a peak of 18 percent in 1981 to roughly 6 percent in the late nineties. Bond yields are headed for around 4¹/₂ percent in both Canada and the U.S. I didn't pick that number at random; it is my estimate of the long-term trend growth in nominal GDP, based on the projected growth of the labour force, productivity and inflation.

FIGURE 10.5

Bond Yields Track Long-Term GDP Growth
(percent)

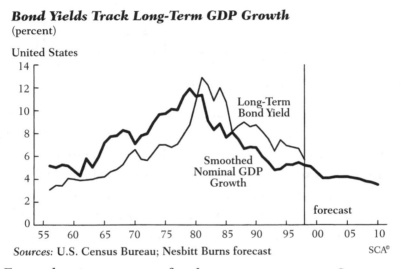

Sources: U.S. Census Bureau; Nesbitt Burns forecast   SCA©

Expect low interest rates for the next twenty years. See any meaningful sell-off in bonds—when bond prices fall, interest rates rise—as a buying opportunity. The general trend in interest rates will be down until they approach a level of about 4¹/₂ percent. If they overshoot that level on the downside, and they might, then expect them to rise; the bond market then would be in an "overbought" position and would correct back to about 4¹/₂ percent.

As always, however, nothing moves in a straight line. Expect volatility. There will be inflation scares. There will be commodity price shocks, weather disturbances, policy mistakes and political developments that will temporarily derail the long-term trends in either direction. See them for what they are: temporary. They will likely be opportunities to profit, keeping in mind that they will ultimately be reversed.

The Stock Market in the New Economic Era

As I have said several times, we are in the early days of an upwave in the economic cycle. Stocks generally outperform other asset classes in an upwave. The fundamental underpinnings for stocks at any time are threefold: interest rates, liquidity and earnings. As we have just seen, interest rates will remain low. They will likely rise intermittently, as they did in 1999, but it will be temporary.

Liquidity is also a strong fundamental support for equity markets and will continue to be so for the next twenty years, as Boomers save for retirement—maybe even longer if the Millennials like stocks as much as Boomers do. In the U.S., most Boomers can no longer rely on defined-benefit pension plans. They do not trust the long-run solvency of the U.S. Social Security System, the government retirement support program. They must save for themselves. The same has begun to happen in Canada as well.

Boomer savings rates are much lower than their parents'; nevertheless, trillions of dollars are pouring into U.S. retirement accounts called 401(k) plans, the equivalent of our RRSPs. In both Canada and the U.S., the net inflow to mutual funds, particularly equity mutual funds, in the nineties has been spectacular (figure 10.6).

FIGURE 10.6

Mutual Fund Assets Soar

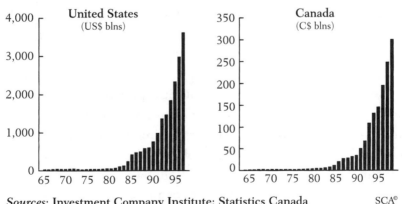

Sources: Investment Company Institute; Statistics Canada   SCA©

Individual investors have been in the process of reassessing their perceptions of the risk of equity investments. Jeremy Siegel, finance professor at the University of Pennsylvania's Wharton School, shows in his book *Stocks for the Long Run* that over twenty years or more, U.S. stocks are no more risky than Treasury bonds or even bills. He writes that "the safest long-term investment for the preservation of purchasing power has clearly been stocks, not bonds." While this has been true for the U.S. financial markets, we will see that it has not been true in Canada, where bonds have garnered greater returns than stocks in the period since 1982.

If Siegel is correct about the U.S. performance, then bonds and stocks should, theoretically, have similar returns, that is, if they do have similar risk profiles over long periods of time. But according to equity-research firm Ibbotson Associates, large-company stocks have been producing average annual returns of 11 percent since 1926, while long-term Treasury bonds have returned just 5.2 percent. Stocks earn so much more because investors, according to Siegel, are irrationally fearful of the volatility of stocks and therefore demand an extra return to compensate for their fears. What has happened since 1982, and especially during the last four years, is that investors are reassessing their fears. They have become more comfortable with stocks. They are requiring a much smaller extra return, or risk premium, to compensate for their fear. It is this declining risk premium that has accounted for the surprising rise in stock prices to levels well above those consistent with the historical relationship between stock prices, earnings and interest rates. The increase in the number of buyers has naturally led to a rise in price. To argue that stocks are overvalued, you must believe that the risk premium will move back up, and it could. This is a matter of psychology. It would take a big event to spook American investors from their "buy and hold" mind-set, but it is possible. Intermittent corrections in stock prices have been evident and are likely to continue. "Rolling corrections," different sectors falling in and out of favour, are also likely. Early 1999 saw, for example, a shift from interest-sensitive and technology stocks to cyclicals as global economic activity was poised to rebound and commodity prices increased. By mid-1999, the tech stocks were rebounding once again.

For the first time in history, American households have more money in the stock market than in home equity. An estimated 60 percent of households own stocks either directly or indirectly. The 401(k) plans, Individual Retirement accounts and mutual funds are democratizing share ownership in America to include many in the working class. According to a 1997 Federal Reserve study, the percentage of stock-owning families with incomes between US$25,000 and US$49,000 jumped by almost 50 percent between 1989 and 1995, to nearly one in every two. The increase was even greater for families making less than US$25,000.

Indeed, the Boomers are largely responsible for bankrolling a good chunk of the explosion in American technology-related new stock issues—initial public offerings (IPOs). In the nineties expansion, technology companies tapped the equity markets for financing. A decade ago it was the consumer and basic industry companies that went public in their drive to upgrade manufacturing to compete with foreign companies in home electronics and other consumer-product areas. The most recent wave of IPOs includes a large number of networking and Internet companies that are building the information highway.

The explosion in Boomer retail investment accounts online and at the brokerage firms, and the growth of the mutual fund industry, have funnelled Boomer funds into the equity markets. This mobilization of funds has fuelled the growth of the public-offering market and permitted emerging companies to find the financing necessary for further growth. This enormous source of venture capital has helped to contribute to U.S. leadership in the technology revolution. In Europe, for example, household investments in stocks are relatively small. Banks dominate the corporate lending business, and European banks typically loan only to well-established, credit-worthy borrowers. Venture capital for newer operations is scarce. In contrast, the American IPO numbers are stunning. Canada, while falling far short of the U.S. numbers, follows a U.S. rather than a European model. A total of $330 billion was raised in the U.S. in the eight-year expansion between 1982 and 1990, but it took only a little more than five years to match that amount in the 1990s, and the total for the decade overall stands at over $1 trillion.

American and Canadian Boomer savings in the stock market are largely invested for retirement, so they are likely valuing growth farther into the future. They are, therefore, theoretically less sensitive to near-term market volatility. The result is higher current valuations and a supply of capital that is generally cheaper than traditional bank credit. Investors are not impervious to stock market movements, however, as the 20 percent downdraft in the U.S. stock market in late summer 1998 showed. It triggered the withdrawal of $11 billion from equity mutual funds in the month of August 1998 alone. That was the first net redemption since September 1990. The following month, however, Americans were pouring money in once again, seeing the sell-off as a buying opportunity. The U.S. stock market retraced its losses in a mere six weeks, helped along by three interest-rate cuts by the Federal Reserve.

The "buy on dips" mentality reigned supreme, as it should. In an upwave, with the demographic support we are seeing, the stock market is the place to be, at least in the U.S. Boomers clearly will continue to be a major source of liquidity for the stock market over the next twenty years. This will help solidify U.S. leadership in the technology revolution, as new companies are able to find relatively inexpensive financing. That does not suggest, however, that the U.S. stock market will not correct. History tells us that the S&P 500 was more than 40 percent overvalued in mid-1999. If investors begin to fear that stocks are more risky once again, we could see a big sell-off. By summer 1999, Internet stocks were down 40 to 50 percent from their recent peaks, only to rebound sharply. As I've said before, markets will be volatile. Expect corrections, but see them for what they are: buying opportunities.

The Canadian stock market is more problematical because of the continued heavy weighting of traditional resource companies, the under-weighting of science and technology companies, the huge Canadian tax burden, the anti-profit sentiment of government and the continued Canadian-dollar risk. If the government were to cut taxes dramatically, as I suggest, and stop subsidizing declining industry, the tides would turn. The Canadian economy and Canadian stocks would take off, just as we have seen in other countries. This is especially so because foreigners are so under-weighted in Canadian-dollar financial assets. Foreigners have shunned Canadian investments in recent years because they fear further declines in the Canadian dollar. If this were to turn around on what they believed to be a sustainable basis, they would be huge net buyers in our market.

Americans have been aptly rewarded for their equity investments: the S&P 500 has surged by a compound annual rate of 18.3 percent since 1982, even with the stunning stock market crash of 1987. In Canada, annual returns have averaged only 11 percent since 1982. Within two years of the crash, the U.S. market had hit new highs; it took six years for our market to do so. For the period 1995 to 1998, annual returns for U.S. stocks were in excess of 30 percent—an unprecedented four-year performance. In direct contrast, the Canadian stock market averaged returns of only 14 percent a year over the same period. Taking into account the sharp fall in the value of the Canadian dollar relative to the greenback, those differences are substantially greater.

The top-performing asset class for Canadian investors since 1982 has been U.S. stocks, followed by long-term Government of Canada bonds (with maturities of more than five years) and then Canadian stocks (figure 10.7). Resource stocks brought down the total returns over the period. In 1999, resource stocks (excluding the gold sector) rebounded on the rise in some commodity prices, particularly oil. This is, as in the past, a temporary phenomenon. Canadian stocks did not always underperform U.S. stocks; from the end of World War II until about 1980, our stock market garnered higher returns than in the U.S.

FIGURE 10.7

U.S. Stocks are Tops
1982–98 (annualized % change)

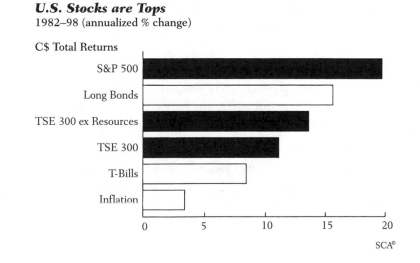

SCA©

Another factor that underpins stock markets is, of course, corporate earnings. Earning disappointments were widespread in Canada from the beginning of the Asian crisis in mid-1997 until early 1999. They finally hit the U.S. in mid-1998 as multinational companies like Coca-Cola and Gillette suffered major reductions in Asian sales, and domestic companies paid the price of higher labour costs with no offset in price hikes. U.S. multinationals were also hurt by the slowdowns in Brazil and Latin America. More recently, U.S. corporate earnings have surprised on the high side and profit growth has rebounded. The same is true for some sectors in Canada as well.

Going forward, it is not reasonable to expect gains in excess of 20 percent year in and year out. Nevertheless, the fundamental underpinnings of the technology revolution—the upwave in the long cycle—as well as low interest rates and strong liquidity will remain an appreciable positive force.

Clearly, the stock market has become a more important factor in household wealth management, in consumer confidence and in spending patterns. Stock market gains influence household spending to a greater degree than ever before, especially in the United States. This is called the "wealth effect." Some have estimated that every time stock values increased by a dollar, about 4 cents finds its way into the consumer spending stream. Alan Greenspan, Federal Reserve Chairman, believes this wealth effect helped to finance the huge Boomer move upmarket in housing in the nineties. Thanks to the surge in the U.S. stock market, household wealth has been increasing by more than 20 percent per year, and wealth as a percent of debt is at a record high. U.S. house prices are also rising, adding to the "feel good" wealth effect.

The flip side of this is that if the stock market were to sell off significantly on a sustained basis, the wealth effect would work in reverse—appreciably reducing confidence and household spending. However, the sell-off would have to be sustained and, as we have seen, individual investors today see sell-offs as buying opportunities. A sustained sell-off—a bear market in stocks—would reduce spending. It is possible that households would become very cautious, reducing spending more when stocks fall than they increased spending when stocks rose. Some think the wealth effect on the downside could be double the effect on the upside—an 8-cent reduction in spending for every dollar lost in stocks. While this may be true, it certainly was not the case in 1987; even with a 20 percent decline in stocks, the U.S. economy remained relatively strong. In any event, we know that volatility will continue and we know that stock values play a larger role than ever before in determining household behaviour.

A Y2K Caveat

I have not mentioned the Y2K problem—the double-zero year-2000 computer programming problem—not because it might not be important, but because it is already "in the market." Everyone is talking about it. Everyone knows that resources—labour and capital—have been diverted from more productive use in an effort to fix the problem. It is estimated that well over $350 billion has been spent to upgrade both software and operating systems. Everyone knows that there could well be substantial, temporary disruptions at the turn of the millennium. The problem has a silver lining, however, in that it forced businesses to abandon outdated, inefficient systems that weren't worth fixing.

We do not know how big these disruptions will be. Could they cause a deep global recession? Perhaps, but the world would see it as an exogenous and temporary shock to the system, similar to a hurricane or blizzard. Economic growth would plunge temporarily but then surge thereafter. The fact that Y2K has generated so much concern is testimony to the technology revolution and the degree to which computers have invaded our lives.

The real risk is that, after the turn of the millennium, the information technology problem could become a legal problem as companies and individuals sue for damages. The U.S. government is attempting to mitigate this effect: the Senate approved a measure that would limit legal liability for companies that take reasonable steps to rectify Y2K problems within ninety days. It also imposed a cap on the amount of damages that a plaintiff can seek from small firms and made it more difficult to file class-action suits. Stock prices of companies facing serious lawsuits will no doubt take a beating. Many firms, however, are protecting themselves in any way possible: disclaimers, temporary pre-announced cessation of service, backup functions, etc. The hype may well turn out to be worse than the reality, but clearly, we will just have to wait and see.

Y2K aside, it is unquestionable that the U.S. is the global leader in the technology revolution. Now, we will look at the reasons why. Canada too could become a world leader; we have many of the necessary ingredients already. We will look at what's missing—what needs to change. And change we will. Just as we conquered the inflation and deficit problems of the past, when many believed we would not, I am optimistic that we will get this right as well.

Part 5

Canada in the Global Economy

The U.S. is the Global Competitive Leader—Why?

The United States is the pacesetter in the technology boom and the global growth leader in the nineties. Compared with just about anywhere else, the U.S. has a large and wealthy consumer base, minimal regulatory impediments, low tax rates, a flexible labour force, advanced infrastructure and innovative capital markets. Massive investments in new technology have worked: computers today are sixty times more powerful than they were a decade ago. IT industries in the U.S. are growing at more than twice the pace of the rest of the economy, making up 8.2 percent of GDP versus 4.9 percent a decade ago. The average annual pay for workers in the high-tech industry in the U.S.— roughly US$50,000—is more than 60 percent higher than the wage for the average worker. Pay in the software field is even higher, on average double the rest of the private sector, and the gap is widening. Silicon Valley software engineers earn about US$90,000 a year, four times what other service-sector jobs pay. Privatization, deregulation and corporate restructuring have worked too. So has the mind-set in the U.S. Americans are risk-takers. They are not afraid to be wrong, to lose. There are problems, however. Let us look first at the problems and then at the strengths.

The Shortfalls

For all the American strengths, there are some weaknesses as well. Generally, they fall into two categories, government and people issues, but there are others. On the government front, the U.S. ranks poorly in its relatively high level of capital and property taxes and in its high average corporate tax rate on profit—although all are lower than in Canada. There is insufficient product liability protection, and environmental concerns remain.

On the people side, the U.S. ranks amongst the worst in alcohol and drug abuse, harassment and violence, youth unemployment, equal opportunity and economic literacy. Shockingly, in the country that boasts the world's best universities and graduate schools and almost the highest level of enrollment in higher education, the U.S. ranks relatively low in overall educational achievement. Clearly, the U.S. is a two-tiered society—the haves and the have-nots. And the gap is widening as the growth in income goes predominately to highly educated, highly trained knowledge workers. Real wages are now rising in all sectors, but the breach remains large. Exposure to computers at an early age is key, and poorer children still do not get enough of that. The dichotomy still falls too much along racial lines, although the situation is improving.

U.S. economic expansion has been good for everyone. Between 1991 and 1997, the share of families with real incomes between $15,000 and $49,999 shrank to 43.2 percent from 45.8 percent. The share of families with incomes below $15,000 also declined, from 13.5 percent to 12.5 percent. Impressively, the share of families earning more than $50,000 jumped from 40.7 percent to 44.1 percent. Concerns that the rich have grown richer and the poor poorer are not borne out by the data. A USA Today/CNN/Gallup poll found that in February 1998, 60 percent of Americans believed that the U.S. economy had never been better in their lifetime—and that includes a lot of Boomers who lived through the record-long Kennedy–Johnson expansion of the sixties.

Other areas of weakness for the U.S. include the low level of domestic savings and the huge trade and current account deficits. The trade balance is the difference between exports and imports. U.S. exports are strong, but imports have been even stronger. The fact is, the U.S. has been the importer of choice for the global economy in the nineties—bringing Canada out of recession in the first half of the decade and helping to forestall an even bigger Asian crisis in the second half.

The U.S. trade deficit exaggerates the poor trade performance. Exports are defined as those products sold outside the country that are produced by American companies located inside the U.S. Those goods and services produced by American companies located outside the U.S. do not count as exports in the trade balance. Consequently, the sales of companies like McDonald's Moscow or Caterpillar Middle East are not recorded as exports of the United States. If you were to add all sales by these foreign subsidiaries of American firms to the trade balance and take out the American subsidiaries of foreign firms, like Honda Ohio, the U.S. would have a large trade surplus. The U.S. has attracted huge foreign direct investment—investment to build U.S. branch plants of foreign companies like Honda. It makes the U.S. current account balance look worse, but it creates jobs and it boosts real estate values and economic activity in the places where the foreign companies locate.

The current account deficit—the net import of capital from the rest of the world—is a problem only to the degree that the world stops wanting American financial assets. The U.S. dollar is the global reserve currency—the currency against which most global prices and transactions are measured; the currency that most central banks and commercial banks hold in reserve in case of financial problems or uncertainties; the currency of choice in troubled places like Russia, Brazil and parts of Asia. In a sense, the rest of the world helps to finance the spending boom in the U.S.

Net holdings of U.S. bonds and stocks by foreigners are huge. The U.S. government bond market is regarded as the global safe-haven market. We saw this in spades in August 1998 when Russia defaulted on its debt. The flight to quality—to the U.S. Treasury bond market— was enormous, taking interest rates down temporarily to thirty-year lows. The euro may give the U.S. dollar a bit of competition in the future, but it will be a long time before it is accepted as a reserve currency on a par with the greenback.

On the infrastructure front, the U.S. is generally very strong, especially in air transportation and computers. However, it ranks low in its relative investment in telecommunications, roads and railways, and it is not self-sufficient in energy or non-energy raw materials. This may be the reason the U.S. biotechnology sector is working so hard to re-engineer and synthesize many basic commodities.

Management is strong, but excessively well paid. American managers rank very high in many measures of competency, creativity and quality, but inordinate remuneration packages at the very top of an organization are a competitive disadvantage. American management does not rank high in international experience or overall productivity, although there is clearly a wide range of competencies.

Finally, while the U.S. is the global leader in science and technology overall, there are areas where other countries have excelled. Among these are digital telecommunications, where Finland is the global leader, and the development and application of information technology, where Finland and Singapore shine. The U.S. also has a relatively low number of qualified engineers, and it scores poorly in basic science education for youth. A recent study by Michael Porter of the Harvard Business School and Scott Stern of the Massachusetts Institute of Technology suggests that the U.S. cannot rest on its laurels. They reported that if current trends continued, by 2005 the U.S. would trail Japan and such upstarts as Finland, Denmark and Sweden because of inadequate spending on basic research and education. The report's findings are being used to support hikes in science and education spending.

Education is a big mixed issue in the U.S. Higher education on the whole is outstanding; indeed, the more advanced it is, the better it gets. There is a growing earnings gap between educational attainment levels. University grads earned 25 percent more on average than high-school grads in 1978, and that gap has now widened to 50 percent. Employers are placing an ever greater premium on skills and knowledge. However, early childhood education through high school does not hold up to the best in the world—far from it. Illiteracy rates are still shamefully high. Remedial programs are increasingly available, but the basic problem has not been addressed sufficiently. A growing community college system is a strong point, particularly for technical and business training. Education innovations—online and on television—are burgeoning.

On-the-job training programs have surged in recent years, with labour shortages in so many areas. The unemployment rate has fallen sharply, especially for high-school dropouts, and more youth are staying in school.

The U.S. Success Factors

Although the problems remain, and some indeed seem intractable, the strengths are without rival. According to the International Institute for Management Development (IIMD)—a prestigious independent think-tank in Lausanne, Switzerland—the United States has had the most competitive economy in the world for six consecutive years (table 11.1). The U.S. economy has been the strongest in the industrialized world for the past decade. It has the largest and wealthiest consumer market, allowing business to make up in volume what they might lose in narrowing profit margins, squeezed by intense price competition. Interest rates, unemployment and inflation are at generational lows. Stock markets are hitting record highs. The U.S. participation in international trade and investment is without rival. The U.S. is a leader in globalization.

TABLE 11.1

U.S. is Ranked Most Competitive Economy in the World

1 United States	6 Switzerland
2 Singapore	7 Hong Kong
3 Finland	8 Denmark
4 Luxembourg	9 Germany
5 Netherlands	10 Canada

Source: International Institute for Management Development, 1999

SCA©

The Tech Giant

It is hard to refute the current U.S. lead in the tech world. According to the *Financial Times* of London, eight of the top ten IT and telecommunications-equipment firms in the world are American (table 11.2); the other two are Nokia of Finland and Ericsson of Sweden. Canada's Northern Telecom is thirteenth and BCE is eighteenth. In their rankings of the top twenty telecommunications companies worldwide, MCI Worldcom was first, followed by AT&T—both American—while Japan's NTT, Germany's Deutsche Telekom and U.K.-based British Telecom rounded out the top five. No Canadian companies made the list—although BCE sold 20 percent of its Bell Canada unit to Ameritech Corp. in 1999, which is part of one of the U.S. telecom giants, SBC Communications. France, Austria, Italy and Spain were represented in the telecom big leagues.

TABLE 11.2

World's Top IT Companies
May 1999 (by market capitalization)

Rank	Company	Country
1	Microsoft	U.S.
2	IBM	U.S.
3	Intel	U.S.
4	Cisco Systems	U.S.
5	Lucent Technologies	U.S.
6	America Online	U.S.
7	Dell Computer	U.S.
8	Nokia	Finland
9	Motorola	U.S.
10	Ericsson	Sweden

SCA©

International research firm Prognos forecasts that the world's most dynamic market sector in the 1997-to-2003 period will be information and communications technologies, which they estimate will grow at an average annual rate of 11 percent. This compares with growth rates of only 2.7 percent in chemicals, 2.5 percent in machine tools, 1.8 percent in the automotive industry, and a mere 0.9 percent in resources. The U.S. is therefore well positioned to remain a global growth leader, dominating the IT and telecom world. Canada, on the other hand, is still far too reliant on the traditional resource sectors and low-tech manufacturing like autos to be a current candidate for growth leadership in the twenty-first century.

Nowhere on earth are there more computers per capita or more computer power per capita than in the United States. An estimated 48 percent of U.S. households have a home computer, the highest percentage in the world, and that number is rising fast. This compares with just under 40 percent in Canada. Internet connections are also very high, at about 30 percent of American households, although surpassed by the percentages in Finland, Iceland and Norway. A Statistics Canada study found that only 22 percent of Canadian households were making use of the Internet in 1998, but that figure has no doubt risen since.

Even so, a 1999 survey shows that Canada is falling behind on the information highway. Australia and Singapore each did a better job in 1998 than we did at turning themselves into information-economy powerhouses. In its third annual ranking, World Times Inc. of Boston and International Data Corp. of Framingham, Massachusetts, scored Canada in tenth spot, down two rungs from our 1998 position. Using such criteria as PC ownership, Internet use, the cost of a local telephone call, newspaper readership, civil liberties and cell phone use, the U.S. was ranked first, followed in order by Sweden, Finland, Singapore, Norway, Denmark, the Netherlands, Australia, Japan and Canada. Australia jumped two spots in the 1999 ranking, while Singapore shot up seven spots. Our per-capita expenditures on all information and communications technology is substantially lower than in the U.S.

These results were confirmed by Canada's drop in the rankings for

U.S. patent issues. In 1996, we were ranked fifth in the number of patents we secured in the all-important U.S. market. In 1998, we had dropped to seventh place, another indicator that we are falling behind in the global technology race. Taiwan and South Korea pushed Canada out of our long-held fifth place. While the quality of patents is arguably more important than the number, the slip in our ranking is troublesome because it suggests we may be losing ground in the fastest-growing area of patent registration—computer software. Topping the list was the U.S. followed by Japan, Germany, France and Britain.

The U.S. also leads in research and development expenditures, number of R&D personnel in business, basic research, the number of Nobel Prizes and intellectual property protection. Much of the development in the defence sector has transferred successfully into private enterprise.

The American Value System

The value system in the United States is particularly well suited to the technology revolution. It is a system based on individual achievement and reward rather than collective achievement. The U.S. model focuses on deregulation, privatization, flexibility and risk taking. In contrast, the continental European system—covering countries like Germany, France and Italy—aims to preserve social cohesion, while the Japanese model fosters loyalty, stability and the collective good. Both of these systems are more risk averse than the American model.

The U.K. and the U.S. were the first to industrialize in the nineteenth century, with the British in the lead back then. The U.K. had the least repressive class structure in Europe, and the U.S. had little class structure at all. Entrepreneurs could enjoy the fruits of their labour and government generally stayed out of the way. Furthermore, the best and the brightest were not coerced into government or military service. Even today, entrepreneurs have second-class status on the Continent. The highest-ranking graduates of French universities tend to enter the government, not business. In Japan, the top graduates of Tokyo University, the most prestigious in the country, head straight for the powerful Ministry of Finance. Not so in the Anglo-Saxon economies; many of our brightest minds go into science, business and the professions.

The work ethic is crucial to overall competitiveness and innovation. The IIMD delineated three levels of worker motivation. "Tigers" are entirely devoted to company life, working more than seventy hours a week. "Cats" focus on work–life balance, working forty to sixty hours a week. "Dinosaurs" thrive on life–life balance; they prefer to work less, under forty hours a week, and convert benefits into time off, sabbatical leaves and other non-monetary rewards.

Asian countries generally fall into the tiger category. This is not such a positive factor for Japan because lifetime employment, unquestioning worker loyalty and large bureaucratic structures often stifled innovation and change. Much of the Anglo-Saxon world falls into the cat category; workers work hard—sometimes too hard—but they do have a life away from the workplace. Finally, a number of countries in Continental Europe have become dinosaurs. For example, France and Italy are reducing their workweek from thirty-nine to thirty-five hours, with no cut in pay. Initially intended to create jobs for factory workers, the law could now be applied to middle managers, software developers, engineers and other skilled workers. If implemented broadly, it could severely undermine France's and Italy's competitiveness. Germany has the highest wage rates and longest vacations in the world. These labour markets are highly unionized, inflexible and restricted, making it very difficult for companies to downsize when necessary or to restructure in a meaningful way in response to global competitive pressures. In consequence, unemployment rates are very high.

Global Leader in Financial Innovation

In the area of finance, the U.S. has no rivals. The quality and scope of financial services is second to none, and the availability and low cost of capital is a primary underpinning for American economic success. The financial markets are the most innovative in the world, with readily available venture capital, active new-issue markets and tremendous stock market dynamism. Wall Street leads in non-traditional financing: high-yield debt (better known as junk bonds), structured finance, asset-backed securities like mortgage-backed bonds, and corporate bonds, to name just a few. Funds have been made readily available even to new companies that haven't yet printed positive earnings. Innovations in the U.S. capital markets in the eighties greatly increased the availability of capital. The junk bond market finances many companies that would be turned away by the banks. The creation of pools of mortgages that were repackaged as mortgage-backed bonds greatly reduced the risk of mortgage lending, thereby lowering the cost to borrowers. The resulting boom in housing activity and related consumer spending on furniture and cars was a significant source of economic growth.

Bank financing, in contrast, is much more important in continental Europe and Asia, where banks lend only to well-established, higher-quality clients. Total bank loans as a percentage of GDP are 116 percent in Germany and 121 percent in Japan, compared with a mere 36 percent in the United States and a somewhat larger 58 percent in Canada. American banks, however, are highly efficient, well regulated and sound.

The household sector in the U.S. holds a larger proportion of their assets in stocks than anywhere else in the world. As discussed in the last chapter, the liquidity available for the stock market is huge, and the stock market itself is the broadest and most diversified in the world. The volume of funds managed by institutional investors—investment counsellors, pension funds and mutual funds—is the largest on the planet. These investors put considerable pressure on U.S. corporations to maximize financial performance.

Corporate Ownership Broadly Based

Most American, British and Canadian firms are financed heavily through the stock market. They are predominantly owned by individuals or their direct proxies—mutual funds and pension plans. In contrast, in continental Europe, Japan, Korea and most of Asia, banks and other corporations dominate corporate ownership through cross-holdings. American CEOs are under intense pressure to perform, quarter by quarter, as measured by earnings and shareholder value. Most CEOs are major shareholders themselves, with stock options a huge component of their overall compensation. In Europe and Asia, the banks and government holding companies that dominate ownership of listed companies have a collegial relationship with management. They don't emphasize quarterly results and they don't rock the boat. This is not all bad; they provide more patient capital where decisions are made for long-term development, not short-term gain. It is more difficult, however, to implement change. The U.S. system provides more discipline and facilitates rapid modification.

Some of the economic problems in Asia today arise from these cozy business relationships. The Japanese *keiretsu*—the large vertically integrated conglomerates that have cross-holdings of equities with other similar groups—are financed by very accommodating banking relationships. Similarly, the South Korean *chaebols* are large family-controlled conglomerates and have similar cross-equity holdings. The banks work with the government to distribute the nation's high level of savings among them. These systems of crony capitalism and nepotism misallocate capital, as has been widely evident in Indonesia, Malaysia, Korea and Japan. In addition, many Asian companies are focused on accumulating assets, not returning profits to investors, and these assets are never to be tarnished by foreign ownership. Reform will not be accomplished quickly.

An Environment Conducive to Change

The United States, with its frontier, capitalist spirit, stands apart in the global economy. It is a nation of immigrants, where the rewards of entrepreneurial spirit or inordinate talent can be reaped by anyone, regardless of pedigree or lineage. This is vividly seen in Silicon Valley, a fifty-mile strip of land from San Francisco to San Jose, where more than 3.2 million people live—people from a wide array of national, social and economic backgrounds. More than seven thousand information technology companies operate there. Eleven new companies are founded every week. In the heyday of the IPO boom, one company went public every five days, creating enormous wealth. In 1997, market capitalization of companies in the Valley exceeded $450 billion, more than the capitalization of the entire French stock exchange. The many stock options distributed to employees have created countless millionaires.

Silicon Valley illustrates the fundamental relationship between competitiveness, technology, risk capital and entrepreneurship. No longer are the traditional competitive advantages of natural resources and low costs the critical factors for success. This has been seen in many other U.S. locales as well. Austin, Texas, for example, is the home of Generation-X billionaire Michael Dell, founder of Dell Computers. The seeds of Austin's high-tech success were planted in 1958 when the University of Texas opened its Computation Center, from which Michael Dell dropped out twenty-six years later. Soon, IBM, Texas Instruments and Motorola established research facilities there. Today, almost two thousand high-tech companies—including three billion-dollar semiconductor plants—employ 20 percent of the workforce of Austin. In fact, since 1990, Texas has added six times more high-tech workers than California, which was also dwarfed by the likes of Washington and Utah.

Other high-tech centres include Salt Lake City, Utah, and Seattle, Washington, home of Microsoft, Amazon.com and RealNetworks. Boise, Idaho, is no longer just a potato town. Giant semiconductor manufacturer Micron Technologies got its start in Boise with the backing of potato king J.R. Simplot. Today, the company employs ten thousand people in Boise. It has been joined by some three hundred other high-tech firms, and more are arriving all the time.

Boston is a hotbed of exotic start-ups, as well as the second biggest recipient of venture capital funding, behind Silicon Valley. Back in the eighties, Boston was the home of computer companies like DEC, Wang and Data General, which bet on the wrong horse, the mainframe computer; when the PC took over, these firms came crashing down. Boston has since recovered, however, through sheer brainpower: it is the home of sixty-five colleges and universities. Today, the city boasts 3,600 high-tech companies, with more start-ups occurring every day. Dorm-room companies are not just a pipe dream; they really do happen in Boston.

In the Virginia suburbs of Washington, D.C., the biggest industry isn't government, it's the Internet. Other high-growth concentrations of specific talent exist in many parts of the U.S.: the medical research community in Houston; the fashion design industry, live theatre, Wall Street and so-called Silicon Alley, all in New York City; and the booming entertainment business in Hollywood, to name a few. These agglomerations of talent in a particular growth industry feed on themselves. They provide the scale to attract the best talent, develop the necessary ancillary businesses and encourage the universities to offer state-of-the-art training, all with little government aid or intervention.

Creative Destruction

Only in the United States are the richest people in the country dominated by the holders of relatively new wealth rather than long-standing family money. Successful start-ups like Yahoo!, Amazon.com and Dreamworks thrive and create new billionaires as others fall by the wayside, often very quickly. Among the *Forbes* magazine list of the richest people in America in 1998, the top five names were virtually unheard of fifteen years ago. They are: Bill Gates, aged 42, of Microsoft; Warren Buffett, aged 68, of Berkshire Hathaway; Paul Allen, aged 45, of Microsoft; Michael Dell, aged 33, of Dell Computer; and Steve Balmer, aged 42, of Microsoft. The next five names on the list are all heirs to the Wal-Mart fortune, the Walton family.

This ever-growing, ever-changing economic landscape is not without its costs. A supercharged economy can also mean intense job insecurity and rapid skill obsolescence—creative destruction. Times of intense innovation are often volatile times, as corporations and workers try to adjust to new technologies. Indeed, some of the deepest downturns in American history came during periods of rapid productivity growth, such as the first half of the twentieth century. Innovation has been fastest in the U.S. economy because it is the most open to the forces of creative destruction.

Reinventing City Economies

The challenge for many U.S. industrial cities, tethered to an obsolete industrial past, has been to evolve or die. Most have risen to the challenge. Pittsburgh, the steel giant of an earlier era, is now a white-collar town—home of Westinghouse Electric. Gone are the steel mills and the depressed coal mines of surrounding Appalachia. Baltimore, once an industrial town as well, has become a regional leader in the financial services industry. It is now the headquarters for T. Rowe Price, the big mutual fund company; Alex Brown, a regional investment dealer bought by Bankers Trust; and U.S. Fidelity and Guarantee company.

The U.S. South has transformed its economic base. It was long dependent on the furniture, apparel, textile, paper and chemical industries—all declining industries that have moved much of their production to cheap labour locales like Mexico. Dozens of cities have diversified away from these low-wage, low-skill sectors to technology-oriented, higher-value-added companies with a much more stable outlook. The Southern states spent millions on mammoth incentive packages to lure new industries to the region. Many foreign multinationals have opened U.S. subsidiaries there. They also invested heavily in flexible community college systems that could tailor classes to the needs of new industries. The results are evident throughout the region.

The states of Virginia, North Carolina, South Carolina and Alabama lost more than thirty-five thousand jobs in the apparel, furniture and textile industries in the past five years. Today, these states are booming with semiconductor plants, auto assembly operations, pharmaceutical companies and new high-tech steel mills that export to markets all over the globe. These states have added about sixty-five thousand new jobs in manufacturing despite the losses in textiles and furniture.

Take Hickory, North Carolina, as an example. Ravaged by the loss of three thousand jobs in the furniture and textile industries in the early 1990s recession, the unemployment rate leapt to 8.3 percent. Since then, these industries have shrunk by an additional six thousand jobs. Hickory's overall economy, however, is booming, and about sixteen thousand new jobs have been added since 1993. In the past five years, two foreign fibre-optic-cable giants, Alcatel SA and Siecor Corp., have built research and development facilities, expanded their plants and brought hundreds of engineers to the region. The fibre-optic companies have also boosted the wages of factory workers. Satellite manufacturing companies and new medical centres are also boosting Hickory's economy and spawning a boom in retail and service jobs. For the first time ever, jobs in service-oriented industries in Hickory outnumber manufacturing jobs.

People are competing for these new, better-paying positions. Enrollment in Catawba Valley Community College has surged 58 percent in the past decade. Last year, Lenoir Rhyne College, Hickory's four-year-old university, added an MBA program. Ron Abst, who started a business in Hickory repairing industrial machinery for the local textile companies in the early nineties, has never been more confident about the economic outlook. Today, his biggest clients are companies like Prodelin Corp., a Hickory-based satellite manufacturer, and Alcatel.

Japan—Falling Behind

Countries with restrictive labour market policies that impede creative destruction lag in the technology revolution. Japan, which until recently guaranteed lifetime employment, could not possibly adjust to the speed of change in today's market. True, Japan has a world-class manufacturing sector, accounting for 24 percent of the nation's output, compared with 13 percent in the United States. However, according to the McKinsey Global Institute, the productivity of Japan's banks, brokerages, retailers and other services is on average two-thirds that of their counterparts in the United States.

These sectors in Japan have barely started the move to the information age, where flexibility and speed matter. One reason is that they tend to be heavily regulated, subsidized and protected from the forces of a cost-competitive global economy. Japan's consensus-leaning, top-down management style is slow to embrace technologies that would shift decision making lower down the management stream. Creativity is stifled. Good ideas rarely make it through large corporations' bureaucratic structures.

Spending on information technology is relatively modest. The Japanese language, for one thing, does not lend itself to keyboard application. Internet service is prohibitively expensive because of the government's monopoly on telephone service. Gifted engineers and executives prefer to work for large corporations rather than for more flexible and innovative entrepreneurial ventures. Even from the earliest days, Japanese primary education focuses on rote learning and conformity.

Permissive attitudes towards immigration, which brings needed skills and out-of-the-box thinking, is also a prerequisite to innovation. Japanese society is, instead, homogeneous, and differences are discouraged, if not shunned. One of the most brilliant elements of the more innovative societies—the multiculturalism of immigration—is missing in Japan, and indeed in much of Europe as well. As we have seen, Japan has a very old population and could really benefit from immigration.

Japan is a very cautious society, where the savings rate is more than twice that of the United States. Whereas a huge pool of available capital might be thought to provide good seed money for start ups in technology, in fact innovation is more likely to come out of a willingness to take risks and an optimism about future possibilities. Japan encourages prudence and frugality by instilling anxiety about the future. The Japanese model does not adapt well to the skills and adjustments necessary in a period of rapid innovation.

It wasn't long ago that Japan seemed to be taking over the economic world. In the early 1980s, when the U.S. was mired in recession, Japan's unique form of state-directed insider capitalism seemed to be outpacing American free market capitalism. Chalmers Johnson detailed the apparent success of Japan in his 1982 book, MITI *and the Japanese Miracle*. Lester Thurow added *Head to Head* and Clyde Prestowitz proffered *Trading Places: How We are Giving Our Future to Japan and How to Reclaim It*. Many others followed. All of these tomes prematurely rang the death knell for U.S. economic hegemony. American paranoia about a takeover by the Japanese ran rampant, particularly when they bought an American icon, Rockefeller Center in New York City.

The doom and gloom prophecies regarding the downfall of the U.S.

economy failed to appreciate the power of free markets. Suffering from what Nobel Prize–winning economist F.A. Hayek termed the "fatal conceit," many in Japan and elsewhere believed that a handful of government planners could out-think millions of private decision-makers. They thought they could pick "strategic" industries, allocate capital in defiance of market signals, and prop up the stock market and real estate values. Their faith in bureaucratic miracles was hopelessly naive. This has become painfully evident in the Asian crisis of the late nineties, as government-supported crony capitalism comes to a devastating end. The demise of Communism as an economic system in Russia and China is also a reflection of this inability of government to do the job of the free market.

Europe at the Crossroads

Europe is in a period of transition. The European Monetary Union is forcing the amalgamation of eleven very diverse economies. Others will soon join. The successes are many, but old-line thinking and policies still remain in countries like Germany, France and Italy. Consequently, the unemployment rate is very high and they have fallen behind in the technology revolution.

This is beginning to change, however, as labour laws are revised, tax rates are cut and capital markets are opened up. Just a few years ago, venture capital money was scarce in Germany, and only giants like Siemens had technological prowess and easy access to capital. Now, upstarts like Inovit, a software maker in Munich, are thriving.

German chancellor Gerhard Schroder has announced plans to cut corporate taxes to a flat rate of 35 percent in 2000, in an effort to attract foreign investors and to improve his country's economy. The Chancellor, speaking at the World Economic Forum's twenty-ninth annual meeting in Davos, Switzerland, said that the corporate tax plan was part of a larger effort to counter the high levels of unemployment in Germany. He said that new jobs would come from new products, new technologies and development of new markets, while spending on research and education are keys to the future.

The move to the European Monetary Union should boost Europe's competitive position, as cross-country synergies can be exploited with a single currency. Examples of this can already be seen. Seattle-based Boeing Co. has lost market share to Airbus Industrie, a European group of four airplane manufacturers. Airbus has taken sales from industry leader Boeing by aggressively discounting its aircraft. The strategy helped Airbus get key orders from United Airlines, US Airways, British Airways and Northwest Airlines. The European jet-maker's market share edged up to around 45 percent as it booked record 1997 orders and cut prices.

Still, the technology gap in Europe is clear. Only 47 percent of businesses in France, Germany and the U.K. had Internet access in 1997, compared with 61 percent in the United States. For households, only 24 percent had computers, half the ratio in the U.S.; less than 10 percent had Internet access, compared with 30 percent in the States.

Britain has come a long way from the onerous labour problems and inefficiencies of the pre-Thatcher years. Today, London is the financial capital of Europe. Much of the trading activity of German and French banks takes place in London, because labour laws are much more flexible, allowing traders to be paid competitively without upsetting the salary schedules of the entire bank. Financial innovation in London is also the most advanced in Europe, and technological innovation is accelerating as well. Today, there are about 1,200 technology companies in the Cambridge area, employing about thirty-five thousand people engaged in everything from computer graphics to molecular genetics.

The 1999 British budget introduced the biggest shakeup of the country's tax system in twenty years. Britain's personal and business tax levels, already well below those in Canada, will be cut further. They have introduced a 10 percent maximum tax rate for low-income earners, cut the basic rate for middle-bracket taxpayers, eased the capital gains tax rate and reduced corporate tax rates on all businesses. The top corporate tax rate is being lowered a notch, from 31 percent to 30 percent. This compares with a total effective corporate tax rate in Canada of 24.6 percent to 39.1 percent (depending on the province) for manufacturers and 38 percent to 46.1 percent for other industries—well above the corporate tax rates in most of the rest of the world (figure 11.1). Gordon Brown, Britain's Chancellor of the Exchequer, says he wants to encourage entrepreneurial activity because of its value to economic growth and jobs.

FIGURE 11.1

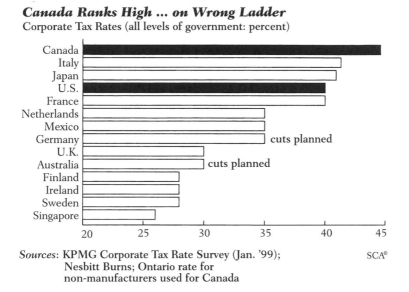

Canada Ranks High ... on Wrong Ladder
Corporate Tax Rates (all levels of government: percent)

Sources: KPMG Corporate Tax Rate Survey (Jan. '99); SCA©
Nesbitt Burns; Ontario rate for
non-manufacturers used for Canada

Tax Cuts Everywhere

Australia's Liberal government has also embarked on comprehensive tax reform. They will introduce a nationwide goods and services tax but markedly reduce personal, corporate and capital gains tax rates. Some 80 percent of taxpayers will pay no more than a top marginal rate of 30 percent on their earnings—compared with over 50 percent in most of Canada. The corporate tax rate will be reduced from 36 percent to 30 percent in an effort to attract foreign capital and prevent Australian companies from moving offshore. These measures will boost an already strong Australian economy. Despite the Asian crisis and the 1997–98 plunge in commodity prices, Australian GDP growth in 1998 was a whopping 5 percent in real terms. Australia, no longer the commodity-dependent nation of the past, is reinventing itself.

Liberal governments around the world are cutting taxes—corporate, personal and capital gains taxes. The list of countries announcing cuts in the past year includes Germany, the U.K., Australia, Japan, Sweden, Denmark, France, Poland, Switzerland, Turkey and Ireland. All recognize the need to create a pro-business, entrepreneurial environment. In the U.S., where tax rates are already significantly lower than in many other countries, the debate on further cuts will be an important part of the year 2000 presidential race.

The Irish Story

A real success story has been Ireland, the Celtic tiger. Mired in economic stagnation, spiralling public sector deficits and out-migration for decades, Ireland now has the strongest economy in Europe. The job market is booming and economic growth has averaged 8 percent since 1993—the highest of any European Union country and one of the fastest rates in the industrialized world. In 1998 the Irish economy grew at an eye-popping 11 percent rate, paced by a 22 percent surge in exports. And it's not whiskey and Waterford crystal that account for this; Ireland is the world's second largest exporter of software, after the U.S., and it supplies about one-third of all PCs sold in Europe. Furthermore, the budget is in surplus and people are moving back, attracted by the enormous job prospects.

Irish officials are confident that they can maintain an average growth rate of 5 percent over the next three or four years, as the demographics continue to be favourable. The net in-migration of young people, returning to their homeland to look for jobs in the rapidly expanding IT, pharmaceuticals and financial services sectors, will swell the labour supply by over 2 percent during the next few years. This is the raw material needed to grow faster than Europe by a significant margin.

No other European city has the boom-town feel of Dublin. New restaurants are sprouting up at a rate of one a week and they are packed, shops are doing a brisk business, help-wanted ads are everywhere and traffic jams are a regular occurrence. Intel now employs four thousand in the Dublin area, which has become Europe's Silicon

Valley. Capital has been pouring into the country at a pace of nearly $100 million per month, including investments by such global giants as Intel, Siemens, Sony, Bayer and Microsoft.

In 1987, Ireland's government set in motion a program of economic liberalization more far-reaching even than Margaret Thatcher's. Government spending was slashed, and now stands at 33 percent of GDP; that compares with an average of around 50 percent for the other ten members of the EMU, 41 percent in Britain, 42 percent in Canada and 31 percent in the United States. Corporate tax rates were also slashed. For exporters and the financial services industry, the corporate tax rate was reduced to a mere 10 percent; this includes most multinational companies operating in Ireland. The top corporate tax rate for all companies, once 40 percent, was reduced to 32 percent with the reforms and was reduced once again in 1999 to 28 percent. When the European Commission ordered Ireland in 1998 to stop favouring exporters with preferential tax treatment, the government shocked its European Union partners by harmonizing downward: starting in 2003, the top corporate tax rate for all companies will be a mere 12.5 percent. Ireland understands the important role the low-tax regime plays in attracting business.

Contrary to conventional wisdom here in Canada, that tax reductions lead to rising budget deficits, revenues surged in Ireland. As tax rates came down, revenues from corporate taxes doubled to 3.5 percent of GDP since 1990. Personal tax rates are still high by U.S. standards but lower than in Canada. Shortly after the reforms, the economy took off. The budget is in surplus and the unemployment rate is at its lowest level in almost nine years.

Ireland has also taken a leading role in educating its workforce. Spending on education has increased almost 40 percent over the past five years. Tuition fees for full-time university and college students who are Irish citizens were abolished in 1997, and the government is working towards implementing free part-time studies as well.

Finland Restructures

Finland is another great success story, with lessons for Canada. It is a country that once was heavily dependent on the forest products industry and trade with the now defunct Soviet Union. Finland has reinvented itself. One of the fastest-growing economies in the EMU, Finland is a global leader in digital telecommunications, with companies like Nokia leading the way. Finland is the world leader in Internet connections, new information technology and cellular mobile telephone subscribers.

The educational system has assisted Finland in its mammoth restructuring. Higher-education enrollment is amongst the highest in the world, as is secondary school enrollment, and Finland ranks third in the overall quality of its education system, following Ireland and Singapore. Finland also ranks first in in-company training programs. Clearly, education has led the way to Finland's renaissance.

Helping too have been its very low corporate tax rates. At 28 percent, it has among the lowest business tax rates in the world—equivalent to the rate in Sweden and only modestly above Singapore's 26 percent rate. But many Swedes are moving to Helsinki because personal tax rates are lower than those in Sweden.

Even socialistic Sweden is waking up. Sweden's sense of economic security has been shaken by the loss of several corporate bastions, such as pharmaceutical company Astra, paper company Stora and the car division of Volvo, to foreign merger partners. When Electrolux, the big Swedish appliance maker, hired a Swede living in the U.S. to set up its data processing division, he insisted on setting up shop in London, where the taxes are much lower. Even mighty Ericsson is moving its headquarters to London to escape the highest personal tax rates in the industrialized world. The brain drain from Sweden is gaining enough momentum to trigger a grassroots drive for lower personal taxes.

Israel—A High-Tech Leader

Education has been a driving force for Israel as well. Israel boasts the world's highest number of engineers, scientists and doctors per capita. One-quarter of the population has a university degree. *Newsweek* magazine named Tel Aviv as one of the ten hot new high-tech cities in the world. Some say that Silicon Valley's most serious global competitor is the urban sprawl around Tel Aviv.

Immigration from Russia gave Israel some of its high-tech talent—computer scientists with advanced theoretical knowledge. More important has been the training of Israelis in the army. The army provided the population—men and women—with important technology training, but it also gave them the self-confidence to innovate, to start new businesses. Microsoft chose to locate its first research facility outside the U.S. in Israel; Intel is building a state-of-the-art research semiconductor plant in Kiryat Gat; and IBM's research facility in Israel is one of only four such centres in the world. Israeli companies themselves are making huge strides in software, biotechnology, semiconductors, digital imaging and the Internet. Many are listed on the U.S. stock exchanges.

Many of the founders of these companies are in their twenties, and these Gen Xers are growing very rich. These whiz kids, like their counterparts worldwide, earn several times more than their lower-tech countrymen. This fast accumulation of wealth is a far cry from traditional Israeli kibbutz socialism, but no one seems to be complaining. Israeli venture capitalists say that sharing the wealth with stock options is today's new brand of socialism.

Other Bright Lights

Since local entrepreneurs and the American giant Texas Instruments discovered Bangalore, India, in the early eighties, the city has boomed. It is now home to 250 high-tech companies, including locally founded multinational software and networking giants Infosys and Wipro. There are an additional one hundred software firms on the outskirts of town. The basis for the boom is the high-tech talent, as India's universities and technical schools are churning out world-class programmers and technicians.

The same is happening in other emerging countries around the world. Romania has become a leader in training programmers who are in demand globally. Taiwan's government provided the seed money for the Hsinchu Science-Based Industrial Park eighteen years ago. This facility, eighty miles from Taipei, is home to hundreds of high-tech companies, some of them blockbusters. Among its many heavy-hitting chief executives is Stanford graduate Wu Tao-yuan, who returned to his homeland and joined Umax Data Systems, a company that now claims 80 percent of the lucrative worldwide scanner market. Hsinchu also has the world's largest semiconductor foundry and the giant PC maker Acer. Many of its engineers and programmers were trained in the U.S. MIT graduates abound.

The Mice That Roared

You don't have to be big to be strong these days; globalization has seen to that. A number of very small countries—Estonia, Iceland, Malta, the Netherlands, Singapore and Slovenia—are outperforming much larger national economies. And remoteness from large consumer markets is not nearly the negative it was in the days before the Internet. The success of small nations results from the same kind of innovation in business and social organization that, in an information age, gives small businesses the edge over large ones. Small countries can have an easier time than bigger entities in adjusting to shocks and taking advantage of new opportunities. When a small country achieves a niche—say, cell phones for the Finns—a world-class prosperity is possible, never mind the tiny home market. This is due to widening world trade.

Take, for example, Iceland. Its 1998 unemployment rate of 2.8 percent was the lowest in Europe, and its economic growth has been among the best in the twenty-nine-nation Organization for Economic Co-operation and Development (OECD). It has the second highest Web usage in the world, behind Finland. The Internet makes citizens of a once remote country feel connected, and it allows them the opportunity to prosper internationally.

Singapore is the smallest country in Southeast Asia and was the least hurt by the region's economic crisis. Botswana, a country of only 1.5 million people, has a higher income per capita than many of its larger African neighbours. The Netherlands accounts for 3 percent of world trade but has only 0.3 percent of the world's population. The Dutch have a conscious strategy of attracting international businesses and institutions. Not only has The Hague, the country's capital, attracted two new international courts in recent years, but it has also lured in a Europe-wide patent office and police force.

New factors are shaping national economic potential. When the critical ingredient for success shifts from natural resources to knowledge, brainpower will win. Shared values and a sense of trust often make it possible for the brainpower in a small country to work together, seizing opportunities more quickly. Iceland, home to only 270,000 people, recently decided to allow a local biotechnology company to market a genetic database of the country's entire population. Icelanders trust that the decision will pay off through the development of a native biotech industry.

Lessons for Canada

There are lessons for Canada to learn from the success of other countries. Globalization can be to our advantage. Canada has a very strong foundation and tremendous potential. We have been advancing on the world competitiveness scoreboard. According to the Institute for Management Development in Lausanne, Canada has advanced from twentieth to tenth place in world competitiveness over the past five years. Notwithstanding this progress, if we are to fully tap into our potential, changes must be made.

Canada—The Fallen Global Growth Leader

A round the country, cities and towns are suffering from the dramatic shifts in the global economy—shifts away from traditional low-value-added manufacturing, natural resource and food production. Just as we saw the demise of the textile, furniture, clothing and paper industries in the southern U.S., sectors all over Canada are feeling the pinch. Plants, mines and mills have shut down, jobs are disappearing and many people are nervous and confused about their economic prospects—people with families, people with children to feed, people with mortgages.

Countries all over the world are facing these problems. Some are reinventing themselves. In Canada, we have only begun the process, and there is much left to do. Corporate restructuring and re-engineering since the mid-eighties has led to job gains, not losses, according to a 1998 study by Industry Canada. Short-term pain leads to long-term gain, according to 568 Canadian companies that underwent some form of restructuring. The report concludes, however, that Canadian companies have not done enough to increase core efficiency. Too many companies hide behind an ever-falling Canadian dollar to make them appear competitive; so instead of investing in technology to raise productivity, they continue along in their old ways, waiting for the next fall in the loonie.

The 1998 OECD study on Canada warned us that we are falling behind—fast. We had the poorest productivity record in the twenty-nine-nation study, and this has been costing us a lot. The report triggered a rash of refuting analysis. A 1999 Statistics Canada study looking at labour and capital productivity growth in Canada suggested that we have outpaced the U.S. in the nineties through 1997. This statistical controversy is unfortunate, because it clouds the real issue—that Canadian living standards are falling relative to the U.S. and relative to most of the nations in the OECD. No one can dispute that nominal GDP per capita in Canada has fallen meaningfully relative to the U.S. since 1985 (figure 12.1). This is due to a number of factors, chief among them being a comparatively sluggish shift to the information economy and excessively tight fiscal policy in the form of high tax rates.

FIGURE 12.1

Canada's Standard of Living Lags U.S.
(US$ thousands)

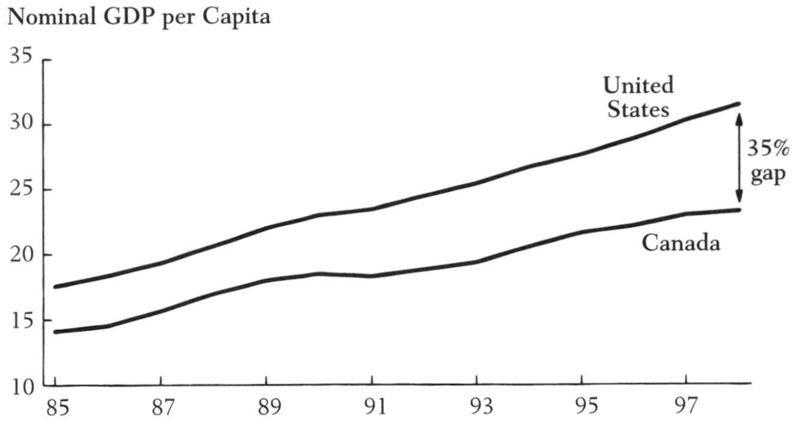

Nominal GDP per Capita

Canada = Purchasing Power Parity (78.5¢ U.S. in 1998)   SCA©
Sources: U.S. Bureau of Economic Analysis; Statistics Canada;
PPP = Nesbitt Burns estimate

If we continue to stand in the way of the global forces of creative destruction—shifting from the old to the new, knowledge-based growth areas of the future—we will fall further and further behind, reducing the economic well-being of all our people. Evidence of this is every-where.

British Columbia—
Major Transformation Needed

The economy of British Columbia has been in recent recession. The unemployment rate is significantly higher than in neighbouring Alberta and the provincial budget deficit has risen significantly. Mines have closed, mills have shut down and businesses have moved away. The minimum wage is the highest in the country and the top marginal income tax rate is second only to Newfoundland's. The province has been the most active in Canada in attempting to stem the tides of change, and the results have been the opposite of what was desired: higher, not lower, unemployment.

Loggers in British Columbia suffered. From the coastal rain forest to the Rocky Mountains, the forest products industry was in crisis. Sales dropped precipitously, and company losses hit a record $1 billion in 1998, according to a PricewaterhouseCoopers study—this on the heels of a very poor showing in 1997 as well. Twelve B.C. mills turned their layoffs into permanent shutdowns. More than fifteen thousand jobs were lost, and many more could follow. And it is not just the mills and factories that were hurting. Job losses have been evident in those sectors that served the thousands of unemployed mill workers. The provincial government budget was also badly affected.

People are finally waking up to the reality that this is not just another bad period. This is not a cyclical phenomenon, soon to be revived by a shift in the economic winds. Commodity sectors globally are facing huge long-term competitive pressure. Supplies are increasing while demand is falling. There are many places in the world that are more cost-efficient than Canada—able to produce forest products and many other commodities more cheaply than we can. Our labour costs are too high, government regulations and fees are onerous, and the environmentalists are (rightfully) more powerful than in many places in the emerging world.

Shipments of lumber products to the U.S. stagnated, despite the booming U.S. housing market, because of the 1996 Canada–U.S. soft-wood lumber accord, a five-year pact. B.C. was also hurt by the Asian crisis, as exports to the region plummeted. Even though the Japanese economy has gained some ground, a sharp rebound in the near future is unlikely. More importantly, Asia is fast developing its own supplies of forest products, and these are much cheaper to produce. In addition, demand in Europe is stagnating as the economy of core Europe remains fairly tepid and very powerful environmentalist forces there disapprove of B.C. coastal logging.

Government efforts to keep people in the mills have been not only unsuccessful but wasteful. Premier Glen Clark has insisted that every single mill and logging job that the NDP government deems viable will be kept alive by government subsidy until the economy bounces back. This cannot work. The forest economy in its traditional sense will not return to its glory days. Pouring government money into decrepit pulp mills is a vain attempt to stand in the way of creative destruction. In 1997, the government spent $300 million to subsidize a pulp mill in the deputy premier's riding. The move temporarily saved seven hundred jobs there, but it took business from several unsubsidized mills in other areas of the province.

In towns like Port Alice on the western tip of Vancouver Island, the situation has been dismal. Almost all of the 1,300 residents depended on the Western Forest Products pulp mill or logging for jobs. All is at a standstill, and pretty much everyone is out of work. The same was true in nearby Port McNeill, Port Hardy, Holberg, Gold River and Campbell River. Some hope that things will improve, but most are coming to the realization that they must move on. Forest products prices will rise temporarily with the global economic rebound. Paper and forest products stocks did quite well in 1999, following a huge downdraft. They have benefited from the sectoral rotation from growth and interest-sensitive stocks to cyclicals in 1999. But, as always, the rebound from an over-sold position will be temporary.

Pulp Mills Everywhere in Trouble

These are not just B.C. problems; the forest products industry domi-nates the economy of many towns in other Canadian provinces. Trois-Rivières and Shawinigan in Quebec are pulp and paper towns where roughly half the population earns less than $15,000 a year; education levels are very low and unemployment rates are in double digits. The same is true in Thunder Bay, Ontario. Reliant on the pulp and paper industry, it was also once the country's grain transportation centre, until the government eliminated the Crow rate subsidy to Western farmers in the mid-nineties. More than a third of the working population earns less than $15,000 a year, a mere 8 percent have university degrees and 12 percent have only a Grade 9 education.

Too much of the Canadian economy is still dependent on traditional resource industries, farming and low-tech manufacturing—all declining sectors. This is certainly true for British Columbia. Forest products have accounted for 50 percent of the province's merchandise exports. Roughly thirty of B.C.'s top one hundred firms are forest product companies, but the number is dwindling.

There is a future for the forest products industry in Canada. However, it does not lie in traditional commodity production but instead in value-added finished-product manufacturing, where talent and technology are applied to the basic product. This switch to specialized goods has already occurred in the United States, Sweden and even New Zealand.

Canada could also excel in biotechnology applied to the forest sector. Breakthroughs are already in place to improve tree stocks genetically and to create synthetic wood products. Forestry companies around the world are engaging in research to find genes that can be inserted in trees to make them grow faster and be more resistant to disease, heat, cold and drought. Scientists at Calgene, an American biotech firm, recently isolated a gene for the enzyme that controls the formation of cellulose in plants. They hope to enhance the enzyme to create trees with more cellulose in their cell walls, producing a more efficient tree for harvesting by the pulp and paper industry.

The possibility of producing lumber from straw was presented at the 1999 meeting of the American Chemical Society in Anaheim, California. Wolfgang Glasser, a wood-science professor at Virginia Polytechnic Institute & State University, believes it may be possible to bypass years of normal tree growth. Instead, just whip up a mix of lignin—the polymeric glue that holds wood together along with the proper proportions of cellulose derivatives from almost any plant, and given the right conditions the molecules will automatically self-assemble into wood-like cells. While the research is still only at the laboratory stage and it will take years for its commercial application, it is reflective of the tremendous technological changes that will impact the forest products sector.

Government and business should work together to encourage this kind of research in Canada. Without it, our forest products sector will continue to decline. Not all companies will survive—only those that can move out of the commodity business. In a world as competitive as ours, the only companies that prosper in a commodity business are the low-cost producers; others either add value by applying technology to the product or they disappear.

The Lure South of the Border

Washington State and Oregon were once every bit as dependent on the forest products sector and fishing as B.C. is today. Washington is now the home of Microsoft, Amazon.com, Boeing and Starbucks. More than 2,500 software companies dot the city and suburbs of Seattle. The high-tech boom has fed on itself as many of Microsoft's stock-option millionaires act as "angel investors" for new companies. Oregon too has attracted high-tech business. Local community colleges provide the necessary training and work closely with business to retrain in areas of need.

One of the problems is that British Columbia is perceived to have an anti-business environment. Tax rates are sky-high, even by Canadian standards. Regulatory practices are onerous, business fees are big, and labour is militant and inflexible. Profit, most definitely, is a dirty word. The NDP government has long supported anti-business, pro-labour policies, to the detriment of all working people.

The business community of Vancouver spearheaded the first business-government summit in the province in late 1998 to address these issues. Not only was the forest products sector in recession, but so was the mining industry. By early 1999, mines were shutting in droves. The Highland Valley copper mine closed, devastating the local economy around Kamloops, and many other mines have done the same. The B.C. government's Job Protection Commission scrambled to save the mines with cost-cutting solutions, but these efforts were fruitless. The global economy has changed and the future for B.C. does not lie in the traditional resource sector. The only way to raise living standards is to redeploy labour and capital to more productive use.

B.C.'s economic underperformance goes far beyond the resource sector and fisheries. The business community is balking. The province's high marginal income tax rates are scaring away many skilled individuals. Some high-tech companies are relocating to Washington State or elsewhere in the U.S.

The Employment Standards Act was another big problem for these companies. It governs workplace practices like overtime hours, and until recently it was not flexible enough to deal with the wild workdays of the high-tech industry, where nine-to-five jobs don't exist. Fortunately, in February 1999, the B.C. government realized the problem and came to the aid of the high tech sector. Under criticism from the B.C. Federation of Labour, the government announced exemptions to the Employment Standards Act for workers classified as high-tech professionals. They are no longer subject to requirements relating to hours of work, overtime and statutory holidays. This is crucial in an industry that is often driven by short-term projects and very tight deadlines. Frequently, penalty clauses require very intense work for limited periods of time. The industry applauded the changes, saying they would provide the flexibility needed to compete.

The future could be bright. High tech is the fastest-growing sector in British Columbia. While still small in revenue terms when compared with the forest products or mining industries, it now comprises roughly 5,700 companies employing 42,000 people. By 2005, employment in the high-tech sector in B.C. is projected to be about 81,000—a welcome prospect.

The unions, however, see it another way. Ken Georgetti, president of the B.C. Federation of Labour, is quoted as saying that he is all for the high-tech industry growth, "but you don't try to attract high-tech professionals by lowering employment standards." He said that

Washington State attracts high-tech workers because it offers higher wages and a better overall employment package. High-tech professionals in Washington State are generally not unionized.

Unions are much more powerful in Canada than in the United States, and nowhere are they more militant than in British Columbia (although Ontario topped B.C. in the average number of days lost to stoppages in the late nineties). Just over 30 percent of Canada's labour force is unionized, compared with 14 percent in the U.S. Unions have been known to strike money-losing companies in Canada and drive them out of business. Unionized workers in Canada spend more time out of work because of strikes or lockouts than workers in any other G7 country. According to the International Labor Organization, an arm of the United Nations, Canada lost an average of 292 workdays annually per 1,000 workers between 1986 and 1995. That was more than forty days higher than the average in Italy, which has a notoriously strike-prone labour force, and it was easily double the average in the twenty-nine member countries of the OECD. Average work stoppages in Canada were a startling five times greater than in the U.S. Stronger, more militant unions in Canada have reduced corporate flexibility, competitiveness and profitability. Ironically, this has increased, not decreased, unemployment.

Workers at two McDonald's and one Starbucks in B.C. have unionized—the first unionized operations for either company in the world. Why would other American companies want to locate in B.C. and risk labour unrest in their other locales? Why would they want the headaches? These companies create jobs, enhance real estate values, increase economic activity in the region. Bigger foreign companies, like Alcatel or Siecor in Hickory, North Carolina, or Total Systems Services in Columbus, Georgia, wouldn't dream of locating in B.C. with its high taxes, restrictive business climate and inflexible labour policies.

B.C. business people find regulatory red tape overwhelming. Stan Fuller, president of Vancouver-based Earls Restaurants Ltd., which operates eighteen popular restaurants in the province, says he will never open another one in British Columbia. The reasons: the highest minimum wage in Canada; high taxation on liquor; and intrusive government regulation and labour laws. Since Earls last opened a restaurant in B.C. almost five years ago, it has opened in Alberta and in Scottsdale, Arizona, with more on track for Phoenix, Dallas and Denver. Business people see the NDP government as unresponsive and lacking understanding. Most of Premier Glen Clark's cabinet is made up of former professors, union activists, teachers, social workers and civil servants, who are unknowledgable or unconcerned about the problems of business.

Why live or locate in British Columbia when just south of you the environment is pro-business, entrepreneurial and booming? For the Canadian health care system? I don't think so. Microsoft has excellent employee health care benefits, and Seattle has an outstanding medical establishment. For low crime? Probably not. Cities in Washington and Oregon have low crime rates and a high quality of life. Jobs are easy to get, and they are clamouring for workers. They will train you, they will relocate you and the tax rates are dramatically lower.

Tax Rates Matter

The lure for well-trained Canadians to these regions is increasingly irresistible. Moving south helped to slash the tax bill for Clearly Canadian, the bottled-water company. They shipped the lion's share of their operation from Vancouver to Burlington, Washington. The tax saving for their employees was huge. For example, the top marginal income tax rate in Vancouver was 54 percent, and it kicks in at incomes of $80,000. The highest marginal tax rate in Bellingham, Washington, fifty miles south, is 39.6 percent, and it is applied only to incomes over $409,000. Sales taxes are 14 percent in Vancouver and 7.8 percent in Bellingham. The capital gains tax rate in Vancouver is nearly twice the 20 percent rate in Bellingham. Mortgage interest is tax-deductible south of the border.

British Columbia has high tax rates even for Canada, but personal tax rates are high relative to the U.S. in most other provinces too. Top marginal income tax rates in Ontario have recently been reduced to 49.6 percent, and they are 52.6 percent in Quebec. The lowest is Alberta's 45.6 percent—kicking in at an income level of $70,000—with no provincial sales tax; the GST of course remains, at 7 percent. In a pioneering development, Alberta erased its existing tax system in the 1999 budget and introduced a flat tax, a single rate for all taxpayers, which is slated to take the top marginal income tax rate in the province down to 41.5 percent in three years. In addition, Alberta has markedly lower minimum wages and corporate tax rates than B.C., no general capital tax or payroll tax, and the lowest gasoline taxes in Canada. The 1999 B.C. budget reduced tax rates for small businesses to levels below those in Alberta, but Alberta appears ready to match the cuts. Its low tax rates and pro-business environment have attracted businesses from other parts of the country, taking the jobless rate down to close to full-employment levels and reducing the youth unemployment rate to levels well below those in its neighbour to the west.

Calgary now boasts more head offices than anywhere else in Canada outside Toronto. Dow Chemical's Canadian subsidiary, for example, moved its headquarters from Sarnia, Ontario, to Calgary in mid-1996, enticed by lower provincial tax rates. They left only a small operation in Sarnia, which still relies on the oil refining and petro-chemical industry for over half the town's employment. The list of companies similarly attracted to Calgary or Edmonton is long and includes: Canadian Pacific, which relocated from Montreal in 1996; TransCanada Pipelines, which moved from Toronto in 1990; Finning International Inc., which transferred from Vancouver to Edmonton in 1997; and Jim Pattison Lease, which moved from Vancouver to Calgary in 1999.

The Brain Drain

Who could blame Canada's top students for being tempted to move south, even if they are educated at taxpayers' expense? It is alleged that Bill Gates himself calls the top graduates in the University of Waterloo computer science program to offer them jobs each year at Microsoft. In fact, it is said he hires more graduates from the University of Waterloo than from any other single school. The folks at the Institute for Computer Science in Toronto say that 20 percent of their graduates intend to head for the U.S. this year.

There is a remarkable amount of controversy around the issue of brain drain. People on both sides present anecdotal evidence of the loss of talented Canadians being a serious or, on the other hand, an insignificant problem. The fact that so many leave at all is meaningful. It is difficult to move to a new country. I know; I have done it. It is difficult to leave friends, family and familiar surroundings for a foreign place, even if the job prospects and tax rates are better. In the past it took dire economic straits to entice people to do so.

Since the 1988 Free Trade Agreement, U.S. restrictions on the issuance of work visas to Canadians have been eased. There is still a quota, however, so out-migration of Canadians south is not as high as it was between 1950 and 1965, when there were no restrictions. Even so, there has been a sharp increase in working visas issued to Canadians, and over the ten-year period since 1988, a decrease in Americans emigrating to Canada. High-skilled workers have been leaving in the nineties to take advantage of greater job opportunities, higher salaries and lower tax rates. Since NAFTA, Canadians can get U.S. working visas more easily. The number issued to Canadians quadrupled over the five-year period ending 1998. Greg Osberg, president of Kaplan Professional, a New York provider of information technology job fairs, told the *Wall Street Journal* in June 1999 that Canadian workers will be the next target for American high-tech companies.

While we do attract skilled immigrants to this country, we lose far too many skilled Canadians. According to Dr. Denis Gagnon, senior vice-president of the Canada Foundation for Innovation, some of our most talented and gifted people are leaving to go to the United States. Since 1993, the proportion of people working at IBM Canada Software Laboratory in Toronto who choose a U.S. employer when leaving the company has risen to 25 percent. Northern Telecom has said it is extremely difficult to attract and keep highly skilled workers in Canada because of the income tax differential. David Burn, Northern Telecom's vice-president of taxation, has been quoted as saying that they have substantive empirical evidence of the brain drain. Engineering executives at Nortel who are transferred out of Canada have a personal bias not to return. Burn says that represents a productivity loss for Canada.

John Roth, chief executive officer of Northern Telecom, warned that the company could leave Canada if Ottawa refuses to ease the tax burden on its scientists and engineers. Roth said that Canada is driving its people away. "We have to follow our people," Mr. Roth is quoted as saying, adding that Nortel is losing up to five hundred engineers a year to competitors in the United States. He added that Canada's personal tax load is such that Nortel, which hires about 25 percent of the country's high-tech graduating class, is having trouble luring staff from Britain, long a plentiful source of ultra-skilled labour. Nortel employs roughly twenty-three thousand people in Canada as part of its global workforce of seventy-five thousand. The biggest problem facing our high-tech sector today is a dearth of highly skilled labour and managerial talent.

The Canadian Medical Association has statistics showing that in 1996, 522 doctors, 1,103 nurses and 352 other health workers—a total of 1,977—emigrated to the United States. The Coalition for Biomedical & Health Research has surveyed Canadian universities with faculties of medicine on this issue. The data show that over the six years ending in 1998, five faculties of medicine have lost 62 faculty or clinical senior members, 232 research technicians, 39 post-doctoral fellows and 68 graduate students to the U.S.

Statistics Canada and others can release study after study telling us there is no brain drain, but we all know otherwise. We know our university-age children may well be attracted to greater job opportunities south of the border. My son recently graduated from Upper Canada College, a private school for boys in Toronto. A record proportion of his graduating class will be attending university outside of Canada—virtually all of the top students—and when you talk to the boys, many tell you they are never coming back. Too many of us have talented, ambitious adult children who have chosen to leave Canada.

The Harvard Business School Club of Toronto has recently begun offering scholarship money to successful Canadian applicants, hoping they will return to Canada after graduation. They are doing this because the proportion of Canadian Harvard Business School graduates coming back to the country has plunged—from roughly 80 percent in the seventies, to 60 percent in the eighties, to only 30 percent in the nineties. The rapid decline has continued over the course of the decade to less than 20 percent in 1998.

A blue-ribbon panel set up by the Liberal government and chaired by Pierre Fortier, head of Innovitech Inc., has concluded that Canada is losing vital, innovative start-up businesses to the United States as a result of high personal taxes and the tax treatment of employee share ownership. The cost to Canada of this out-migration of high-skilled talent is severe. As discussed in chapter 6, we are already projected to have a slower-growing labour force than the U.S., as our youth population—the Millennials—is proportionately smaller. Our manufacturing productivity is considerably below the U.S. and we spend more per capita on education than they do. So it is very costly for us to lose some of our most highly skilled, productive people. We are losing managers, engineers, financial analysts and traders, professors, doctors, lawyers, scientists, nurses and programmers in high numbers. Yes, we do have in-migration as well, but we would have that anyway, and we need all the high-skill workers we can get to raise our potential growth rate.

In a knowledge-based economy, high-skilled people are our most important resource, and they are in global demand. We cannot afford to lose them.

More Declining Businesses

The East Coast fishery has been in deep decline for many years. Only half the forty thousand people who worked in the fisheries industry in the late eighties remain. Government attempts to help the jobless become less reliant on the sea have been disappointing. The auditor general has reported that attempts to retrain existing fishermen have failed. In large measure, this failure is a mystery. Why has the U.S. South so successfully re-engineered while Newfoundland remains depressed? Continued reliance on government income-support programs might be one answer, along with a reluctance to retrain or relocate and a dearth of foreign investment in the region.

In St. John's, Newfoundland, for example, the unemployment rate is just over 9 percent. Two major processing firms, National Sea Products and Fish Products International, have dramatically scaled back operations. Former fishing towns across Atlantic Canada have been devastated. Burgeo, Newfoundland, once the home to 3,000 residents, has dwindled to 1,800 over the past decade as the fish have disappeared. Families boarded up their homes and left a town that has nothing more to offer. The local fish plant, Seafreez Foods, which once employed 500 people, is gone.

Biotechnology Revolutionizes Food Production

In fisheries, food production and livestock breeding, breakthroughs in genetic engineering and alternative growing methods will appreciably increase the world's food supply and slash food prices. The number of people working in today's farms and fisheries will decline dramatically, continuing a process that began with the Industrial Revolution in the eighteenth and nineteenth centuries. To attempt to stand in the way of this is to live in denial.

The federal and provincial governments of Canada, nevertheless, continue to subsidize depleted wild fisheries. This encourages people to stay in places where there are no jobs. The unemployment rate in Newfoundland is still the highest in the country, at 17 percent. The economy there has been helped by Hibernia, the oil exploration project, but there are still a disheartening number of people waiting for the fish to return.

The future of bioengineering in the agriculture sector is also spectacular. As an example, scientists have already used bioengineering as a partial substitute for traditional chemical treatments for insects and disease. Tissue culture research will move more agricultural production indoors. Researchers have successfully grown vanilla, orange and lemon vesicles and cotton cells in indoor vats of nutrients. Genetic research on animals has made cloning possible. Scary as all this genetic tampering is, it is dramatically increasing food supplies, putting downward pressure on prices.

Subsidizing Another Declining Industry

Canada maintains its subsidies for traditional farming, unwilling to accept the reality that the number of farmers will continue to decline. In 1906, 85 percent of Canadians were involved in food production; today, less than 1 percent of the population feed us all, and that number will fall further. The government announced in late 1998 that it would devote up to $900 million over two years to help rescue farmers from the dramatic decline in global pork and grain prices. Hog farmers were hurt by the substantial decline in Asian demand for their product. Saskatchewan was the hardest hit of all the provinces, feeling the effects of the global decline in demand for pork and grain, as well as being caught in the crossfire of the grain-subsidy war between the United States and Europe, which drove prices down further. Farm income in the province dropped sharply. Grain and hog production accounts for about 30 percent of Canada's total farm output and involves almost ninety thousand farm families.

These subsidies are stop-gap, band-aid measures to slow an inevitable process. The U.S., Europe and Japan, as well as most other countries, also subsidize and protect their farmers and resource sectors. Nevertheless, many farmers are destined to leave the land, whether we like it or not. The pork industry is undergoing the same transformation the poultry business went through in the eighties. Big producers in the U.S., like Murphy Farms and Premium Standard Farms, are building giant, low-cost hog factories in a war for market share, but demand hasn't kept pace with the expansion in capacity.

Saskatchewan has taken a leadership role in the development of biotech research applied to agriculture and livestock. The University of Saskatchewan in conjunction with a consortium of private biotech companies is making great strides in agribusiness development; but the traditional farm business is a declining one.

All Resource Businesses at Risk

The Canadian government finally pulled the plug on the coal business in Cape Breton, Nova Scotia, in early 1999 after thirty years of decline and losses of $1.6 billion. The Cape Breton Development Corp., the federal crown corporation that ran the mines since 1967, had only one customer for its high-sulphur coal, Nova Scotia Power. The mine had been a constant drain on federal money and the number of workers had fallen from 13,000 in 1960 to just 1,670 at closing. The uproar in the media over the mine closing was deafening. A mock funeral was staged for the CBC cameras and a tearful woman, Edna Budden, accompanied by her husband, Van, aged forty-five, a miner for twenty years, vividly depicted the human costs. The unemployment rate of Cape Breton was already 19 percent. The Buddens have two unemployed children, aged twenty and twenty-one. "What are we to do?" they implored. "Surely we can't move away, but there is nothing here." How could the feds close the mine? How could the government be so heartless? The viewer is meant to ask.

Why were the workers at the Devco mine in Cape Breton so surprised? How could they have sat by year after year, watching the workforce and the region decline, and not have done something to take care of themselves and their children? The archaic patronage-driven economic development model of the government encouraged them to believe that they should stay, that things would eventually come around. These government subsidies to declining sectors do no one any good. They cost billions of dollars and actually exacerbate the jobless problem by discouraging change and innovation.

Any strong, growing economy will experience a natural churning in labour markets—out with the old businesses, in with the new. Think of the stagecoach business when the railway arrived. Imagine the stagecoach lobbyists demanding that the government do something to protect them. If the government had continued to subsidize stagecoaches, people would have been shocked thirty years later that they had to find a new line of work, that their children might have to move to where the jobs are. All the billions of dollars wasted on Devco could have been better spent on tax incentives to lure growth industry to the region, and on training programs for workers so that people wouldn't have to leave to find work.

The fact is that human history is a history of migration, of change, of moving from depressed areas to where the economic prospects are better. Canada is a nation of such immigrants.

There is no question that all traditional commodity businesses are at risk of substantial further decline. Information technology applied to the life sciences is revolutionizing all resource sectors. Be it genetically modified trees, biofuels, fuel cells, improvements in mining or the creation of myriad synthetic products to replace non-renewable resources—all traditional resource businesses are at risk. Technology has also increased supply around the world, making it possible to find new sources and to economically capitalize on these sources. This is true in fossil fuels, in mining and in most other raw materials production and extraction.

Furthermore, the demand for basic commodities is decreasing. Fibre optics and synthetic products have reduced the need for many basic commodities. Low inflation has even reduced the demand for gold, which is no longer seen as the only reliable store of value in times of trouble. You don't need as much lumber to build houses and skyscrapers as you used to. Some would say that the most important commodity in the technology revolution is sand. The demand for sand is huge, but the price is nearly zero.

FIGURE 12.2

Real Commodity Prices in Long-Term Downtrend
(GDP deflator adjusted: 1801 = 100)

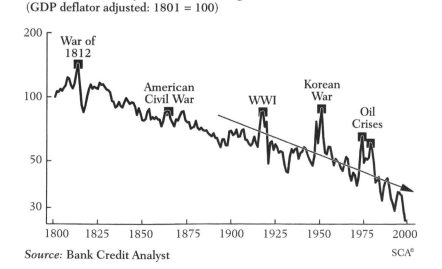

Source: Bank Credit Analyst

SCA©

Real commodity prices have been declining for the better part of two hundred years (figure 12.2). With the exception of world wars and oil crises, commodity prices have consistently trended downward. Canada was lulled into thinking its future lay in natural resources by the OPEC-induced rise in resource prices from 1973 to about 1980. Over that inflationary period, the Toronto Stock Exchange rose 164 percent compared with a 65 percent gain in the U.S. S&P 500. Even in Canadian-dollar terms, the U.S. market underperformed at a 98 percent total return. Canadian resource stocks gained a whopping 225 percent. Those days are long gone, however, never to return on a sustained basis. Commodity prices may rise intermittently, as they did in 1999, but see this as temporary.

What is in short supply is knowledge. Knowledge applied to traditional commodity businesses is one area where Canada can, and should, shine. We are already making headway in some of these fields—geophysical exploration, oil exploration, alternative fuels, advanced extraction techniques and agritech—but so much more could and should be done. No longer can we rely on our endowment of natural resources and fertile land to ensure economic prosperity.

Other Declining Sectors— Low-Tech Manufacturing

When we refer to low-value-added or low-tech manufacturing, we mean that little advanced skill or knowledge is applied in the production of the product; it can easily be replicated by competitors. Most of the jobs in this kind of manufacturing are relatively low-skill, and are either automated out of existence or moved to places where low-skill labour is much cheaper. That is what we have seen in so many American cities that once relied on textile, furniture, apparel and other low-tech businesses. We see it in Canada as well. Even the automotive industry, the backbone of manufacturing in central Canada, is a declining business and is considered relatively low-tech. Sure, there are many computer chips embedded in today's cars, but the automobile is the high-tech product of the early 1900s, not of the new millennium.

Global excess capacity in auto products is large and growing; production cutbacks are already evident. As we discussed earlier, growth in this sector will be moderate in comparison with the high-tech world of IT and telecommunications.

Too many regions of Canada still rely on low-tech manufacturing. Sydney, Nova Scotia, is poor and getting poorer. Like Appalachia of old—the former coal mining and steel region around Pittsburgh, Pennsylvania—Sydney is a coal mining town and it also relies on Sydney Steel, a perennial money-loser that continues to be propped up by government subsidies. Average personal income in Sydney is 30 percent below the national average, and more than one-third of the population does not have a high-school education.

Sault Ste. Marie, Ontario, has been battered by the loss of eight hundred jobs as Algoma Steel Inc. closes two of its steel mills and goes out of the business of making steel pipes and structural steel for construction. The oil and gas industry had been one of the biggest purchasers of steel pipes, but demand is down sharply. Steel prices fell with the surge in global supplies. There has been a flood of cheaper, imported steel into the Canadian market.

Other examples abound. Wallaceberg, Ontario, had been dependent on its largest employer, U.S.-based glassware producer Libbey Inc., for more than one hundred years. The company recently shut down its Wallaceberg operation to move to Mexico, where labour is much cheaper, taking 560 jobs with it. A similar thing happened in Halifax when the Volvo car assembly plant decided to cut costs by moving to Mexico; two hundred jobs were lost. Chicoutimi, Quebec, is also dependent on blue-collar, low-skill jobs, and the labour force there is getting poorer. Twice as many people in Chicoutimi have less than a Grade 9 education as have a university degree. The jobless rate has been double-digit for a decade. Brantford, Ontario, has yet to recover from the shutdown of the Massey-Ferguson tractor plant more than a decade ago. It was the city's largest employer, and nothing has replaced it.

The human toll represented by these stories is heartbreaking and shocking. The fact is that too many people depend on social welfare payments, with little hope of satisfying employment. Local and federal governments should lure other businesses to depressed regions, retrain and relocate workers, and provide incentives for education. The old and infirm must be taken care of through government assistance, but able-bodied Boomers, Xers and Millennials need the opportunity for a future. The regions can be revitalized. There are good news stories, many of them, but they are still too few.

Foreign Direct Investment Plunges

In many ways, our economic decline has been self-inflicted. We were so fearful of losing our Canadian identity that we discouraged the very thing that could have promoted our economic well-being: foreign investment. Can you imagine Ireland today being fearful of Intel's or Citigroup's investment in its country, or the U.S. trying to keep Daimler Benz from buying Chrysler, Deutsche Bank from buying Banker's Trust, Honda from opening plants all over the country? Much of the rebuilding in the U.S. South has been through the development of foreign companies.

The history of Canadian fear of foreign, particularly U.S., investment is long, beginning with the National Policy of Sir John A. Macdonald more than a century ago. The establishment of FIRA (Foreign Investment Review Agency) in the 1970s caused a disastrous reduction in foreign direct investment, the shadow of which remains today. A 1998 United Nations report on world investment paints a grim picture for Canada. The growth in the nineties in foreign direct investment in our country— investment by foreigners not in stocks and bonds, but in start-up and existing business operations—lags that in the rest of the world (see figure 12.3). It was a mere 21 percent, compared with 233 percent for Ireland, 167 percent for Mexico, 83 percent for the United States, 73 percent for the Netherlands, 70 percent for Australia and 35 percent for the United Kingdom. Our share of global foreign direct investment has more than halved in the past decade. Global flows continue to increase while Canada's share continues to decline. We are significantly underperforming our NAFTA partners in attracting new foreign business, yet the outflow of Canadian business investment continues to surge.

The recent flurry of high-profile foreign takeovers of Canadian businesses has raised a renewed spectre of Canada losing its identity. People warn of a foreign-owned economy, particularly a U.S.-owned one. But the spate of U.S. deals involving companies like Club Monaco, Bell Canada, Newcourt Credit, JDS Fidel, MetroNet and others is occurring in an environment of increasing globalization. The fact is that merger and acquisition activity by Canadian firms abroad has been far greater than foreign activity in Canada. According to a KPMG study, in 1998, Canadian firms did 403 foreign merger and acquisition deals valued at US$41 billion. The U.S. component was 265 deals, totalling US$24.3 billion. This compares with U.S. companies doing 170 deals here, worth US$12.7 billion. So while it is true that inbound foreign investment has risen recently, it continues to decline considerably as a share of overall global flows.

FIGURE 12.3

Canada's Foreign Direct Investment Lags
1990–97 (percent: US$ terms)

Foreign Direct Investment Growth

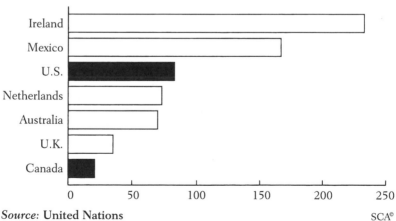

Source: United Nations   SCA©

Foreign control of the Canadian business sector as a share of operating revenues is now roughly 30 percent, compared with 25 percent in 1988. U.S. control by this measure went from 17 percent to 20 percent. When based on the share of assets, however, the figures have been quite stable, at around 21 percent since the late eighties. In some sectors, such as construction, minerals, metals and energy, foreign ownership has declined.

Foreign direct investment is important for Canada. The government would prefer "greenfield" or start-up operations rather than takeovers, although takeovers are beneficial as well. In 1996, a new agency, Investment Partnerships Canada, was created to persuade foreign companies to invest money in this country. The federal government estimates that a $1-billion increase in foreign direct investment would create forty-five thousand new jobs and increase GDP by about $4.5 billion over five years. There have been some successes. Among them are the $250-million planned investment by Swedish-owned Astra Pharma Inc. in Mississauga, Ontario.

Whether it is acquisitions, mergers or start-up operations by foreigners, Canada benefits. Takeovers often bring stronger management with global expertise, new technology, more capital and more efficient production and distribution. International business potential is strengthened. Government reports show that foreign-controlled firms in Canada generally exhibit stronger revenue growth and more rapid business expansion than domestically owned firms in the same field. For example, the $80-million takeover of Club Monaco of Toronto by Polo Ralph Lauren Corp. of New York will give the Canadian clothing chain the financial muscle for further global expansion. Merrill Lynch's takeover of Midland Walwyn has already expanded the business, created new jobs, transferred technology and research, and enhanced revenues. Foreign ownership often increases competition, benefiting consumers and creating a climate that encourages domestic firms to restructure and enhance productivity.

The effect on the country's standard of living would be profound, according to the Conference Board. In France, for example, foreign direct investment tripled between the early eighties and the early nineties, when research incentives were hiked and corporate taxes cut. The tax rate fell from about 50 percent to 32 percent.

Canada's corporate tax rates have been a substantial deterrent to attracting foreign investors, particularly for new business operations. Effective corporate rates are the lowest in the resource sector, but where we need to attract business—in the growth industries—they are non-competitive with the U.S. and most of the rest of the world. Although we have very generous R&D credits in Canada, this is not enough. Figure 12.3 showed the surge in foreign direct investment in Ireland, where corporate tax rates have been slashed to attract business. Personal tax rates in Canada are also far too high. You attract high-tech talent with a good quality of life, low taxes and advanced infrastructure: universities, airports, leading-edge telecommunications and a critical mass of other high-tech companies.

Tax Gap Widens

The *coup de grâce* for Canadian economic-growth leadership was the widening of the tax gap in relation to the U.S. and much of the rest of the world that began in 1980 and has accelerated ever since. Today, personal tax rates in Canada are not only higher than in the U.S., but they are above the average of the twenty-nine countries in the OECD (figure 12.4).

FIGURE 12.4

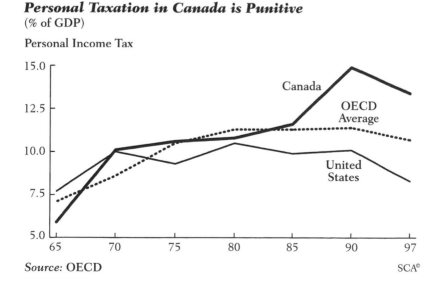

Personal Taxation in Canada is Punitive
(% of GDP)

Personal Income Tax

Source: OECD   SCA©

The inflation surge in the seventies and early eighties reduced household purchasing power in both Canada and the United States. The massive corporate restructuring that eliminated many high-paying, low-skill jobs in transportation, mining, manufacturing and the resource sector generally compounded this. By 1982, however, very tight monetary policy in the U.S. had broken the back of inflation and commodity prices started to fall. The commodity sector has been in long-term decline ever since, with only very brief periods of respite.

A Growing Competitive Disadvantage

A combination of factors caused the Canadian growth advantage to fade. More restrictive labour policies and more militant unions, as well as higher tax rates, compounded the loss of foreign business investment under FIRA. Labour laws and policies in Canada tend to impose a higher regulatory burden on employers. Minimum wages tend to be higher, and regulations regarding hours of work and overtime tend to be more restrictive, as do notice and severance rules. Labour laws encourage the formation and retention of unions. The very high cost of the social safety net and benefits packages are financed in large measure by payroll taxes, which raise the cost of labour and drive jobs out of the country. Regulatory practices too are more restrictive, and interprovincial trade barriers remain a deterrent to growth. The ongoing political uncertainty in Quebec has had a negative influence on economic growth and has certainly taken its toll over the years on the Canadian dollar and on the cost of capital. We remain far too reliant on natural resources, traditional farming and fishing, and low-skill manufacturing.

We have not invested sufficiently in technology; there is a meaningful "technology gap" between Canada and the U.S. Our manufacturing labour productivity has fallen well below that in the United States. However, productivity is notoriously hard to measure and causes a good deal of controversy. The measures of indisputable importance are living standards, economic well-being, and consumer and business confidence. The fact is, real U.S. per-capita income grew at double the Canadian rate in the 1990–98 period.

Canada is also the only country in the OECD other than Sweden whose economy has not shifted away from manufacturing and towards services in recent years. Most Canadian manufacturing is still low-skill and low-tech. Canada continues to employ a higher share of labour in low-value-added, low-technology manufacturing than the other major industrialized countries. What is of even greater concern is that there has been little improvement over the past twenty-five years. The indicators of structural change in manufacturing show only a very modest shift towards high-tech business since the mid-seventies. This is in direct contrast to the other countries.

Figure 12.5 shows that the fastest-growing sectors in U.S. manufacturing in the past decade have been the machinery, electrical and electronics sectors, commonly known as high tech. These are the sectors with the greatest productivity growth. In contrast, the fastest-growing sectors in Canadian manufacturing have been relatively low-tech sectors like furniture and food processing, where productivity growth is relatively slow. So the real growth problem in Canada is not that each of our businesses is unproductive; productivity growth in Canadian furniture, transportation equipment, petroleum and chemical products manufacturing exceeds that in the U.S. The problem is that the level of productivity growth in these sectors is relatively low, at only about 5 or 6 percent annually, compared with more than double that pace in the high-tech sector.

The good news is that we have become more international in our business dealings, with a growth in exports since the introduction of the FTA and NAFTA. The increase in the openness of the Canadian economy to international trade, especially with the United States, should have already led to a strong exchange of technology and meaningful R&D spillovers. Instead, Canada has a very disturbing innovation and technology gap with the U.S. We have exhibited a relatively slow uptake of new technology, low levels of R&D expenditure and a reluctance to restructure business and retrain and redeploy labour.

FIGURE 12.5

Canada, the High-Tech Laggard
Real Output Growth, 1998 vs. 1989 (% change)

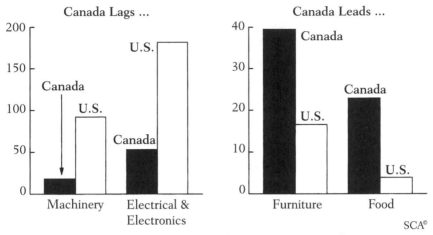

Sources: U.S. Bureau of Economic Analysis; Statistics Canada

Too many businesses in Canada have hidden behind the protection of the ever-falling loonie to make their products look more competitive in the U.S. They have not been forced to restructure, retrain and invest in new technologies to compete on a global basis. While import prices have been falling in the U.S., owing to the devaluation of many overseas currencies, import prices are rising in Canada, reflective of the late-1998 plunge in our dollar. This means that domestic producers of import-competing products do not face the degree of price competition that their American counterparts face.

Canada is ranked tenth in overall global competitiveness by the Swiss-based International Institute for Management Development—nine spots behind our most important trading partner, the United States, the partner that accounts for more than 80 percent of our exports. The U.S. is not only our most important trading partner, it is virtually our only sizable one. Number two is Japan, and trade there fell sharply in recent years, with prospects over the near term being unencouraging.

Slowing Potential Growth

The bottom line is irrefutable. Relative to other OECD countries in general, and to the U.S. in particular, Canada has a high share of small- and medium-sized companies that are less innovative, less internationally oriented and, as a result, less competitive than in other countries. Our disappointing productivity performance is bad enough, but it is compounded by the dramatic slowdown in the growth of the labour force. This slowdown is the result of two things: demographics and discouraged workers. The demographic factor is partially shared with the U.S.; labour-force growth in both countries peaked in 1982 as the youngest Boomers entered the job market, but the slowdown was markedly greater in Canada. Moreover, the slowdown in the growth of the labour force here is also reflective of a decline in labour-force participation, as many people have become too discouraged to look for work. Some of this is acceptable, to the extent that more young people are pursuing higher education to improve their job opportunities. But others have just plain given up. Participation rates in the U.S. have never been higher.

This Canadian disadvantage is compounded by slower growth in the capital stock, which has reduced our potential pace of economic expansion—the strongest sustainable non-inflationary growth we could expect if the economy were running on all cylinders. This potential growth rate has fallen from 4 percent to just over 2 percent in the past thirty years. This means a reduction in living standards—a reduction in our economic well-being.

We have already suffered a major decline in living standards. It will get worse unless we do the following:

- increase productivity through education, training, research, restructuring, innovation and investment in technology;
- allow the forces of creative destruction to operate—don't subsidize declining industries and sectors;
- improve the mobility of labour, goods and services between provinces;

- remove interprovincial regulatory impediments and trade barriers;
- provide incentives to attract foreign business;
- increase our labour-force growth by encouraging workers with viable job opportunities;
- halt the brain drain;
- attract high-skill immigrants;
- increase our capital stock—production facilities, high-tech infrastructure, machinery and equipment, commercial buildings and investment dollars;
- roll back the inordinately high average tax burden of businesses and individuals, and reduce high marginal income tax rates;
- reduce payroll and capital gains taxes.

The Failing Loonie

The Canadian dollar has fallen sharply to reflect this relative competitive disadvantage. For the better part of twenty-four years—with the exception of the period of very high interest rates, from 1988 to 1990—the Canadian dollar has been in long-term decline. In 1998, the Canadian dollar fell relative to all the world's major currencies owing to the Russian debt default and further declines in commodity prices. Prime Minister Chrétien told us that it was a good thing; it would boost tourism. Most economists in the country said that it was a necessary shock absorber, preventing a more dramatic decline in the economy due to commodity price cuts. This kind of thinking perpetuates our dependence on commodities and low-tech manufacturing, and denies the necessity to restructure our economy so that we may prosper in the future. Manufacturers and exporters generally applauded the decline, once again avoiding the sorry fact that we are not as competitive as our major trading partner. A falling dollar moves us onside only temporarily; as long as we are under-represented in the high-growth sectors of the future, our relative economic performance will continue to decline. Our currency will have to depreciate again and again to reflect this relative underperformance vis-à-vis the U.S.

If devaluation were a good thing, Thailand would have been booming. If a 69-cent dollar were a positive economic development, how about a 50-cent dollar, 25 cents, 10 cents? We all know it is not a good thing. It reduces the value of the money we earn, the money we invest. It is the equivalent of a national pay cut. It means it costs more to buy the products we import, many of which are essential to our well-being. It costs more to buy food—orange juice, grapefruit, pineapples, bananas, and all the fruits and vegetables we cannot produce in the Canadian winter. It costs more to buy technology—software and hardware. It costs more to travel outside the country, and Canadians are great travellers. Sure, it is good for tourism; but tourism is only 1 percent of our GDP. Many Canadian tourism hot spots set their prices for foreigners anyway, which means they're sky-high for Canadians. Have you seen prices in Whistler or Banff lately?

Falling Living Standards

The fall in the Canadian dollar has taken a huge toll on our economic well-being. Living standards in this country—as measured by GDP per capita—have descended to a shockingly low level. In U.S.-dollar terms, while rising recently, they are still very near the average for the OECD countries (figure 12.6), down substantially from earlier years. And this doesn't even tell the whole story, because it doesn't account for the higher tax burden in Canada. The complete picture is seen in figure 12.7, which shows that per-capita income after tax in Canada has fallen to less than one-half the level in Connecticut, 60 percent of the level in New York State and California, and below the level in Arkansas, West Virginia and Mississippi, traditionally very depressed U.S. states. Even our richest city, Toronto, has after-tax income per capita that is barely above the level in Arkansas, and 30 percent below New York State. And look at Montreal: whoever says the loss of head offices and a talent drain don't matter should look at the relative income levels of that metropolitan area.

This is scandalous. We should all be outraged, given the inherent potential wealth in Canada, the enormous human and capital resources at our disposal. How could this have happened?

FIGURE 12.6

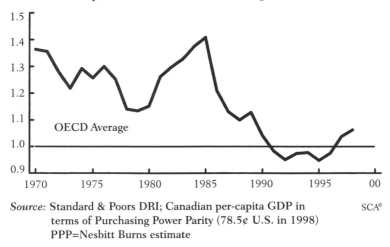

Canadian Living Standards in Decline
(US$ terms)

Canadian Per-Capita GDP Relative to OECD Average

Source: Standard & Poors DRI; Canadian per-capita GDP in terms of Purchasing Power Parity (78.5¢ U.S. in 1998) PPP=Nesbitt Burns estimate

SCA©

FIGURE 12.7

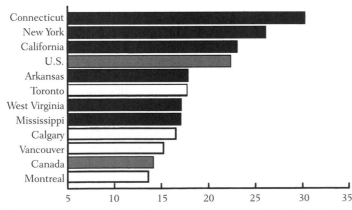

Per-Capita Income after Tax—Canada Lagging
1998 (US$ thousands)

Canada and Canadian Cities=Purchasing Power Parity (78.5¢ U.S. in 1998)
Sources: Bureau of Economic Analysis; Statistics Canada
PPP=Nesbitt Burns estimate

SCA©

Cut Tax Rates

First and foremost, we must cut taxes—all taxes, business and personal, for everyone. The yawning tax gap drives people away, drives capital away and drives business away. As the tax gap has widened, our relative growth has waned, our relative jobless rate has risen and our relative stock market performance has plunged (figure 12.8). Yes, we have balanced the budget; we even have a surplus and are paying down debt, and that is great. But tax cuts would not jeopardize our hard-won gains on that score. Look at Ireland. Tax cuts would encourage foreign and domestic business investment, spur household spending and saving, and boost the stock market. I estimate that about one-third of the decline in household savings in this country is a direct result of the rise in household tax payments. Tax cuts would boost income, profits and stock market valuations sufficiently to increase tax revenues overall. More of the economy would shift from the public to the private sector. It has worked in so many other countries: the U.S., the U.K., Finland, France and Australia, to name a few. It has worked in Alberta, and more recently in Ontario.

Traditional economic theory says that reduced tax rates mean reduced tax revenues; but new-age thinking, sometimes called supply-side economics, says that lower tax rates could mean higher tax revenues because so much growth is created. Supply-side economics was the underlying principle of the Reagan tax cuts in the early 1980s. The new theory was seen by some to have failed because the U.S. budget deficit ballooned over the next ten years. When Ronald Reagan left office the deficit had gone from roughly $75 billion to $155 billion, and by the time his successor, George Bush, left office, the deficit was an eye-popping $290 billion. Did this prove that supply-side economics was bunk? No. The reason for the large deficits was Reagan's dramatic increase in U.S. defence spending. That policy turned out to be the right thing, because it might have contributed to the demise of the Soviet Union, the opening up of the Eastern bloc and the end of the Cold War.

FIGURE 12.8

The Link between High Taxes and High Unemployment
(percentage points)

Canada minus United States

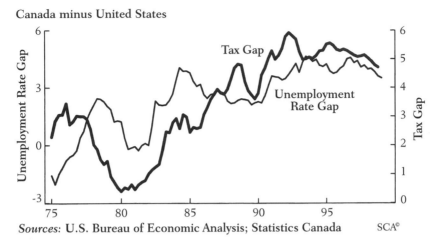

Sources: U.S. Bureau of Economic Analysis; Statistics Canada   SCA©

As an aside, there are those who would argue that the Reagan "Star Wars" defence program had only a minor influence in bankrupting the Soviet Union. That instead it was the surge in oil prices in the late seventies followed by their subsequent collapse in 1986 that wreaked havoc on the Soviet economy. This is particularly ironic and noteworthy for Canada. If volatility in commodity prices could bring down the so-called "evil empire," what could it mean for a bunch of nice guys in Canada?

In any event, the U.S. defence buildup masked the true effects of the U.S. tax cuts. In 1986, President Reagan cut the top marginal personal income tax rate from 50 percent to 28 percent, and the top corporate tax rate from 46 percent to 34 percent. Tax revenues surged 11 percent the following year and an additional 7 percent in 1988. The tax reductions touched off a multi-year economic boom, with strong job creation and increased business investment.

The same thing happened in Britain. Top marginal income tax rates were slashed from 60 percent to 40 percent in 1988. Revenues surged 9 percent the following year, a full percentage point stronger than the average annual gain in the previous five years. The U.K. has been a top economic performer for most of the nineties, in large measure due to the tax cuts. Britain in the seventies and eighties had been a tax-heavy economic laggard. It is no coincidence that the U.S. and the U.K. managed to cut taxes dramatically and balance their budgets without imposing substantial spending restraint. There is a lesson in this for Canada.

Examples of tax cuts that pay for themselves can be found closer to home. The Harris government cut personal income tax rates in Ontario by 30 percent since 1995. Many thought this would drive revenues down and keep the budget deficit close to $10 billion; but look what happened instead. Ontario has enjoyed one of the strongest GDP growth rates in the country, in some measure due to the confidence boost brought about by the tax relief package. Skeptics back in 1995 argued that the Ontario government would lose roughly $5 billion in revenues as a direct result of the tax reduction. But 500,000 new jobs were created and 3 percent average economic growth was generated, so that Ontario's revenue stream is now more than 15 percent higher than before the tax cuts were implemented. Indeed, even personal income tax receipts—where the relief was most heavily concentrated—have climbed almost $2 billion over the past four years. And the government has reduced the budget deficit ahead of schedule. Moreover, because of the growth-led revenue surge, the Ontario government did not fully implement its planned spending cuts; program spending has in fact increased 3 percent since the Tories took office. The Tory victories in the last Ontario and New Brunswick elections were further confirmation of growing grassroots support for tax reduction.

We have already cut federal government spending in Canada, and now we must cut tax rates as well. We should eliminate the 5 percent personal surtax on Canadians earning more than $65,000; it was meant to be temporary anyway—at least that's what we were told in 1986, when it was first introduced. We should also reintroduce the full indexation of the personal tax system for inflation. Further cuts to Employment Insurance (EI) premiums would restore balance in the EI account, currently in huge surplus. EI premiums are paid by employers and employees and are a direct tax on jobs, discouraging badly needed employment gains.

These are just housekeeping issues, however, and their implementation would still leave the top personal marginal tax rate unacceptably high, at around 47 percent. What we really need is a substantial move to bring down the tax burden for all Canadians, so that the top rate would be closer to the U.S. level of 40 percent. To get there, I recommend that the marginal rates in all three personal income tax brackets be cut by three percentage points—to 14 percent for low-income, 23 percent for middle-income and 26 percent for high-income earners. This would amount to a 12 percent average personal income tax cut, which could be phased in over three years. Even with this reduction, the top rates would kick in at income levels substantially below those in the U.K. and the U.S.

The capital gains rate should be cut back as well, to 50 percent of the top income tax rate from 75 percent today. This would effectively reduce the top marginal tax rate on capital gains to around 20 percent, about the same as in the U.S., and would encourage a more entrepreneurial, risk-taking attitude in this country, which would ultimately boost the stock market, capital formation and household wealth. Entrepreneurs and business executives today frequently receive stock options as a large measure of their compensation. Many have been reluctant to realize their stock- or bond-market gains because they would be required to fork over almost 40 percent of the gain to the government. A cut in the tax on such gains would quickly translate into higher, not lower, revenue growth for the government. In the U.S., capital gains tax rates were last reduced in 1997, and the annual revenues from this source ballooned from US$67 billion to roughly US$100 billion. The revenues generated by the positive effect on the stock market and the enhanced incentive to realize gains more than offset the loss from the actual cut in the tax rate itself. This also happened the previous time the U.S. reduced capital gains tax rates, from 40 percent in 1978 to 20 percent in 1982; the government's revenue more than doubled. It is no coincidence that the great bull market in stocks began in 1982 amid this historic cut in the capital gains tax rate.

Corporate tax rates in Canada should be reduced meaningfully as well. A five-percentage-point cut in the general rate would put Canadian industry on a competitive footing with the United States. Why not give our business sector the tools it needs to compete in an international setting, where corporate tax rates are coming down virtually everywhere?

The initial cost of this entire tax package is roughly $17 billion. This may sound radical, but this prescription is an essential ingredient to help rejuvenate an economy and stock market that have lagged behind most of the industrialized world for almost twenty years. The tax relief will not push us back into budgetary deficit, as Finance Minister Martin fears, because of its powerful multiplier effect on the broader economy, which is so vividly evident in other success stories around the globe and here in Canada. Job creation would be stronger, income growth more robust, business start-ups would grow, foreign direct investment would surge and business investment would rise. So would the stock market, which would give a huge lift to household wealth, consumer confidence and spending power. The growth surge resulting from the tax cuts would in a matter of two or three years, maybe less, increase budgetary surpluses, not reduce them. This would give us *more* money to spend on health care, education and other social programs. The empirical evidence is there; only the political will is lacking.

Human Capital Development

The knowledge-based economy in Canada is still relatively small by international standards. We must emphasize this sector if we are to share in the prosperity of this upwave. The knowledge-intensive sectors are wide-ranging, encompassing far more than just the computer hardware and software fields. It includes all businesses that apply technology and knowledge to their ongoing enterprises. It includes applications of technology to the life sciences, food production and the resource business. It includes knowledge-intensive businesses like financial services, law, medicine, pharmaceuticals, universities and other educational institutions, consulting—the list could go on and on. It does not include traditional food production, traditional natural resource production, low-value-added manufacturing or low-skill services—the historical underpinnings of the Canadian economy.

High on our national agenda should be the promotion and attraction of knowledge-based businesses, the creation of incentives for their development and relocation in Canada. Also, importantly, we must train our labour force to provide the high-skilled services needed in the technology revolution. We have a very high level of public spending on education in Canada compared with most of the rest of the world, but we have a disturbingly poor return on that spending. For example, 13 percent of the adult population in Canada in 1996 had a university degree, compared with 20 percent in the United States. The high-school dropout rate remains relatively high: 25 percent of Canadian adults did not complete high school, compared with only 14 percent in the U.S. Furthermore, literacy levels continue to be surprisingly low here compared with other countries. In 1997, a record 67 percent of high-school graduates went on to university or college in the U.S., compared with 60 percent in Canada. More emphasis on vocational training and job-relevant skills might help keep students in school. Community colleges have become the bricks and mortar of a national training system in both countries.

Regional differences in literacy and educational attainment are glaring. East of Ontario, the proportional representation of university graduates falls the farther east you go. In Newfoundland, three times as many people had less than a Grade 9 education as had university degrees, according to a 1998 Statistics Canada study. The literacy rates and level of completed formal education are decidedly lower in Quebec, the Northwest Territories and the Atlantic provinces than elsewhere. The most unfortunate finding of the government study was that the relative educational trends are not changing among younger generations. Language barriers are an added problem in Quebec because they reduce labour mobility.

These factors, along with a continued reliance on seasonal work and the resource industry, go a long way towards explaining the relatively high unemployment rates in some parts of Canada. Better coordination of educational curricula between regions and improved mobility of labour are crucial to addressing regional economic disparity; so is further effort by provincial governments to attract new businesses to their region. Local community colleges could work with new businesses to train the labour force.

There is a shortage of high-tech labour in Canada. International Data Corp Canada Ltd., a Toronto-based research firm, reported in early 1999 that continuing shortages of skilled high-tech workers have caused project delays for 60 percent of the country's large companies. The research firm also found that 43 percent of companies in the transportation, utilities and communications sectors said the labour shortage slowed their overall growth. It is estimated that the 175 largest high-tech companies in Canada planned to hire ten thousand people in 1998. The most recent data suggest that all the country's computer science and electrical engineering programs combined produce fewer than five thousand undergraduates each year.

There is a lack of advanced manufacturing technology workers as well. Douglas R. Greer, a retired general manager for SKD Co. in Brampton, Ontario, has been on a one-man mission to get this message across. He believes there is a grave shortage of high-tech machine-tool designers in Canada, forcing many durable-goods manufacturers like the auto industry to import machine tools. Because of this labour shortage, Canada has been unable to capitalize on opportunities that could translate, according to Mr. Greer, into thousands of well-paid, semi-skilled jobs. Ontario produces only three hundred toolmaking graduates annually, most of whom lack the academic qualifications necessary for the high-tech demands of today's durable-goods manufacturers. General Motors has terminated all apprenticeship training programs in Canada, and the Big Three's collective agreements provide for contracting out of tooling to independent tooling manufacturers, which generally means that the work goes outside the country. Almost every manufacturing firm in Canada—from the automated production systems of modern agriculture and food processing, to mining, petroleum and the forestry sector—is affected by the shortage of competent toolmakers. With fewer than eight thousand fully qualified journeymen toolmakers, we are rapidly approaching an untenable shortage.

Software developers and computer programmers also continue to be in particularly short supply. While the high-tech industry in Ontario estimates it will create up to fifty-six thousand new jobs over the next five years, only twelve thousand will graduate from the province's universities. The shortages are immense in Quebec as well and there is little in-migration of these workers to the province. In 1998, there was an estimated 40 percent shortfall in tech-trained workers there for the 1,816 new job openings. Between 1996 and 2001, demand for IT professionals is expected to grow by 20 percent per year.

Ontario's universities have an insufficient number of spaces for new students in computer sciences and engineering. In 1997, there were 12,500 places in these fields, causing the schools to turn away a large number of very qualified students. The University of Toronto, for example, had 3,566 applicants for engineering, with only 800 available spaces. At the University of Waterloo, 3,816 applied for only 780 engineering spots. The same is true all over the country. Each time a bright, eager student—sometimes with an average in the high eighties—is rejected by a Canadian university, it represents a lost opportunity to strengthen our competitive position.

Current government funding policies make training students in technology fields a losing proposition financially for the universities. It costs the provinces more to train engineering and high-tech students than traditional humanities, commerce and social science students. Surely Canada's premier high-tech companies like Northern Telecom, BCE, Newbridge Networks, Corel, the chartered banks, Mitel, Telus and the like would subsidize these additional costs through outright donation, co-op programs and student loans.

Ironically, many of these companies have resorted to hiring foreign workers—a real tragedy when youth unemployment in this country stands at over 15 percent. Canada's high-tech sector launched a major overseas recruiting initiative in 1997 in an attempt to hire thousands of new foreign software workers. Our government has relented to private sector pressure to make it easier for these workers to enter the country quickly on temporary work permits. Indeed, the federal government announced in late 1998 that it was extending indefinitely a pilot program that relaxed the immigration rules for high-tech workers. Most of these workers come from India, Pakistan, Malaysia and South Africa. Industry Minister John Manley said that the reason for extending the program was to help fill the dire skills shortage in the technology sector; this is critical for the development of the Canadian IT industry in the global, knowledge-based economy. There is a huge shortage of IT executives too. Veteran high-tech executives are in extremely high demand and short supply globally. Many are lured elsewhere because of better pay and lower taxes.

IT departments in Canada's major companies are desperate for qualified workers. In a late-1997 survey of high-tech companies alone, 88 percent responded that they faced a shortage of skilled workers. The Software Human Resource Council—an Ottawa-based research facility jointly funded by the private sector and government—estimated that there were fifteen thousand vacant programming jobs in Canada. That number has risen sharply more recently. American companies face an even bigger shortage and are aggressively recruiting in Canada.

An international study by management consulting firm Towers Perrin found that executive compensation in Canada, though rising, still lags well behind U.S. pay scales. Compensation for senior managers in Canada is falling further behind U.S. levels, putting Canadian companies at a competitive disadvantage and increasing the pressure to staunch the flow of employees south of the border, the report added. Towers Perrin found in its 1998 Worldwide Total Rewards survey of twenty-three countries that the average total remuneration for a chief executive in Canada was just under $500,000 a year, compared with $1.07 million in the U.S. The gaps are proportionately even wider at the executive levels below the CEO. According to the Ontario Institute of Chartered Accountants in Toronto, the U.S. job scene is hugely attractive, in terms of both relative compensation and relative tax rates. The U.S. has eased restrictions on immigration of tech-skilled workers to address their shortages. For Canadians, it often takes only three to five days for U.S. work visas to be processed. Most who leave on work visas get permanent working papers, or green cards, within a few years of arrival in the U.S.

Clearly, progress requires a high degree of interaction between educational institutions and the private world of business. If the private sector and universities and community colleges are working well together, the market incentives can guide researchers and teachers towards valuable new areas. An example of this process was seen in the U.S. years ago, when the opportunities in the emerging petroleum refining industry led to the creation of schools of chemical engineering.

Political Leadership Needed

The government must create an environment that fosters change and progress. That means we must allow old, unprofitable, declining businesses to die. We must divert the money we use today to subsidize these businesses to the development of new high-tech opportunities. Creative destruction must be allowed to occur. A new and improved product usually replaces an old one. Workers who produced the old product have to shift into some new activity. At best, this results in a spell of unemployment; at worst, it can lead to a permanent loss of income. The job market in a vibrant economy is in a constant state of turnover; indeed, the turnover accelerates during a period of rapid economic expansion.

Innovation and change inevitably create winners and losers. Job losses and pay cuts are the most visible and politically powerful symptoms. But we know that for society as a whole, innovation and technological change offer large net gains. If we had not tolerated disruption in the past, we would still be travelling by horse and wagon.

Many older firms and sectors need to shrink. No amount of fiscal or monetary stimulus will change that. If government policy measures delay the process, as they have in Canada, they make things worse; they have perverse effects in the long run. They reduce the competitiveness of the economy as a whole; they drain precious resources from otherwise more profitable and efficient use; and they keep people in dead-end jobs and ensure the demise of whole regions. There is a growing recognition, for example, that the high levels of long-term unemployment in Europe may be the unintended consequence of the very policies designed to fight unemployment and recessions in the first place. A much more productive approach to policy is to make the adjustment process as efficient and painless as possible, and to maintain the conditions that lead to rapid entry of new firms that compete for workers.

This requires political leadership. Each year, an agitated electorate voices new demands for security and protection from disruption. Government efforts to provide this protection have corrosive effects on markets and on that essential ingredient, competitive spirit. Leaders must give people the confidence to compete. They must encourage people to believe that economic change brings genuine opportunity, that the risks are real but manageable.

A nation that creates a policy stance fostering the process of creative destruction can count on sustained economic growth, on being a global growth leader in the upwave of the technology revolution. But a nation that tries to resist change by protecting inefficient firms and sectors will impede the flow of goods and ideas, and will fall further and further behind.

Take Care of Yourself

Many of us will suffer losses and setbacks in our careers, but that does not mean we are down for the count. Who among us wins every time? If you are in a declining industry, get out. If you are in a dead-end job, get out. If you live in a dead region, move. That's easy for me to say, you think. Well, the alternative is worse. We are a nation of immigrants. Our forefathers made remarkable sacrifices to come to a new country where nothing was guaranteed. Our relocation would be far less painful and traumatic than theirs. There are tremendous educational opportunities available in Canada today, for little cost; take advantage of them. There are many regions that are growing, many businesses that are clamouring for workers. We will look at these success stories in the next chapter.

Great Canadian Success Stories

The potential is huge for a major revival in Canadian growth leadership. The necessary ingredients are here; what we need now is the will to change, the will to envision a new economic paradigm that says change is good, globalization is good, competition is good. We can compete and excel, but we cannot continue to be mired in the past. Past is not prologue; it never has been.

Profit is not a dirty word. Profit is the necessary ingredient for progress, prosperity, growth and job creation. There is still a mistaken belief propagated by the schools, media and the press, and embedded in the Canadian psyche, that people who do things for profit are greedy or underhanded. But only a profitable company can create sustainable, high-paying jobs. The more profitable a company, the more investment capital it can attract to respond to growth opportunities in the future. Profit is a sign of achievement; it means someone has produced something of value that other people are willing to buy. Employees and shareholders alike reap the rewards of this success. It is the engine of growth in the economy.

Reinvention and Restructuring—Calgary

We have accomplished much already. Take, for example, the economy of Alberta and the oil patch. In the early eighties, falling oil prices and global recession led to an enormous bust in the energy sector. The economy of Calgary, and of Alberta as a whole, collapsed. When oil prices fell to twelve-year lows in 1998 and early 1999, Calgary fared much better. To be sure, layoffs and exploration cancellations took their toll, but the diversification away from energy-related business in the region has helped. So has the substantial restructuring in the oil industry itself.

In 1986, roughly 60 percent of all provincial corporate tax revenues in Alberta came from the oil and gas sector; today, that has slipped to about 22 percent. Over the period 1993 to 1998, 105,000 jobs were created in Calgary, 22 percent of which were in business services, 20 percent in manufacturing, 14 percent in construction and 11 percent in transportation, according to a Royal Bank study. Calgary has attracted more than seventy thousand people in the past three years. The jobless rate has fallen to just over 5 percent and there are labour shortages everywhere—in the skilled building trades, high-tech energy sector, computer programming and more. Smed International, a fast-growing high-end office furniture maker, hired about 1,200 people in 1997 and still had more than 150 job vacancies in 1998. The labour shortage did not deter British-based Chroma-Colour International, the world's leading manufacturer of paint for animation cells, from opening an office in Calgary. They chose Calgary after considering such U.S. cities as Phoenix, Denver and Portland. Quality-of-life considerations and tax incentives were fundamental to the decision.

Calgary now has the second highest number of corporate head offices in Canada, behind Toronto. The move of corporate headquarters has been notable, and none more so than the 1996 move of Canadian Pacific from Montreal—the largest corporate move in Canadian history, shifting more than 1,200 workers. The reason given by CP executives was that 80 percent of CP's rail, petroleum, coal and hotel operations were located in the West. Although they didn't publicly state it, the much lower tax rates didn't hurt either.

More than 1,100 high-tech firms are now located in Calgary, employing more than thirty thousand people. Calgary is home to a booming telecommunications industry. Northern Telecom is one of the city's largest employers, having established two wireless phone plants there in the past five years. One of the new Calgary businesses is WestJet Airlines, a cut-rate airline that has carried more than 2.5 million passengers to nine Western Canadian cities since early 1996. The significant growth in air traffic stimulated the economy, especially in car rentals, hotels, golf courses and restaurants.

Calgary has also become the hub for distribution and warehousing in Western Canada. Combining a major international airport, the Trans-Canada Highway, and CN and CP railways, the city has become the gateway to the so-called Canamex corridor. This is the area that links Calgary to Salt Lake City, Utah—a new and growing high-tech city—and continues all the way south to Guaymas, Mexico.

The energy industry itself has diversified and strengthened. It has cut the fat and reduced operating costs to the point where it can stay in business when commodity prices are low, and cash in when prices rise. Technological innovation has raised productivity and reduced costs. Shifts to natural gas and high-tech production techniques have also helped. Streamlining and labour efficiencies are evident. And companies have learned to use financial technology, hedging oil price declines in the futures markets. Pipeline construction will be another engine of growth. Oil executives say that the industry was hurt by low oil prices, leading to the slashing of capital spending projects, but it is much leaner and better capitalized than in the eighties. Even so, as the oil price collapse lingered, companies like Amoco Canada, Canadian Occidental Petroleum and Gulf Canada announced layoffs, taking the total of job cuts to well over a thousand in 1998 and early 1999. The oil services sector was negatively impacted as well. There was some uptick in the gas business, but not enough to offset the slowdown in oil. Oil prices moved up at the end of the first quarter of 1999, but oil executives today don't count on sustained rising prices to make money.

The overall growth in Calgary presented its challenges. Office vacancy rates plunged. Indeed, the pressure on the city's infrastructure was huge. Housing starts were strong for years, and downtown office space was so tight that the addition of three new towers eased the vacancy rates only marginally.

Edmonton Contributes to Alberta's Success

Edmonton too has made an amazing comeback. Alberta's capital city was hit hard by the government cutbacks and layoffs in the early nineties. In 1993, the unemployment rate was 11.2 percent, compared with just over 6 percent today. The city has seen a rise in population and stepped-up commercial building. The reason for the success is technology.

The heart of Edmonton's economy is the oil and gas industry, followed closely by mining, manufacturing, advanced technology, farming and forestry. Above all, Edmonton is a service, supply and research centre for the energy sector. Since 1995, the city's economy has been boosted by the successful innovations in extracting heavy oil from the northern Alberta oil sands. The results have been spectacular—estimated to contribute more than $22 billion to the Alberta economy over the next decade, with companies like Syncrude Canada Ltd. and more than fifteen others claiming their share. Even with the extended oil price collapse, Suncor was in recruitment mode, planning to hire eight hundred people in the next few years to staff its $2.2-billion oil sands expansion in Fort McMurray, Alberta. Other firms, however, put their oil sands projects on hold or downsized them substantially until oil prices came under some sustained upward pressure.

The positive spinoffs from the oil sands development to date have been huge. Finning International Inc., a $2-billion-plus Vancouver-based supplier of Caterpillar heavy equipment, decided to move its head office to Edmonton to be closer to the action, shifting 190 jobs along the way. Finning rents, sells and leases equipment for the oil sands project, as well as for the agriculture, construction, forestry and mining industries. The truth is, however, that Finning's relocation was motivated as much by a desire to escape the high taxes and regulatory red tape of British Columbia as it was by the need to be closer to the oil sands. Jim Shepard, the Vancouver-born CEO of Finning, was so concerned about the anti-business climate in B.C. that he helped spearhead a business summit of eight hundred representatives from small, medium and large companies in the province.

Important to Edmonton's ongoing prosperity is that it is not just an energy resource town. The University of Alberta works closely with the business community for their mutual benefit. Spearheading this endeavour has been James Murray, the director of the university's Industry Liaison Office. Murray, a former professor of geological sciences, believes that one solution to reduced governmental R&D funding is to commercialize made-on-campus inventions. Since his arrival in 1994, royalties for products and services that the university has produced have surged from $927,000 in 1995 to more than $4.2 million. More than forty-eight spinoff companies were born and more than 1,255 direct jobs generated. Biotechnology has been a huge success. Biomira Inc., one of North America's foremost cancer-treatment research facilities, got its start with research developed at the university. Edmonton is now home to a whole fleet of biotech firms. The university provides on-campus incubation space, crucial to fledgling companies, keeping them close to the originating research labs and key people while giving them a dedicated space in which to develop their technologies towards commercial applications.

Technology is the Key to Resource Sector Success

Future growth potential will be unlocked in all resource sectors as businesses apply technology and skill to base-level products. Processed manufacturing in forest products—high-value-added specialty products—can become our forte. Biotechnological breakthroughs will also add to our potential competitive advantage. To date, however, the Canadian forest products industry remains extremely low-tech, dampening significantly the economies of British Columbia, Quebec and other areas.

B.C. is not without its success stories, however. Ballard Power, located in Burnaby, is a great example of a high-tech energy resource story. It develops and manufactures fuel cells that convert hydrogen and oxygen directly to electricity. This kind of fuel can be used in power plants, mass transit buses and automobiles. The possibilities on the auto side are huge, as fuel cells allow for zero-emission cars. This has not been lost on General Motors and Daimler-Chrysler, customers of and investors in Ballard. Buses powered by the Ballard fuel cells are already running in Chicago and British Columbia.

Other alternative-fuel successes are clearly in sight. Petro-Canada has bought a 10 percent stake in the ethanol division of Ottawa-based Iogen Corporation, a private biotechnology company owned by the Foody family. Iogen is a world leader in the production of enzymes for industrial use. The natural enzymes are extracted from a fungus that lives on dead wood. Iogen pioneered the commercial use of enzymes in the pulp and paper industry to reduce the toxic effluents in the bleaching process. With support from the National Research Council and Natural Resources Canada, Iogen developed and commercialized these natural enzymes that can be used to bleach pulp in place of environmentally unfriendly chlorine. The enzymes are also used to bleach textiles. All stonewashed Wrangler jeans use Iogen's enzymes. There are many other uses for these enzymes, which have been sold to help in the beer-brewing process and to make animal feed more easily digestible.

Potentially the most exciting use of the enzymes is to break down agricultural and forest waste products—such as wood chips, hay, straw and ultimately paper—into sugars that are fermented to produce a type of ethanol that Iogen says can cut auto emissions more than 90 percent compared with conventional gasoline. The fermentation itself produces a by-product that can be used as a fuel and burned to power the entire process. In the works for many years, they believe that this is a unique breakthrough technology, far superior to its competitors' ethanol, which is produced from corn. Corn-produced ethanol is more expensive and has emission levels only slightly lower than gasoline. Unlike the Ballard fuel cells, which require a change in the engine structure of the motor vehicle, Iogen's ethanol simply replaces the fuel currently in use.

Canada's commitment to the 1997 Kyoto agreement to reduce greenhouse gas emissions could be a boon to Iogen's ethanol business. Iogen's challenge is to reduce the cost of commercial production of the ethanol. For now, fuel made with Iogen technology would cost about

5 to 10 cents more per litre than conventional gasoline. Improving technology will likely make the product competitive very soon. Fossil fuel companies like Petro-Canada know they need to invest aggressively in new technology to stay competitive under the international rules to reduce emissions. It was announced in early 1999 that Iogen and partner Petro-Canada would jointly invest another $15.3 million to build a demonstration plant before marketing the ethanol. In less than two years they expect to begin building the world's first plant to produce ethanol from natural fibre, a $200-million venture.

The mining industry has produced its own high-tech successes. Rio Algom, headquartered in Toronto, is a global leader in bio-leaching copper ores. Bio-leaching is the process by which natural bacteria literally consume copper sulphides and oxygen to excrete copper oxides and ultimately copper cathode plate—the desired end product. Process innovation in Rio Algom's Cerro Colorado mine in northern Chile has set a new standard in biotech mining.

Noranda, Inc., the copper mining giant headquartered in Toronto, found a way to make its Horne smelter in Rouyn-Noranda, Quebec, more profitable by mining electronics. Each year, fifty thousand tons of discarded computers find their way to Rouyn-Noranda, home of the biggest smelting and recycling plant in North America, the Horne smelter. Noranda, an expert extractor, has figured out how to retrieve the precious metals found in old computers. A load of computers can contain up to fifteen ounces of precious metal per ton, fetching as much as $2,000.

The Horne smelter's real vocation is copper. The smelter churns out 5 percent of the world's output each year. Copper ore found naturally always contains some precious metals like platinum, palladium, selenium and tellurium in addition to gold and silver, which Noranda has to separate. With this expertise, Noranda made the move into mining electronics.

Old computers and related equipment pour into this recycling giant from as many as eighteen countries. Noranda has an alliance with Hewlett-Packard Co. Its subsidiary, Micro Metallics of San Jose, processes all obsolete HP machines from all over the world and then sends the processed equipment to the Horne smelter for metallurgical recycling. Noranda is trying to strike the same deal with other computer makers and believes the Y2K problem is a boon to their business, increasing the number of discarded machines worldwide. Noranda's Horne smelter is a global leader in electronic recycling. Its only competition is in Europe, where Boliden, the Canadian-Swedish conglomerate, and Union Menière of Belgium run similar plants.

Canada's mining industry is at the leading edge of other innovative developments, including remote tele-mining (mining below the ground surface using above-ground sensors and remote equipment), geo-sensing, laser-guidance systems, and 3-D animation and simulation applications. The use of advanced robotics and telecommunications devices will improve safety and reduce costs, as well as enhance productivity. Inco, in Sudbury, Ontario, is running pilot projects in tele-mining that have already shown encouraging results.

Agra-Tech—Huge Potential Growth

Like so much else, the future of food production lies in the technology revolution. We can be proud of our agra-tech accomplishments. The Canadian Food Inspection Agency has approved more than thirty-four genetically altered vegetables and grains for consumption. These include canola, corn, tomatoes, cotton, potatoes and soybeans. Nearly 20 million hectares of genetically re-engineered foodstuffs were planted in 1998 in Canada and the U.S., a threefold increase in two years.

While much of Canadian agriculture and fishing is of the traditional low-tech variety, Saskatchewan has made significant strides in the high-tech sector. Saskatoon has become a leader in agricultural biotechnology with its path-breaking Innovation Place. Adjacent to the University of Saskatchewan, Innovation Place is home to roughly one hundred private biotech companies, employing more than 1,600 people. These companies work closely with the faculty and students of the university in the areas of agriculture, information technology, resource sciences and life sciences, which are the university's areas of greatest strength. Leading discoveries include the first genetically manipulated crop and the first genetically engineered animal vaccines. Innovation Place contributes roughly $200 million each year to the Saskatchewan economy, and that figure is growing rapidly. About 30 percent of Canada's agricultural-biotech industry is located in Saskatchewan. Between 1922 and 1998 the average house price in Saskatoon jumped 40 percent, boosted by the flourishing biotech industry.

Even Low-Tech Manufacturing Can Adjust

There is no reason why old-line, low-value-added manufacturing companies can't reinvent themselves. In fact, there are a few companies in the U.S. that were founded nearly three hundred years ago and, having made significant readjustments, are still in business today. For example, J.E. Rhoads & Sons has been around since 1702, when it began manufacturing buggy whips. This company would have disappeared long ago if it hadn't been for the smart management in the 1860s who saw the railway coming and knew that buggies would be a relic of the past. They retooled the factory to make conveyor belts.

The Dexter Company opened for business in 1767 as a gristmill in Windsor Locks, Connecticut. Innovative managers understood the concept of corporate re-engineering. They saw that milling was a dying industry, so they closed the mills and started to produce stationery. From there they switched to tea bags, and from tea bags to glue. Today, they make high-tech coatings and adhesives for airplanes.

My great-grandfather's brother, Jake Bloom, a Lithuanian immigrant with no formal education, founded a company at the turn of the last century that produced cedar chests—wooden boxes on legs that protected woolen blankets and sweaters from moths and damp weather. When World War I broke out, he transformed his factory in Philadelphia to produce coffins for the U.S. Army. He made a fortune.

While the textile industry has been declining in Canada and the U.S. for many years, the Tiger Brand and Cambridge Towel companies, both in Southern Ontario, have prospered by investing and reinvesting in leading-edge technology. Even modern technology companies are forced to restructure in this fast-changing world. Early in 1999, telecom giant Northern Telecom, based in Brampton, Ontario, bade farewell to its remaining assembly plants. Nortel has long recognized that telephone equipment manufacturing has become a low-margin commodity business that is best left to cheap-labour locales in the Far East. They have now completely bowed out of traditional manufacturing and abandoned a legacy of telephone assembly work that dates back to the firm's beginnings in 1895. Today, more than 75 percent of Nortel employees are engaged in R&D, sales and marketing. Just ten years ago, that number was 45 percent.

Retailing Turnaround and Successes

While the defeats in Canadian retailing have been notable, some nimble retail business managers have successfully re-engineered. Loblaws Companies Limited, Canada's largest retail and wholesale food distributor, has recovered smartly from its ailing days in the early seventies. Galen Weston took over the money-losing family-owned company in 1972. He raised money by rationalizing assets and installed new senior management, starting with two McKinsey & Co. consultants, former university roommate David Nichol and Richard Currie. One of the most highly acclaimed aspects of the Loblaws turnaround was its private-label program. The No Name product line was launched as a price leader in 1978, with immediate success. In 1984, the program took a dramatic and innovative leap forward with the creation of their President's Choice brand—the first large-scale private brand that offered a premium product line in direct competition with national brands, offering superior products at lower prices. Loblaws is now a highly profitable destination retailer, and the Loblaws private-label program is considered among the best in the world.

Turnarounds have also been evident at Canadian Tire, Sears Canada and Holt Renfrew, to name a few. Roots Canada and Club Monaco are among the best in their class worldwide. Chapters and Indigo rival anything that U.S.-based Barnes and Noble or Borders have to offer. Smaller retailers have established booming businesses: Toronto-based Wm. Ashley, offering china, crystal, silver and a real-time bridal gift registry on the Internet; Pusateri's, a gourmet food emporium where service is king; and Sporting Life, the always crowded sports clothing and equipment retailer that appeals to Boomers and Millennials alike. These are but a few examples.

Quick-witted management that is prepared for change and looking for opportunity has always been essential for survival. This is not new. We've seen substantial repositioning by companies such as Seagrams (into entertainment), Famous Players (mega-theatre-plus complexes) and High Liner Foods (from National Sea Products). Sometimes whole towns have to re-engineer themselves. We have seen this in Barrie, Ontario; in Summerside, Prince Edward Island; and in Moncton, New Brunswick, to name a few.

Booming Barrie

Barrie is tucked along the shores of Lake Simcoe, one hundred kilometres north of Toronto. It was long considered a pit stop on the road to Toronto's cottage country—the Muskokas and Algonquin Park. That is changing, as Barrie now is one of the fastest-growing cities in the country. Its population has taken off, from 70,400 in 1994 to 91,000 today, benefiting from a boom in retail services and manufacturing. A string of big-box retailers has moved in, attracting Boomer shoppers on their way north. These retailers include Wal-Mart, Costco Wholesale, Home Depot and Business Depot.

The auto parts sector has been key to a manufacturing boom, triggered by the opening of a Honda plant in nearby Alliston. Yachiyo of Ontario Manufacturing Inc., a Japanese parts maker that produces gas tanks and metal struts, opened an operation in Barrie in 1990 specifically to supply the Alliston factory; it now employs more than two hundred people. French auto parts manufacturer Bertrand Faure started an operation four years ago. The company, which makes reclining mechanisms for car seats, has grown rapidly. They chose Barrie because of its affordable land, skilled labour force, quality of life and good transportation system, with easy access to Southern Ontario's auto assembly plants.

High-tech companies have also come to Barrie. Prodomax Industrial Automation International Ltd. designs and builds very sophisticated robotic assembly, welding and machining systems. Sales have exploded and so have jobs: Prodomax employs more than 125 workers. Engineers at the plant enjoy the affordable housing, clean air, easy commutes and child-friendly environment. The marina, yacht club and proximity to cottage country are appealing as well.

Summerside Averts Disaster

The local air force base in Summerside, P.E.I., had long been a large and secure source of economic stability for the town of roughly fourteen thousand inhabitants. In the summer of 1989, the Mulroney government closed the base, sending 1,200 people looking for new jobs. Many left town. The federal government helped by awarding Summerside the national processing centre for the GST, but the community knew this was not enough to ensure ongoing prosperity. They took action. On the site of the former air force base they created Slemon Park, an immense industrial facility. In addition, they lured new businesses to the region by forgiving all provincial and local income, property and sales taxes for corporate residents. They have since attracted a wide range of companies in manufacturing, telecommunications, retail and tourism. The town's population is now growing.

Atlantic Turbines Inc., a company that overhauls Pratt & Whitney airplane engines, is one of four aerospace companies that have located at Slemon Park. The other three are AlliedSignal Aerospace Canada, Testori Americas Corp. and Wiebel Aerospace Inc.

Canada's Aerospace Successes

Our aerospace industry is one of Canada's great successes, having accomplished much since it was privatized a decade ago. Over the past ten years, aerospace companies in Canada have grown more rapidly than in any other OECD country. The industry has edged out Japan to become the world's fifth largest in terms of sales in 1998, and it is on track to eclipse Germany and take the number-four spot in 2000. Still ahead of Canada are the U.S., Britain and France.

The industry's contribution to the economy is huge, representing more than sixty-four thousand high-paying jobs. The average weekly earnings for all manufacturing industries is about $748; aerospace employees earn close to $940. Huge research dollars are spent by this sector, too. The industry invested $1.4 billion in 1997. On average, aerospace companies invest close to 11 percent of total sales in R&D initiatives. For example, Pratt & Whitney, the airplane engine manufacturer, is second only to Northern Telecom in R&D expenditures. Other top R&D companies in the field are Montreal's Bombardier, with its Canadair and de Havilland aircraft divisions, and Montreal-based CAE Inc. The world's largest supplier of aircraft flight simulators, CAE is seeing its business surge. It is the world leader in the design and production of military flight simulation equipment, supplying close to 70 percent of the global market. Committed to investment in innovative products, CAE consistently puts between 10 percent and 20 percent of its sales into R&D.

Canada has also been a global leader in the development of military aerospace technology. We have developed some of the most advanced space communications systems and are renowned for our space robotics technology. Canada is a leader in satellite communications and earth sensing equipment as well. A world leader in space robotics for almost thirty years, Spar Aerospace developed the world-renowned Canadarm Robotic Arm for the U.S. space shuttle program and was in the process of developing the next generation of space robotics for Canada's contribution to the international space station Alpha. Spar, however, fell on hard times and has been reorganizing, selling many of its units, including the Canadarm, to a U.S. firm. Another Canadian company, COM DEV International, is a leading designer, manufacturer and distributor of satellite communications technologies for processing wireless signals. Of the eighty-one communications satellites launched in 1997, sixty-seven had COM DEV products on board.

Canadian companies also supply world military markets with unique, specialized defence equipment and technology. For example, the Canadian Marconi Company is at the forefront of design, manufacturing, sales and support of high-tech aerospace electronics. The company is most famous for its Doppler Radar Systems, which use radar beams directed at the ground to determine an aircraft's velocity, providing crucial navigation information.

New Brunswick

Thanks to former New Brunswick premier Frank McKenna's tax incentives and state-of-the-art infrastructure initiatives, call centres have flocked to Moncton and elsewhere in New Brunswick. New Brunswick was the first province or state in North America to establish a broadband fibre optic network and to fully digitalize its telephone system. It was the first place in the world to have telephone access to shopping, banking and information services. It was the first Canadian province to introduce multi-tenant electronic kiosk service, letting the public renew vehicle registrations, purchase licences and access government information interactively. It was also the first Canadian province to make computer literacy a high-school graduation requirement. It is not surprising, therefore, that New Brunswick has become the call centre capital of North America. Its bilingual workforce has contributed as well. Moreover, local community colleges have successfully developed programs targeted at call centre training.

In 1995, the Royal Bank opened a seven-hundred-person call centre network. UPS, Xerox, CP Hotels, Northern Telecom, Federal Express and Purolator have also located call centres in New Brunswick in recent years. The unemployment rate in Moncton is a respectable 7.4 percent. The city has led New Brunswick and the rest of Atlantic Canada in business growth over the past four years. The population is rising and real estate development has picked up.

The Creation of Tech Centres

The key to Canada's future prosperity is a leadership role in the technology revolution. The seeds of such leadership have been planted—in aerospace, in information technology, in biotech, in agra-tech, in telecommunications, software and more—but further steps must be taken, and soon. Success stories abound in virtually every Canadian city centre—from Vancouver's QLT, a world leader in light-activated drug technology, to Winnipeg's CanWest Global Communications Corp., Canada's largest private broadcaster, to Ottawa's Silicon Valley North in Kanata, to the technology triangle around Kitchener-Waterloo, Guelph and Cambridge, Ontario. There are several key elements to the development of any high-tech hotbed, and these are outlined below.

1. A MAJOR RESEARCH INSTITUTION

The importance of this has been evident in both the U.S. and Canada. In 1939, Stanford University professor Frederick Terman persuaded recent graduates Bill Hewlett and Dave Packard to start a firm in the area. This was the beginning of Silicon Valley. To this day, half of Silicon Valley's revenues come from Stanford-seeded companies. Similarly, the Massachusetts Institute of Technology (MIT) has spawned four thousand companies employing more than a million people, according to a 1997 BankBoston study. MIT success stories include Lotus (now owned by IBM) and Firefly (purchased by Microsoft).

The universities are a major provider of the tech sector's most crucial raw ingredient, knowledge workers—the life scientists, engineers, computer scientists, programmers and others that make it all happen. The same university–business synergies evident in the U.S. are percolating here in Canada. The University of British Columbia is giving birth to biotech companies with its world-class genetic research. QLT is a tremendous contributor to cancer and eye disease treatments; it was founded in 1981 by a group of scientists from UBC who were frustrated at the lack of government funding available for their projects. UBC has also spawned money management firms through graduates of their quantitative money management program. MacDonald-Dettwiler and Associates Ltd., a systems engineering firm that builds ground stations for satellites, was founded in 1969 by John MacDonald, a former engineering professor at UBC. The company now employs nine hundred workers and has sales of $120 million.

We have already discussed the success of the University of Alberta's and University of Saskatchewan's initiatives to commercialize their high-tech research. Both have generated high-tech companies that are at the leading edge in their fields. Sheridan College, near Toronto, is a global leader in technical animation, spinning off talent for companies like Disney and Dreamworks.

No star shines brighter in the techno-education galaxy than the University of Waterloo. Bill Gates has said he hires more people from Waterloo's computer science department than from any other university in the world. An alliance between the University of Waterloo, Sir Wilfrid Laurier University and Guelph University, along with private sector companies, has created Canada's Technology Triangle (CTT). It has already spun off two hundred companies in the area, employing two thousand people—including the likes of Open Text, a leader in the development of application platforms for intranets, and Research In Motion, a leading international developer, manufacturer and marketer of low-power modem technology.

Another fast-growing success story in the CTT is Automation Tooling Systems (ATS), renowned worldwide for its application of innovative technologies and robot-automated systems. With three plants in Cambridge employing 1,400 people, job growth is expected to be more than 20 percent in the next year. Over the past five years, sales have soared at a 40 percent annual clip. Its total workforce has mushroomed to 2,600 in eighteen different facilities worldwide. Its customers are global names like Gillette, Ford, General Motors, Northern Telecom and ITT. Klaus Woerner, winner of Canada's 1998 Entrepreneur of the Year award, founded the company in 1978.

Woerner praises the University of Waterloo and Conestoga College for introducing new programs to train young workers. He recently donated $1 million to Conestoga College, the largest donation the college has ever received. ATS has long hired grads from Conestoga's mechanical engineering program, especially those specializing in robotics and automation. The company has also donated money to the University of Waterloo to establish the ATS Mechatronics Laboratory. Mechatronics combines expertise in computer, electrical, systems design and mechanical engineering.

A new National Capital Institute of Technology was slated to begin operation in the summer of 1999. Dubbed—maybe wishfully—the "MIT of the North," the Ottawa institute is expected to boost the number of people learning information technology by 40 percent in 2000. The institute will have no actual campus, but will use facilities and teaching staff from both Carleton and Ottawa universities and the National Research Council.

2 . AT LEAST ONE BLOCKBUSTER SUCCESS STORY

A tech centre needs at least one global success story to attract the critical mass of talent and capital required to propagate and entice other businesses. A brand-name company draws in world-class talent and generates a stream of veterans who leave to start their own companies. This has certainly been evident in Seattle, where Microsoft has unwittingly become the mother to a slew of spinoffs known locally as Baby Bills. In Helsinki, the Nokia wireless telecommunications company has created a hotbed of tech activity.

In Canada, this process is nowhere more evident than in the western suburb of Ottawa called Kanata, known to some as Silicon Valley North. This area is home to more than eight hundred tech companies employing 50,000 highly skilled people generating more than $8 billion in revenue. In addition, an estimated 95,000 jobs are indirectly associated with this thriving sector, providing work for a total of 145,000 people, and that number is rising fast. Today, the region is home to a diverse array of established and emerging companies in the fields of telecommunications, new media, systems integration, PC manufacturing, data communications, networking products, life sciences, aerospace and defence. The mega-hitters in the region include

Northern Telecom, Newbridge Networks, Mitel, JDS Uniphase, SHL Systemhouse and Corel Corporation.

Northern Telecom—with seventy-five thousand employees throughout the world and twenty-three thousand in Canada—already recruits about 25 percent of all Canadians with undergraduate degrees in electrical engineering and computer science, and 30 percent of the masters and doctoral graduates in those disciplines. Nortel still finds that it has to recruit foreign students to fill all its Canadian job openings, as our universities pump out insufficient numbers of high-tech workers. Canada is the favoured location for the research operations of Nortel, Newbridge and others because of the very generous R&D tax credits offered here.

Today, Newbridge ranks in the top three vendors of frame relay telecommunications equipment worldwide, an industry growing at a 10 percent annual rate. It is the leading vendor in the Asynchronous Transfer Mode (ATM) wide-area network equipment market, a technology that is revolutionizing the field of global broadband networks. ATM is a high-speed switching technology that can be used for data and voice communications simultaneously. The company is set for expansion, with plans to increase the local workforce by three to four thousand workers by 2001. Mitel, a master of telecom chip design and manufacturing, was one of only two Canadian companies named in the 1998 *Business Week* list of the top one hundred global technology firms; the other was Montreal-based Teleglobe, a provider of low-cost international long-distance services across North America, Europe and Asia. JDS Fitel merged with U.S.-based Uniphase in the summer of 1999 to become a world-leading fibre optics company. It has carved out a lucrative niche with its wavelength division multiplexer technology that makes fibre optic networks more powerful. Its major customers include Northern Telecom, Lucent Technologies Inc. and Ciena Corp. JDS Uniphase is at the leading edge of the building of the Internet infrastructure. If the company remains in the forefront through ongoing R&D, growth in this area will be enormous for years to come.

There are other tremendous success stories in the Kanata region. Software giant Cognos Corp. is taking advantage of the explosion in demand for Internet-related technology. It is developing Web-based applications for its core product, business intelligence software. World Heart is a global leader in artificial-heart research. It will soon begin production of its artificial heart-assist device, HeartSaver. Animal testing has been conducted and human trials are next. The HeartSaver is a left-ventricular device that is implanted in a patient's chest cavity either permanently or until a transplant organ becomes available. Heart failure is the leading cause of death in North America and Europe. Only a few thousand organs are available for transplant each year, so artificial heart-assist devices will be in huge demand.

The booming technology sector in Kanata, which has grown more than 56 percent over the past five years, has been a boon to the Ottawa region, more than offsetting the depressing effects of the cutbacks in government jobs. The population of Ottawa is rising and the importance of civil service jobs is shrinking. In 1976, federal jobs represented 32 percent of the employment in the region, compared with 18 percent twenty years later. For many tech companies, there are a variety of benefits to being in Ottawa that go beyond access to skilled tech labour. They include close proximity to the seat of political power and to major government-funded research bodies like the National Research Council.

3. High-tech talent

Whether they come from existing blockbuster companies, a university or, in the case of Tel Aviv, the Army's Central Unit for Data Processing, smart new talent is like oxygen to a high-tech firm. Only a place with a rich talent pool can claim to be a tech centre. An example: after years of bragging about how even a remote location like North Sioux City, South Dakota, could incubate a world-class computer manufacturer, Gateway gave up and relocated its headquarters to San Diego; they had simply exhausted the Sioux City workforce. It takes a critical mass of talent to sustain a tech centre. New talent will flock there if they see opportunities in a range of existing companies and hot start-ups.

The labour shortage in Canada's high-tech sector is getting more acute. According to Carol Stephenson, the chairwoman of the Information Technology Association of Canada, our high-tech industry is expected to generate at least thirty thousand jobs over the next two years. There will be a strong demand for project managers, senior software developers, technical consultants and systems engineers. While the universities and colleges are responding by expanding their computer science and engineering programs, they are not able to keep up with demand. A growing number of U.S. companies facing similar shortages are anxious to hire highly skilled Canadians, exacerbating the shortage in this country. A 1999 survey conducted by Ottawa-based Personnel Systems found that 78 percent of computer science and engineering students in Canada are willing to take jobs in the United States. With NAFTA, it is easier for an American firm to bring in a Canadian than, say, a European, and there are no language barriers. Higher salaries and lower taxes are key lures, according to David Rocheleau, a senior consultant with Personnel Systems.

4. VENTURE CAPITAL

The U.S. has very advanced capital markets that have become increasingly friendly towards tech start-ups, small-business financing, venture capital needs and initial public offerings (IPOs). The Canadian government has provided incentives for venture capital funds like Working Ventures that loan seed and growth money in exchange for a piece of the action. These labour-sponsored funds lent $1.8 billion in 1998.

Established in 1990, Working Ventures pools money from union pension plans and individual investors to loan to early-stage and developing businesses all over Canada. The fund has more than $700 million under management, making it one of the largest single sources of venture capital in North America. Individuals investing in such funds are given a 15 percent federal tax credit and a matching provincial tax credit. If placed in an RRSP, this investment and the credits would add to the income tax reduction. In addition, Working Ventures shares qualify as a "small business property," which allows shareholders in most circumstances to bump up the allowed foreign content in their RRSPs by three times the value of Working Ventures shares held in their RRSPs. This increases the maximum amount of foreign content an investor can hold in an RRSP account from 20 percent to 40 percent.

These have been powerful incentives to attract capital into the fund; indeed, Working Ventures currently has more money than what they consider to be appropriate investment opportunities, given their risk profiles. A portion of the fund is still invested in short-term securities.

Tech executives themselves often provide the seed money for new start-ups. Known as "angels" in the high-tech world, these newly minted millionaires often see potential in hot new companies. Merchant banking operations, small and large, are also popping up everywhere. Be they spinoffs of large chartered banks or the creations of wealthy entrepreneurs looking for lucrative investment opportunities, money is available for some in exchange for an ownership cut. The banks themselves have developed tech-focused lending operations, recognizing the need for seed, venture and growth capital in these businesses.

Boomers also are funding the high-tech boom. Hot new tech IPOs are in huge demand in the U.S. The Internet craze has taken some of these new issues to the stratosphere. Yahoo!, an Internet search engine, had a market value of $41 billion in early 1999, bigger than Boeing, bigger than Anheuser-Busch, bigger than Monsanto, Kellogg, Colgate-Palmolive or Seagram. Even after a sizable correction the stock remained overvalued by any standard measure. Boomers are saving for the long term and are willing to discount earnings well into the future. Science and technology mutual funds were the top performers in 1998 and the first quarter of 1999. Money came pouring in. Even with tremendous volatility in the sector—big ups and downs—household investors in North America are a huge source of capital for tech companies, particularly in the U.S. The challenge of finding money is still there for small business operators, but it is much easier in the U.S. and (to a lesser degree) Canada than overseas.

The dearth of venture capital in Europe and Asia has been an important factor holding back the tech sector in those regions. Big money in London, Paris, Frankfurt and Tokyo just isn't accustomed to funding propeller-heads. The banking systems are generally closed to all but the highest-quality borrowers, and household money is still locked up in bonds and deposits. Households invest relatively little capital in stocks or mutual funds. This will change, however, as we have seen in Israel, where big venture capital funds have helped seed a start-up culture that is weaning the country from its traditional unionized, state-run, kibbutz-based mentality.

5 . INFRASTRUCTURE

High-tech companies and their star executives need a large and sophisticated supporting infrastructure, from easy access to international airports and state-of-the-art telecommunications systems to all the amenities of home and entertainment. On this score, Bangalore, India, does not reach the mark despite its large supply of programming talent. The cyberindustry needs lawyers, investment bankers, foreign exchange specialists, analysts and accountants specializing in high-tech business. They need Web designers, desktop publishers, animators, advertising firms, printing firms and a wide array of other business and banking services. Essential is high-speed fibre for Internet connections. These companies must lure to their locales expensive talent that is in global demand, so all the amenities of high-quality living must be there.

6 . COMPETITIVE TAX RATES — CORPORATE AND PERSONAL

The example of Ireland shows the power of low corporate tax rates to draw companies to a region. When Ireland lowered its corporate tax rate for exporters to a mere 10 percent, foreign direct investment in the country boomed and tax revenues actually rose. Regulatory practice and a flexible labour force are also important considerations. Too much government regulatory restriction or excessive union power is a major deterrent.

The high-tech tax war within Canada has crystallized the importance of corporate tax rates in location decisions. Quebec is successfully luring high-tech companies to the province through major tax incentives. Companies from nearby Kanata and Nepean, Ontario, are making the move to Quebec to take advantage of a host of tax breaks. These breaks include: refundable tax credits for the production of multimedia titles; tax credits for scientific R&D; a two-year partial capital tax holiday on some new investments; venture capital funding; and the development of four tech facilities—in Montreal, Quebec City, Hull and Laval—that offer additional tax incentives, including a five-year holiday from income, capital and payroll taxes. Tenants are also eligible for 40 percent tax credits on every dollar paid in wages to eligible employees and on specified equipment expenditures. Companies with fewer than fifty employees are exempt from the French language requirements of Bill 101.

The lure was too much for Vorton Technologies Inc., a software company based in nearby Nepean, Ontario. The company will make the twenty-five-kilometre move across the Ottawa River and save itself more than $100,000 a year. Vorton is just one of a growing number of tech companies on the move in search of a better deal on taxes and other costs. At least three other companies from the Ottawa area have made the short move to western Quebec, and Hull officials have been in discussions with a dozen more. Overall, taxes in Quebec are still quite high, but the province has been the most aggressive in using tax incentives to attract high-tech companies. For example, foreign-controlled non-manufacturing companies pay a provincial corporate tax of 9.15 percent, well below the average of 16.1 percent for the other nine provinces. Quebec now claims that it is the cheapest place in North America to conduct research—aided, of course, by the weak Canadian dollar.

Quebec isn't the only province using the tax system to attract business. We have already discussed the interprovincial tax battle for call centres and film production. Most provinces now offer R&D credits to top up the federal deduction. Indeed, a 1998 OECD report criticized Canada for the generosity of its research credits, saying that companies like Northern Telecom and Newbridge conduct research in Canada to take advantage of the tax breaks but locate much of the rest of their business elsewhere, a problem for Canada. Our overall corporate tax structure has, as we have seen, been a primary factor in discouraging foreign direct investment.

Personal tax rates are also a crucial consideration. We've seen the allurement of Alberta, with the lowest personal tax rates in the country. Compared with the U.S., where top marginal income tax rates are 39.5 percent and kick in at annual income levels of close to $409,000

Canadian, our tax burden is onerous. Top marginal tax rates here are roughly 50 percent in most provinces, and they kick in at annual income levels of a mere $70,000. Furthermore, mortgage interest is tax-deductible in the U.S., and capital gains tax rates of 20 percent are roughly half the rate in Canada—a huge consideration for tech employees and execs with stock options. Canadian companies have to pay up big-time to lure talent, and American companies are loath to move north. Importantly, the flow goes the other way: much-needed talent and business operations leave Canada to move south.

7 . THE ENTREPRENEURIAL MIND-SET

Attitude is probably the most important ingredient in U.S. supremacy in the high-tech world, a crucial factor in the success of Silicon Valley—the gunslinging, macho, "I can do anything" attitude that creates billionaires. Outside the United States, the value system often encourages the very things that Silicon Valley loathes: aversion to risk, big bureaucracies, government regulation and intervention, fealty to one employer and the willingness to work within a strict hierarchy. These factors have been the death knell for the innovative spirit in Japan and Europe.

Efforts to grow hothouse tech cities like Sophia-Antipolis in the south of France have been largely unsuccessful because of attitude. While government tax breaks and government funding may lure some name companies to the region and get some start-ups going, the real gel for success was missing—the "big-swinging-chip" attitude that balloons dorm-room and garage operations into billion-dollar IPOs.

Obedient, cautious populations do not engender this attitude. A surefire killer is a government that is bent on controlling the free market of ideas. Singapore has made this mistake. With arguably the best science and math education system in the world, and an advanced high-bandwidth infrastructure, Singapore has failed to incubate creative, imaginative local tech companies. Big Brother government does not instill or encourage the necessary breakout thinking so essential to real success in this field.

Is this a problem for Canada? I hope not, but the answer is mixed. Government must get out of the way. Most importantly, government must encourage innovation and change, not discourage it by subsidizing declining businesses and taxing away the incentives for success. Government can nurture an environment where the educational institutions work with the private sector to innovate and create value; where profit is not a dirty word, and where success is valued and rewarded.

Every Canadian kid must be told from birth that he or she can be or do anything, can accomplish anything, can lead the world in anything—that we are capable of being the best in anything. No dream is too big, no roadblock too high. This can-do, risk-taking, world-beating attitude arises in the home, the schools, the culture. Self-reliance and self-esteem must be nurtured. The winning attitude is action-oriented, impatient, questioning and optimistic. The seeds of this are certainly here.

An Amazing Canadian High-Tech Family—The Foodys

Patrick Foody Sr., a vigorous sixty-nine-year-old self-made millionaire, emigrated from Ireland to Canada as a young man in 1952. He had an engineering degree from Queen's University in Belfast and worked initially in the mining and grain industries in Montreal. That is where he met Helen. Born on a farm in Manitoba, she was awarded a full scholarship to McGill University to study math, the first in her family to earn a university degree. Their marriage has been fruitful, to say the least. They had five sons in six years, and a sixth son four years later. They were committed to giving their sons the best education possible.

In time, Pat ran a successful Montreal engineering firm, Techtrol Ltd. He had other business interests too, and was one of the original financiers of the mega-successful Ottawa tech firm SHL Systemhouse Inc. All that in one lifetime would have been enough for most people, but not for Pat Foody.

In 1978, when the world was mired in oil crisis and fearful of an ongoing shortage, he started work on the development of an alternative energy source, ethanol, derived not from traditional sources like corn and wheat, but from waste products—the ultimate in conservation. Most others were betting on the potential of alternative fossil fuels like methanol, which was made from coal, and, later, on nuclear power. They were also counting on offshore and northern oil exploration to bolster fuel supplies. Pat Foody was convinced that ethanol produced from waste fibres would be a revolutionary and immediate success. He threw himself and his millions behind the project. Success was far from immediate, however. It has been more than twenty years since Pat Foody first began researching his ideas, and ethanol production is only now about to begin.

Foody's work is the inspiration and driving force behind Iogen, a company we discussed earlier, which has a strategic alliance with Petro-Canada. Located on the fringes of the Ottawa airport, Iogen is Canada's largest producer of industrial enzymes. Its annual revenues are estimated at between $10 million and $20 million, and the hook-up with Petro-Canada will further accelerate growth. It has not been an easy venture, nor an overnight success. Of the $40 million Iogen has spent on ethanol research over the years, more than half has come directly from Pat Foody's own pocket. Pat has called it an expensive hobby that sometimes caused even Helen to question his business judgment.

But this story gets even better. Pat Foody's six sons are every bit as driven as their dad. All have been outstanding students and have clearly demonstrated their own entrepreneurial spirit, risk-taking mentality and drive for excellence. Iogen is run by three of Mr. Foody's six sons: thirty-nine-year-old Brian, Iogen's president, who oversees all the research efforts; thirty-seven-year-old Patrick Jr., who is chief operating officer; and younger brother Kevin, who is responsible for textile product sales. While Patrick Sr. has never run the company himself, he still takes an active interest. Each week he drives for ninety minutes or so to the Iogen plant from his riverfront home in the town of Hudson, west of Montreal.

Brian began researching enzymes at the age of twenty-three, having graduated from MIT with two undergraduate degrees, both in engineering—civil and mechanical—and one master's degree in mechanical engineering. He earned these three degrees in four years, a remarkable feat. His brother and partner, Patrick Jr., earned two degrees in four years.

The other three brothers, Michael, Daniel and Tom, work together on their own, very different kind of high-tech project, a company called

Visual Edge Software, Ltd., a privately held firm established in 1985 and located in Montreal and California. Visual Edge's corporate mission is to help customers implement or change business processes that span enterprise-wide software applications like SAP and Peoplesoft. They develop custom business software to help with financial, human resource, treasury and project management. Visual Edge's software technology has been integral to the systems architecture of major companies like Hewlett-Packard, Sun and DEC.

Michael Foody, president, founded the company; his brother Daniel is chief technology officer and brother Tom is chief financial officer. Michael earned a master's degree in electrical engineering and bachelor's degrees in both computer science and computer engineering from Rensselaer Polytechnic Institute (RPI) in Troy, New York, all in four years. Daniel holds both bachelor of science and master of electrical engineering degrees from Cornell University. Not to be bested, Tom has an undergraduate degree from RPI plus a master's from Stanford University and an MBA from the Sloan School of Management at MIT.

Can you imagine what Pat and Helen's tuition bills were like? Patrick Sr. told a reporter from the *Ottawa Citizen* that one year they were a staggering quarter of a million dollars. You can believe it. Here is a man who understands the importance of education, and a family that gives new meaning to "high achievement"—a terrific example of what is possible at the outer limits of the envelope.

Part 6

What All of This Means to You

What the Upwave Means to You

T he world is in the midst of a technology revolution. Change is rapid and accelerating. We are all affected—our businesses, our jobs, our families, our children, our institutions. It is exciting and it is frightening, but ultimately it is very positive. As I discussed earlier in the book, we are in the early days of an upwave in the long cycle. I expect a twenty-five-year period of tremendous economic growth and prosperity. Recessions may occur, but they will be relatively mild and short-lived. Inflation will remain moderate.

The technology revolution ensures that productivity gains will continue. Increasing returns to knowledge—knowledge begetting more knowledge—accelerate the pace of these gains and keep inflation at bay. Indeed, deflationary forces will continue to surface. Product prices will continue to fall in some sectors because of innovation that increases commodity supply and reduces costs. And inflation will remain relatively low because of mounting global competitive pressure as price differentials become more and more evident. The Internet allows for easy comparison shopping on a global level. The establishment of the euro as the single currency for the European Monetary Union enhances the transparency.

Businesses, in order to stay alive, must continue to innovate, to invest in technology and to increase efficiency and productivity. Firms are streamlined, restructured, re-engineered; all excesses are eliminated. High-paying, low-skill jobs are going or gone—replaced by computers or cheap labour in foreign countries. All rote, repetitive human operations will be replaced by computers, robots, technology. The winners are the knowledge workers, those who add value that cannot be replicated by a computer. Workers who analyze, synthesize, innovate, create, synergize and transform facts and figures into insight and actionable recommendations will win. Those who help others increase their productivity will win. That doesn't mean that everyone must have a chemical engineering or computer science degree to make it in this new world. It does mean, however, that each of us must add unique value. Cookie-cutter jobs are a thing of the past.

Reinventing Business

The same is true in business. If your company produces a commodity product—one that is easily replicated by another company—you had better be the low cost producer or you will be out of business. Even more preferable would be to add technology, knowledge and skill to create something unique about your product or process. Rio Algom uses bio-leaching. Noranda is recycling computers. Petro-Canada is investing in alternative fuels. Ballard Power has created a clean-engine option for automobiles. Saskatchewan's agra-tech research improves the quality and productivity of food products. The successes are many, but improvement must be ongoing.

The speed of change requires businesses to constantly innovate. This is particularly so because breakthrough technology is difficult to create but easy to copy. What is new today is an easily replicated low-margin product or service in the not too distant future. Yesterday's sources of Canadian competitive advantage—the traditional natural resource and low-tech manufacturing sectors—will drag us down in the future if they are not transformed. Creative destruction must be ongoing and rapid. Alan Greenspan, Chairman of the Fed, called creative destruction the necessary churning in a growing economy that results in the efficient use of labour and capital, increasing productivity and living standards.

Government Should Foster Creative Destruction

Government efforts to slow the pace of creative destruction are self-defeating. The very subsidies that are aimed at saving jobs ultimately lead to higher, not lower, unemployment. This is readily apparent in Germany, France and Italy, where labour laws that restrict layoffs and downsizing have only succeeded in creating or perpetuating double-digit unemployment. In the U.S., where layoffs are surging and creative destruction is rampant, the unemployment rate is around 4 percent, the lowest level in a generation, and the average duration of unemployment is near a record low.

Technological innovation ultimately creates jobs, it doesn't destroy them. It is the fuel for growth, productivity and rising living standards. Without innovation we would all still be living at subsistence level. Nevertheless, throughout the ages people have been fearful of change, fearful of innovation. The term Luddite originates from the eighteenth-century British textile worker Ned Lud, who destroyed his employer's stocking frame, fearful that it would replace his job. The original Luddite revolt occurred in 1811. English weavers protested the arrival of mechanized looms, viewing them as a threat to their livelihood and way of life. They destroyed the machines with hammers and burned the factories in a futile attempt to save their jobs.

The upheaval of innovation is very painful, to be sure, but in every case the innovation allows the economy to grow stronger, creating ever more jobs. The Industrial Revolution in North America in the mid-nineteenth century gave us the railway and mechanized production. Costs of production and travel plunged, and real family purchasing power surged, as did the quality of manufactured goods, food and services. No one today questions the positive spinoffs of these developments, but at the time they were just as frightening to displaced old-tech workers in, for example, the stagecoach business as the computer is today. Unfortunately, people will continue to be displaced by innovation. Traditional secretaries, travel agents, old-style librarians, telephone operators, tellers, order-takers, sales personnel, intermediaries and distributors of all sorts, middlemen and middle managers—

all will be replaced by technology, unless they add value, insight, analysis, research, advice. Certainly, technology alters the very nature of these jobs.

Think of an example in my business—the selling of stocks and bonds. With the growing popularity of stock trading on the Internet, the future for traditional brokers might look bleak. Why pay higher commissions to deal with a traditional broker when you can trade for a fraction of the cost on the Internet? Old-time order-taker-type brokers will disappear; in many ways, they already have. However, there is the opportunity to become investment advisers—trusted financial consultants who provide research, analysis, advice and insights; advisers who understand their clients' needs, risk profile and goals, and help them to construct a savings plan and portfolio consistent with these. The e-trade on the Internet cannot replace this service. However, investment advisers must be far better trained than brokers, and the training must be ongoing as financial innovation is rapid. The same is true for all financial services personnel who work with the public: insurance agents, mutual fund salespeople, financial planners, bankers.

New jobs will be created in droves. The occupations that are lost will be replaced by hundreds of others: computer scientists, programmers, technicians, graphic artists, desktop publishers, Web site designers, Webmasters, technical writers, call centre/Internet reps, information specialists, network administrators, biotech scientists and technicians—and the list goes on. New businesses are being created at a record rate, businesses we would never have dreamed of just a few years ago. How many new electronic-commerce businesses are there? Biotech firms? Cellular phone companies, satellite companies, pharmaceutical breakthroughs? Thousands, if not tens of thousands. The wealth that is created by these new businesses is without precedent. In the United States between 1993 and 1998, household net worth increased by 50 percent. Jobs are easy to get, even with surging layoffs. Consumer confidence has zoomed. No wonder Bill Clinton has been so popular.

There are those who lose from change, at least in the short term. The social safety net—unemployment insurance and welfare—is important for those who are truly in need, infirm, elderly, handicapped or otherwise unable to provide for themselves. For others, government monetary assistance should be seen as temporary, not as a way of life. For those who are able-bodied, public money is far better spent on incentives to entice new growth businesses to depressed areas, on relocating and retraining people for the many jobs that go unfilled. The money is better spent on lowering taxes.

A Reality Test

The truth is that we all must take care of ourselves, take action to maximize our own potential and that of our children. If you are in a dead-end job, get training and upgrade or, if that is not possible, get out. If you live in a depressed area with no sign of improvement, move. If you are in a declining business or industry, exit. How do you know if you fall into one of these categories? Take this quiz.

If you answer yes to any of the following questions, think about taking action.

- Has your overall compensation been stagnant for the past few years?
- Is your compensation set without consideration of merit or your personal performance?
- Is your firm continually downsizing?
- Is your employer in financial trouble? Has your firm been consistently unprofitable?
- Is your employer dependent on government subsidy?
- Could a computer do your job?
- Have any of your co-workers been replaced by technology?
- Are you fearful of being finished at forty, fifty, sixty? Are you fearful of being replaced by a twenty-eight-year-old?
- Are you fearful of your economic future?
- Do you feel obsolete?
- Are you among a minority in your business that is computer illiterate? Are you computer-phobic, thinking it is too difficult to learn?

- Do you let your secretary deal with the computer, reading and sending your e-mails, calendar and research material?
- Could your clients or customers replace your company's or your services with an Internet supplier?
- If you quit your job today, would it take you more than a few months to find at least as good a job in your region?
- Do you work in a traditional resource business—forest products, energy, mining, fishing, agriculture—where a low-value-added commodity is produced and little new technology is used?
- Do you work in a low-tech manufacturing company that would have trouble selling its product if the Canadian dollar were to strengthen too much?
- Is the local unemployment rate dramatically above 8 percent, the national average? If so, has it been for long?
- Is the population of your region in long-term decline?
- Is your region dependent on just one industry? If it were to shut down, would the local economy be devastated?

If you answer no to any of the following questions, think about a change.

- Have you used the Internet in the past three months, or do you work with or for someone who has?
- Do you provide a service that is highly valued? Is your boss upset when you unexpectedly take a day off? Is anyone?
- Does your company provide training programs for employees or encourage people to take courses and upgrade their skills?
- Have you been improving your skills and knowledge base? Are you committed to lifelong education?
- Do you have a global perspective? Does your boss? Does your company?
- Have you kept up in your field? Is it necessary?
- Are your skills in demand?
- Is your business committed to ongoing technological innovation?
- Is there a growing market for your company's product or services?
- Is there a growing market for your product or services?

- Has your company reinvented itself to get ahead of the competition in recent years? Does it have a strategic plan?
- Are there growth industries in your region?
- Are there good schools, community colleges or universities in your region?

Some of these questions might sound harsh, but think about them. In some cases you may only need to re-jig your skill set and mind-set. In other cases, more dramatic action might be called for.

Create a Plan

If your answers to these questions suggest a potential problem, begin the process of rethinking your options, planning your strategy. There are enormous opportunities out there.

BECOME COMPUTER LITERATE

Anyone today can learn to use the computer. Thanks to Windows technology, it is as simple as clicking on a picture—no kidding! Self-help tutorials are available online, on tape, in books. Someone can quickly show you the basics. You can learn to use e-mail in twenty minutes. If you are computer-phobic, break through the fear. If your employer offers training, take it, regardless of how senior you are. For those fifty-something senior executives who don't know how to use the computer on your desk, you are making yourself look obsolete.

Even as electronic commerce is poised to bring sweeping changes to virtually every industry, fewer than one-third of CEOs in the U.S. consider themselves Web-literate, according to a Pricewaterhouse-Coopers survey of more than eight hundred CEOs. Only one in four surf the Web regularly, and 69 percent describe their Internet sophistication as fair or poor. It is certain that the numbers are no better in Canada.

This Luddite behaviour causes serious problems. The vast majority of these same chief executives know that electronic business will be central to their future; if they don't know that, they are kidding themselves. How can top execs learn to navigate in the cyberworld if they don't get their fingers dirty on a computer keyboard? Those who don't get down to some serious, hands-on Net prowling may soon find themselves with little else to do. While we are living in a brand new economy, some are mired in the Middle Ages, bleeding their patients.

You can learn to be proficient enough in remarkably little time. Ask for help. Pretty soon you will be surfing the Net like the rest of us, amazed that you waited so long.

STAY UP-TO-DATE IN YOUR FIELD

A wealth of knowledge in every field is available on the Net. Easy self-help books are available to teach myriad skills. Read the global publications in your field. Read the newspapers—not just Canadian, but American as well, even if just the Sunday *New York Times*. For those of you in business, the *Wall Street Journal* and *Business Week* are invaluable for a U.S. and global perspective. *Canadian Business* has good Canadian coverage. Also excellent are the *Financial Times* of London and the *Economist* magazine (which calls itself a newspaper). If you are in the financial world or have U.S. investments, *Barrons* is a must. *Wired* has the latest on the high-tech world. Every business has its own trade publications; read the best ones for your sector. See my Web site at **www.sherrycooper.com** for other reading suggestions. Take advantage of training opportunities offered by your employer.

IF A JOB CHANGE IS NECESSARY, RETRAIN AND MOVE ON

Every community college and university in the country is offering courses in fields where jobs are available and labour is in short supply. Courses are offered on the Internet and even on television. Check my Web site to see a list of innovative new educational opportunities in Canada.

Many fields are open to people without a university or college degree. Kenneth Gray and Edwin Herr describe many high-skill, high-paying job opportunities for the non-degreed in table 14.1. Their 1995 book *Other Ways to Win: Creating Alternatives for High School Graduates* offers a whole host of career options and training alternatives for those who do not have a university degree. By the way, included among this group are Bill Gates and Michael Dell—billionaire founders of their own companies, and college dropouts.

TABLE 14.1
High-Skill/High-Wage Jobs for the Non-Degreed

Health Occupations
Dental Assistant
Dental Hygienist
Emergency Medical Technician
Home Health Aide
Licensed Practical Nurse
Medical Laboratory Technician
Medical Record Technician
Optometric Technician
Radiology Technician
Surgical Technologist

Service Occupations
Accountant
Agribusiness Sales
Automatic Office Manager
Commercial Design
Computer Graphics Specialist
Criminal Justice and Corrections
Data Processing Manager
Fire Fighter
Law Enforcement/Protection
Paralegal
Professionally Trained Chef

Crafts and Construction
Construction Drafting
Construction Project Manager
Heating/Air-Conditioning
   Technician

Plumbing, Pipe-Fitting Technician
Precision Welding
Specialized Carpentry and
   Installation
Specialized Interior
   Finishing/Install

Manufacturing
Computer-Controlled Equipment
   Operator
Equipment Operator
Drafting Technician
Electronics Engineering Technician
Electronics Lab Technician
Engineering Technician
Manufacturing Systems Operator
Manufacturing Technician

**Technical Service, Repair and
Installation**
Specialty Auto Mechanic
Airframe Mechanic
Avionics Repair Technician
Biomedical Equipment Technician
Computer Systems Install/Repair
Electromechanical Repair
   Technician
Telecommunications Install/Repair

Source: Gray, Kenneth C., and Herr,
   Edwin L.

BUSINESSES STAY ON TOP

If you are a business owner or executive, you must be ever ready to change, shift course, reinvent. Use technology to your advantage. Get on the Internet. Add value to your product to differentiate it from your competitor. Know what your competition is up to and get ahead of them.

Remember the buggy whip company that became a conveyor belt manufacturer, or the gristmill company that shifted to stationery, tea bags, glue and now high-tech adhesives. These companies have been in business for three hundred years. The ones that are slow to change disappear, even in the technology field. Those that bet on mainframe computers rather than PCs and couldn't make the transition failed. Even IBM and more recently Apple have had their problems; but quick-witted innovative management made the necessary shifts. Renaissance is possible in businesses, in regions and in careers, as we have seen. The key is a willingness to change, to think outside the box.

Hire the best people and ensure that they remain well trained. You will keep them if you reward their contribution and provide continuous growth potential. Knowledge workers want challenge, a team environment and the opportunity to keep learning and growing. The old-time hierarchical management structure doesn't work for them. They don't want or need someone looking over their shoulder monitoring and altering their work. It stifles productivity, creativity and innovation. They also want to reap the rewards of their efforts. That is why stock options have become such an important component of compensation for many growth companies.

Remember: Me, Inc.

Remember that, regardless of what you do for a living, you are first and foremost the president of your own personal services company, one with tremendous global competitive pressure, one with no assurance of tomorrow's success except through a commitment to constant improvement and innovation. You have to be the best at what you do, the most efficient, the most productive and reliable, the most insightful. You have to add the most value, or sooner or later you will be overtaken by the competition or replaced by lower-cost, higher-value service elsewhere.

You must be on the lookout for opportunity—to grow, expand, increase your expertise and knowledge. You must be committed to ongoing study in your own and related fields. That's not easy. It requires a huge commitment of time and energy to stay on top of an ever-expanding body of knowledge. Most people do not, which makes it an even greater competitive advantage for those who do. Every mega-successful person I've ever met or heard about reads, often voraciously. Remember, you put yourself in a small minority if you ever read a non-fiction book in your field, and if you read one a month you are extremely unusual and advantaged.

Let me recap the important trends and economic realities:

- Expect interest rates to remain low. Labour force growth will continue its downward trend in Canada and the U.S. for the next twenty years, which will keep the lid on nominal GDP growth, contributing to continued moderate levels of inflation. This means you have to save more for retirement and invest it in riskier assets like stocks to increase your returns.

- Begin saving early—the sooner the better, the younger the better.

- As long as Canadian tax rates remain meaningfully above those in the U.S. and the Canadian government continues to subsidize declining businesses, standing in the way of creative destruction, expect the Canadian stock market to underperform the U.S. and many others around the world in the long run. The only exception will be relatively brief periods when commodity prices are under upward pressure. The 1999 rise in prices of commodities like oil and base metals reflected a strengthening in Asian economic activity. It is great for the Toronto Stock Exchange and the Canadian dollar while it lasts, but it won't last for very long. Happily, resource stocks are not our only hope. We have world-class Canadian companies in many fields, as we have discussed, but even their valuations—their price-earnings multiples—are typically well below those in the U.S. and U.K.

- Similarly, as long as we are relatively non-competitive, expect the Canadian dollar to remain relatively weak except during temporary periods of commodity price inflation. Until we create an environment that will attract more foreign business, expect the Canadian dollar to remain weak.

- Expect volatility in all markets. In 1997 and 1998 it was Asia and Russia. In early 1999 it was Brazil and Latin America. The U.S. stock market will gyrate, sometimes very painfully, but the long-term trend will be up. See sell-offs as buying opportunities. The bigger the sell-off, the bigger the opportunity, as long as you invest regularly—biweekly, monthly, quarterly. Invest for the long run and buy a diversified portfolio of stocks. Don't try to time the markets. Put your base savings on automatic pilot. We will discuss this in further detail in the next chapter.

- There is a lot of hype in the U.S. stock market. Look at the Internet craze, for example. In very early 1999, Yahoo! had a bigger market cap than Boeing. As wild as this is, and as much criticism as has rightfully been levelled at the hype, the fact is that the Internet is real. Fifty thousand people visit the Yahoo! site each day, and that number is rising rapidly. Internet connections are increasing speedily. Some analysts have estimated that traffic on the Internet doubles every one hundred days. The Internet blue chips include America On Line, Yahoo! and Amazon.com. Yes, these stocks have astronomical valuations and are extremely volatile. A major correction in these stocks began in early 1999; Yahoo! and Amazon.com quickly retraced 50 percent of their gain only to rebound once again. More corrections will come. Rolling corrections, from sector to sector, will also be evident.

  The surge in U.S. stocks in general in the past decade—particularly the large-cap stocks—has been based on real value, competitive advantage, world-class innovation, low interest rates, low inflation and huge liquidity. It is not a bubble in the sense that the Japanese stock market was in 1989. The Nikkei back then was based on bank stocks, stratospheric real estate values and cross-holdings. The underpinnings for the U.S. stock market are more sound. But do expect volatility and big corrections periodically.

- Do not assume government or big business will take care of you in your old age. Work as long as you can. Most of us will want to work beyond age sixty-five. Save for retirement. Max out your RRSP contributions first. Invest regularly, not once a year during RRSP season. Invest as much as you can in foreign assets, particularly U.S. stocks. The limit is now 20 percent of your RRSP, but there are a growing number of legal ways around this restriction; more on that in the next chapter.
- In an upwave, stocks generally outperform other asset classes.
- Financial assets outperform real assets, but I continue to believe that residential real estate, including family homes, will hold their value and even appreciate. Boomers like space, and home is where the office is these days. Furthermore, empty nests often aren't empty indefinitely, thanks to the boomerang of university-grad offspring.
- With overall inflation remaining low—and deflation underway in some sectors—it pays to get out of debt. In the old days of rampant inflation, you paid down debt with depreciating dollars. That is no longer true.

What Every Canadian Citizen Can Do

As we have seen, Canada's relative economic performance in the global economy has deteriorated. The good news is that we can fix this. We can once again grow at a pace sufficient to fully employ all of our people. We can enjoy tremendous economic prosperity like so many other technology leaders around the world. A strong, competitive economy is the foundation for raising our standard of living.

As Canadian citizens, we must encourage our government to: foster an environment of creative destruction; stop subsidizing declining industry; allow new to replace old; let competitive pressure do its job; permit the free market to work; and nurture co-operation between the universities and colleges and the private sector. Above all, we must demand that our tax burden be reduced.

Barry W. Pickford, Vice-President of Taxation at Bell Canada, testified to the House of Commons Standing Committee on Finance in December 1998. He said that the majority of manufacturing companies in his industry are

> subsidiaries of multinationals, primarily based in the U.S., so their bosses are in the U.S. and quite often they take the better people from Canadian companies. Those are the ones who get promoted and get an offer to go south. Now I don't say that the move is necessarily made because of lower income tax, but they don't come back because of that ...

The issues surrounding the tax burden are huge. In a knowledge-based economy, skilled labour is our most important resource; never before has it been so critical. Knowledge is the key to our future economic prosperity, to our developing a strong and competitive economy. We must invest adequately in our own human capital, make the changes necessary to attract and keep skilled labour, and encourage foreign investment as well.

Some Specific Recommendations to Your Elected Representatives

PERSONAL TAX RELIEF

- Eliminate the 5 percent surtax on high-income earners, which kicks in when a taxpayer's basic federal tax exceeds $12,500 or around $65,000 a year in income. It is a huge incentive-killer. It was introduced as a temporary deficit-reduction measure in 1985. Total initial cost: $650 million.
- Reduce Employment Insurance (EI) premiums to help offset the scheduled rise in Canada Pension Plan premiums. These are both federal payroll taxes paid by employers and employees. The government has already reduced the EI premiums and offered a

premium holiday for all firms hiring young people in 1999 and 2000 because the EI fund is in huge surplus.

- Reinstate full inflation indexation of the tax system. Bracket creep—the movement into higher tax brackets because of any inflation less than 3 percent—has increased the tax burden for the lower and middle classes. Total initial cost: $840 million.

- Reduce the federal income tax rates for all brackets by three percentage points: from 17 percent to 14 percent for lower-income Canadians; from 26 percent to 23 percent for middle-income earners; and from 29 percent to 26 percent for higher-income taxpayers. Total initial cost: just over $11 billion, plus the effects on provincial revenues that are tied to basic federal income tax. Quebec and Alberta have established provincial income tax systems that are not tied to the federal system, so they won't lose revenues when federal taxes are cut. Manitoba has threatened to do the same.

- Raise the threshold for the highest marginal tax to at least $80,000. The OECD has criticized our income tax system as the most progressive in the industrialized world. Marginal tax rates that are very high discourage work, saving, investment and productivity growth. No other country has marginal tax rates so high at such a low level of income. Canadians today hit the highest marginal tax rate at a middle-class income level of roughly $63,400 in salary and interest income, depending on the province. In the U.S., a taxpayer would hit their (significantly lower) top tax rate at an income of about $409,000 Canadian. Total cost: estimates range around $500 million.

- Take steps to phase down the capital gains tax rate, currently at around 38 percent for the top income tax bracket, depending on the province, compared with 20 percent in the U.S. This is a huge incentive-killer for entrepreneurs and is a disincentive for wealth accumulation and retirement saving. The government could create a lower tax rate for capital gains on securities held for longer than one year to encourage investment rather than trading. The initial cost of this would be negligible.

- The 20 percent Foreign Property Rule for RRSPs should be raised. The House of Commons finance committee recommended that it be raised two percentage points per year for five years. The markets are doing it for the government anyway, as financial institutions create a wide array of products that legally circumvent the rule. Canada represents less than 3 percent of the global financial marketplace. Our stock market and our currency have underperformed most of the rest of the industrialized world, penalizing Canadians who are required to hold 80 percent of their retirement savings in Canadian securities.

- Increase the contribution limits for RRSPs and RPPs. At a maximum annual contribution level of $13,500, Canada's tax-favoured retirement saving vehicle is far less generous than in the U.S. or the U.K. Only a small percentage of Canadians use their maximum RRSP room, which suggests that this change would not cost much in the way of tax dollars forgone. It could be an important incentive for higher-income earners to prepare for retirement, and it would level the playing field for those most likely to be lured to the U.S. The Retirement Income Coalition—made up of members in the public and private sectors, including the Canadian Federation of Independent Business, the Financial Executives Institute and the Canadian Teachers Federation—recommends that RRSP contribution limits be phased up to $27,000 per year beginning immediately.

CORPORATE TAX RELIEF

Canada offers very attractive tax incentives for R&D. The OECD suggests they are too generous because firms carry out research here but locate their production, sales and marketing in the U.S., where corporate tax rates are lower. The Conference Board of Canada argues that the positive impact of our R&D tax incentives on marginal investment decisions is largely offset by the high burden of overall business taxation. Canada's corporate tax burden is one of the top three impediments to investment. According to the Conference Board's survey of executives of transnational companies, a favourable taxation environment is needed to compensate for some of the drawbacks of locating a business in Canada: the vast geography with a relatively small population base, severe weather and political uncertainty.

- The 1998 OECD survey of Canada estimates that large Canadian manufacturers face a marginal effective tax rate—measured as the general corporate rate less tax credits—of 25.5 percent on new investment, a rate exceeded only by Germany and Japan, both of which are slated to cut their tax rates. The U.S. rate is 21.5 percent. In the service sector the Canadian differential is even larger, which is particularly troublesome because so much of the knowledge-based economy is in the service sector. For service companies, Canada's 32.2 percent rate is far higher than the 19.9 percent levied on similar firms in the U.S. The gaps are huge in terms of the general tax rate as well, a significant competitive handicap. The general corporate tax rate (federal and provincial combined) is 43 percent (38 percent to 46.1 percent, depending on the province) for non-manufacturing firms— 50 percent higher than in the U.S.—and 35 percent (24.6 percent to 39.1 percent, province to province) for manufacturers and processors. The effective tax rates are lowest in the resource industry, an incentive structure based on old-economy thinking.
- The Mintz Committee report, commissioned by Paul Martin, recommended bringing more corporate economic activity within the tax net base by rescinding preferential treatment in some sectors, while unifying and lowering the tax rate to an internationally competitive level. This is vital for the fast-growing knowledge-based economy.

Tax rates, because they are so visible, often become the main terms of comparison in investment location decisions. High taxes are an investment barrier for existing Canadian companies and for potential foreign investors.

- Tax incentives are a powerful tool for attracting business; we should use them. They include tax holidays (used in Singapore and Taiwan), low corporate income taxes (Ireland and Hong Kong), as well as reductions in profit-insensitive taxes such as property or payroll taxes.
- The government should reduce the general corporate income tax rate by five percentage points. Total initial cost: $3.9 billion.
- Improve the tax environment for commercializing and adopting innovative products, processes and services. This can be done through a lower overall corporate income tax rate; faster depreciation write-offs for high-tech machinery and equipment; and strict intellectual property rights.
- Federal, provincial and municipal tax authorities must work together to foster a pro-business, high-growth environment.

POSITIVE BUDGET RESULTS

While these tax measures will not immediately pay for themselves, the boost to overall economic activity they would engender would quickly enhance tax revenues. We have seen this in Ireland, the U.S. and the U.K., as well as Alberta and Ontario. As long as the federal government keeps program spending and transfers to the provinces under control, our hard-won elimination of budget deficits would not be endangered. Over the longer run, tax revenues would surge, providing more, not less, money for much-needed social spending.

A strong, competitive economy is essential to our future health and well-being. We have all the necessary ingredients to be a global leader in the technology revolution. As a citizen and as an individual, you can make a difference. Encourage your elected representatives at all levels of government to adopt these policies. Write, fax, call or e-mail your Members of Parliament (check my Web site for names and addresses and a sample letter), urging them to foster an environment conducive to growth, innovation and economic prosperity for all.

Your Own Financial Game Plan

Too many people allow the random events in life to determine their fate. They have no concrete, measurable goals, so forces that seem to be beyond their control buffet them about from year to year. I have found that written goals are a very powerful tool for achievement. Goals about every aspect of life—education, career, family, friends, finance and fitness—provide a profound sense of direction and accomplishment. Each year, on January 1, I write down my goals for the next year and for five years hence. I make them as concrete, specific and measurable as I can. I write them in the present tense, as though they have already been achieved, and carry them around all year in my briefcase. I have a file of them going back years. I rewrite them as the year goes by, sometimes as often as daily, particularly when I seem to be faltering or losing initiative.

How I Got into This Goal Thing

I know this may sound a bit compulsive to some, and certainly, I don't achieve all of my goals, particularly in my predetermined time frame, but my track record is pretty good. This habit started when I was an eighteen-year-old freshman at Goucher College, a small liberal arts college for women in Baltimore. I was twenty-five pounds overweight and had been fighting a weight problem all my life. I was a cute-chubby baby, toddler and young girl, but by the time adolescence set in, cute-chubby had become more than pleasingly plump. This was not surprising, since in my family—on both sides, Mom's and Dad's—expanding waistlines is a common trait. Teenage girls are very sensitive about their weight, however, and I was terribly self-conscious. I hated gym, I hated wearing a bathing suit and I especially hated comparisons with my thin friends. Try as I did, with crash diets and Metrical—a liquid diet fad of the time—the pounds just kept mounting.

Finally, at the age of eighteen, I had had enough. I went to see Dr. Stanley Miller, a kindly old internist who had known me for years. I took the diet he gave to diabetics and heart patients, prescribing so many ounces of protein, carbohydrates and fat for each meal—and I began to set goals. I saw him every Saturday morning for months for a weigh-in and pep talk, my own self-constructed Weight Watchers program. I weighed myself almost daily and kept meticulous records. For a while I even wrote down everything I ate, right down to the number of grapes. I bought a calorie counter and memorized it. I studied food and nutrition books. I started to exercise, although I didn't really become committed to that until twenty years later. Within six months I reached my goal: I weighed 105 pounds (I am only five foot two).

Ever since, for more than thirty years, I have jotted down my weight once a week in a special fitness calendar—an in-my-face reminder of my genetic heritage. Ten years ago I started keeping a record of my workouts as well, on the same calendar. I have more than thirty of these annual pocket calendars—a kind of "This is your fitness life, Sherry Cooper." I know I peaked at a whopping (for me) 142 pounds when I was pregnant, I know that it took me two years to take it all off, and I know the ups and downs of vacation eating, anxiety eating, celebration eating and dessert splurges ever since. I know how much harder it is to maintain my weight the older I get, how much more I need to exercise, since I have never been able to fully deny myself all the good food and wine I enjoy so much.

I realized that if this strategy worked for my weight and fitness goals, it would work in my career, financial and personal life as well. Indeed it does. The mere fact of writing down goals and reviewing them seems to make them happen, or at least open up avenues and possibilities for achievement. Discussing them with family, close friends or colleagues helps, too. Just writing them out and saying them aloud makes them real, not fantasy. This is the "ask and you shall receive" principle. The biggest deterrent, I find, is fear of failure. If I get through that and push on anyway, I can do it.

If I think I can, I can. Brian Tracy, a motivational writer and speaker whose many books and tapes I devour, says that anything you can "conceive and believe, you will achieve." That is my credo.

Career Goals

I took my first economics course when I was a sophomore in college because I had a hole in my schedule at ten a.m. and Econ 100—Principles of Economics—was offered at that time. We used Nobel Prize–winning Paul Samuelson's *Economics* textbook, and I was hooked. I was nineteen and I set a goal to become an economist, to get a Ph.D. by the time I was twenty-five (I overshot that goal by two years due to illness). Never mind that I had never met an economist other than my professor and wasn't really sure what they did; never mind that I had never met anyone with a Ph.D. prior to university and wasn't sure what you had to do to get one. Nothing was going to hold me back. I was committed.

The other thing I wanted more than anything else was to be financially self-sufficient as soon as possible. That meant I had to get a fellowship and a job to go to graduate school. My father thought a Ph.D. was an outrageous idea—he later changed his mind—so I didn't want him to help pay for it. I did get a fellowship and a teaching job. I had no money. The rent on my furnished one-room apartment took more than half my monthly income of $400, but I didn't care. It never occurred to me to go into debt. I just ate a lot of canned soup and drank jug wine. I'll never forget the taste of Cribari Rosé, $4.00 a gallon.

My starting salary at the Federal Reserve was $20,000 a year. I was on my way. I felt rich and, in 1977, I probably was. At least I could afford to eat more than canned soup.

Over the years, my goals have broadened and sometimes changed. They often include my husband and my son, but they are always very concrete and specific. At the start of every year, I review them and construct my new one-year and five-year plans. Writing this book first showed up on my 1995 five-year-goal list; I just made it.

Your Life Goals

So much is written today about financial planning and retirement planning, yet it is all so confusing. The more I read, the muddier the water gets. No one can tell you exactly how to invest your money for maximum return—stocks, bonds, cash, mutual funds. All that the financial gurus can do is look at probabilities. But will history repeat itself, or is it really different this time? No one can tell you precisely how much money you will need for financial security, and no one can tell you how long you will live. There are no cookie-cutter, one-size-fits-all solutions, and no one can predict the future, your future, with any certainty at all. We must all make assumptions and operate with uncertainty. I will attempt to delineate what I think we do know, and where the options and decisions arise.

Start Now

We know that the sooner you set your career and financial goals, the better. You can change them as you go, but if you have no plan, you will allow random influences to push you around and may just end up going nowhere. I'm not suggesting you can plan everything. If someone had told me in 1980 that I would move to Canada in 1983 and stay there, I would never have believed it. But in the context of my wanting to be a successful, financially self-sufficient economist, it made sense. If I had not found an economist job in Canada that I was excited about, I wouldn't have come. So set your career goals in a concrete, specific but flexible way and list the actions you can take to further those goals— education, networking, skill development—actions that move you along the path. Don't underestimate the value of the people you meet along the way, especially potential mentors and role models.

And remember, it is never too late. My mother took her first full-time paying job when she was fifty. She had done volunteer charity fundraising work and bookkeeping for my dad for many years, but she never earned her own paycheque until she became the administrator of the Women's Division of the Associated Jewish Charities in Baltimore at fifty. She had an office and a staff, and travelled to Israel and

Morocco on business. She used all the skills she had acquired over the years and attained a good deal of self-satisfaction and self-esteem doing it. We were very proud of her, especially my dad, who originally was quite upset that she felt she needed to work. When my dad died nine years later at age sixty-two, my mom had something of her own to fall back on. Moreover, it was her health benefits that paid for my father's multi-month stay in the intensive care unit at Johns Hopkins Hospital and his private nurses afterwards.

Many people have lifelong dreams of starting their own businesses, working from home or getting another degree. Many have discovered that, for them, the rewards of corporate North America are unsatisfying or simply not enough. What was right for you at thirty may not be right for you at forty or fifty. People are changing careers, sometimes more than once. For those of you who feel out of sorts with your current path, I recommend Marti Smye's new book *Is It Too Late To Run Away and Join the Circus?*

The Pay-Yourself-First Mentality

While most people starting out in their careers find it difficult to think about retirement, the fact is, the sooner you get in the habit of paying yourself first, setting aside a portion of each paycheque in savings, the more easily you will achieve all of your goals. Having a nest egg gives you the freedom to pursue your goals in the future, be they buying a house, educating your children, taking a dream trip around the world or changing careers. You are less likely to spend money if it has already been taken out of your chequing account.

The very act of self-discipline, of even a small amount of self-denial—postponing your immediate gratification for larger and more important goals—will become habit-forming and incredibly satisfying. I find that the path to achieving goals, the journey, is the really fun part; once you get there, it's time to move on to the next one. Not that it's necessarily a letdown. The day my dissertation committee accepted my final defence of my thesis and called me doctor was a fabulous day, believe me. But the process, the climb to the summit, is the stuff life is made of. Truly successful people are willing to set aside time, energy and money to achieve their goals, both short-term and long-term. Successful people need and pursue new challenges.

Difficult to Save

As we have seen, the growth in Canadian family disposable income has slowed significantly in the past twenty-five years. Even many two-income families have trouble making ends meet. Our tax burden has grown appreciably since the mid-eighties. Any Canadian with taxable income of around $65,000 and up pays the top marginal income tax rate of roughly 50 percent. Canadians also face the highest property tax rates in the G7 countries. To protect living standards, we have gone increasingly into debt. So it is not surprising that only 13 percent of the maximum RRSP room is used and that personal savings rates have plummeted. The Canadian Association of Insurance and Financial Advisors—financial planning experts—cited their clients' personal debts as the greatest impediment to increased retirement savings contributions in 1999.

Nevertheless, saving is crucial to your financial well-being because only you can take care of yourself. Only you can ensure your future financial security. Saving buys comfort, freedom and peace of mind. For that, it is worth making sacrifices along the way, but it takes self-discipline and a plan.

For today's Generation Xers, in the early stages of careers and families, saving is the key to ultimately owning a home, paying off school loans and creating financial security. Work towards saving 15 percent of your gross income. Do it by saving an additional 1 percent every six months if necessary, but get started. Pay yourself first. Have your bank or your employer automatically deduct from your chequing account or your paycheque a pre-specified amount that rises over time to 15 percent of your gross income. Put the money in an RRSP. Depending on your tax bracket, you will receive a tax refund of up to half the money back. In some cases, your employer may match a part of your RRSP contribution. If you have another kind of registered pension plan where you work, you may not be allowed the maximum RRSP contribution of 18 percent of income up to $13,500 annually. Save anyway, in a taxable investment account.

Your investment choices are varied. Indeed, the plethora of invest-ment options is head-spinning. That is why it is important to get advice from a professional investment adviser or financial planner who is willing to take the time to understand your risk profile and life cir-cumstances. There is no universally applicable investment plan. The younger you are, the more risk you should be willing to take to enhance your returns. However, make sure the risk–return trade-off is there. As you will see in the next chapter, the average annual rate of return on resource stocks over the past sixteen years has been below that on Treasury bills—no kidding. Over the same period, bonds have outper-formed stocks in Canada, and dividend mutual funds—funds invested mostly in banks, utilities and pipeline companies' stocks that pay divi-dends—have beat the Canadian diversified equity funds. With interest rates having fallen so far in the past sixteen years, it is unlikely that bonds will outperform stocks in Canada over the next sixteen years, but historical performance suggests that, in the past, investors were not rewarded for the risk they were taking.

Keep in mind also that risk has as much to do with the investor as the investment. How risky an investment seems depends on what price you paid, when you will have to sell, how well you understand it and whether you bother to look at the daily price changes. For each investor, risk is what you make it, so it is important to know your own risk tolerance. See my Web site (**www.sherrycooper.com**) for a per-sonalized quiz to help you assess your individual risk profile.

The Key is Saving

First of all, you need savings. I used to think that the key to a fat invest-ment portfolio was putting together the right mix of investments and selecting the best stocks, bonds and mutual funds; but the real key is good savings habits. The fact is, if you don't save a healthy amount each month and invest on an ongoing basis, it doesn't matter whether you earn 8 percent a year or 18 percent.

Non-financial decisions, having precious little to do with money, often have a larger impact on your economic well-being than you might imagine. If you smoke, drink heavily, fly into uncontrollable rages, eat to excess and never exercise, you probably won't need an impressive retirement nest egg. If your only hobby is shopping and you need possessions to prove your value in the world, you will likely find it tough to be a good saver. If you get divorced, you will probably lose 50 percent of your net worth, more than was lost in the brutal stock market crash of 1973–74. If you have six kids, you may have to revise your financial goals. I'm certainly not saying that you shouldn't have kids, enjoy a bottle of wine, splurge a little or extricate yourself from an unhappy marriage. Keep in mind, however, that these ostensibly non-financial decisions have a profound financial impact.

Credit Card Debt Trap

If you have serious trouble saving or are deeply in debt, there are free counselling services available to help. Anyone who regularly has monthly debt payments in excess of 20 percent of after-tax income is probably headed for trouble. Credit card debt is the most dangerous of all. Credit cards are a wonderful convenience, giving a thirty-day interest-free loan and sometimes even frequent-flyer points; but if you spend more than you can afford to cover in full each month when the bill arrives, then get rid of your cards. Credit cards encourage you to spend before you have the money; interest rates on credit cards are very high; and running up too much credit card debt can be financially ruinous.

Pay down all credit card debt as soon as you can. Start with the highest-rate loans and work your way down. You can also get the help of a bank to consolidate your loans, probably at a lower monthly rate. If you are tempted to run up any more credit card debt in the future, use debit cards only; they automatically deduct any expenditure from your bank account. If the money isn't there, you can't spend it. That is the beauty of automatic savings deductions: you pay yourself first, and once the money is gone, you are less likely to overspend.

Some Painless Ways to Live Beneath Your Means

If you want to grow rich or if you simply want financial security, you must spend less than you earn. It is as simple as that. Many people find this enormously difficult, suggesting that they will save next month, next year, when the kids grow up, when the boss gives them another raise. For most people, saving is a residual—the last off the bottom, not the first off the top. Here are some ideas to help.

- Keep track of what you spend. Save your credit card receipts and add them up each week. I use only one credit card and keep a file of my receipts. Each week, I check my current bank account balance—the one I use to deposit my paycheques and pay my bills—and subtract all outstanding cheques and credit card receipts. If you are aware of what you spend, you will tend to spend less.
- Pay in cash whenever possible for incidentals and unnecessary splurges. The experts say that psychologically it is harder to spend hard currency than to charge to a credit card.
- Use a debit card instead of a credit card if you cannot keep yourself from spending more than you can pay off in full each month.
- Have two bank accounts: a chequing account and a savings account. Deposit your paycheque into your chequing account and have the bank take 15 percent of your gross income off the top and automatically send it to your RRSP or investment vehicle(s) of choice. If saving 15 percent of your income is too much, start with less and work your way up. I have my paycheque automatically deducted each pay period for my current-year RRSP contribution, which goes in part into my company RRSP plan and in part into my self-directed RRSP. That takes care of $13,500 of my annual saving. For the remainder, my account is automatically deducted monthly and invested in mutual funds. Once the balance gets large enough, you can consider a more individualized form of professional money management.

  I do invest directly in individual stocks, in what I call my trading account, which is separate from my core holdings. I see them as an attempt to enhance the returns of my core portfolio—

more successfully at some times than at others. To be honest, I also do this because I enjoy it. Sometimes the entertainment value is costly, however, and I would never risk my core holdings on relatively speculative stocks.

If you receive income other than your regular paycheque—bonuses, commissions, interest, dividends—don't forget to deduct two things off the top: the tax you will owe if it is not already withheld, and your 15 percent pay-yourself-first savings. Put the tax in your savings account until it is due; there is nothing worse than getting an unexpected tax bill. Invest the 15 percent savings or use it to pay down debt.

Use the chequing account to pay your regular monthly bills. Use the other account to save for those lumpy expenditures, including vacations, property taxes, quarterly estimated tax payments, car and house insurance, summer camp fees for the kids, a new car, clothing, school tuition and the like. Don't forget gifts and charitable contributions; I have my United Way contribution deducted from each paycheque. Where possible, request to pay infrequent bills on a monthly basis. If this is not possible, pay yourself in your savings account each month so these bills don't come as a surprise. Don't forget those seasonal expenses either, like snow removal in the winter and garden upkeep in the summer. Estimate all of these irregular expenses, add them up and divide by twelve. Transfer this amount each month from your chequing account to your savings account to cover these expenses.

Also, remember to keep a balance for unexpected disasters: a flooding basement, leaking roof, broken pipe, new transmission, bad sales quarter, smaller-than-expected bonus or temporary job loss. You should keep the equivalent of roughly three months' expenses in fairly liquid form—a money market mutual fund, Treasury bills or the like. With interest rates so low, I just keep it in my savings account.

- Restaurant meals and vacations are two areas where spending often spins out of control. Eating out is estimated to cost five times more than eating a home-cooked meal. The markup on a restaurant's bottle of wine is often staggering. Don't get me wrong, I love to eat out. When my husband and I were first married, we randomly split our household expenditures. As it turned out, I paid the grocery bills and he paid for restaurants. Being the generous person that he is, we ate out three nights a week. About three years into our marriage, we revamped the finances, once again pretty much randomly splitting expenses. This time, I had shifted property taxes to him and I got the restaurant bills. Now the same person paid for groceries and restaurants. What a shock! I realized we were spending more on one restaurant dinner than on a week's groceries and wine. The Coopers now dine out less often.

People frequently go overboard on vacations too. Set up a budget and save in advance for your vacation, and don't buy stuff you don't need when you're away. Did you ever wonder why there are always jewelry stores in expensive hotels and resorts? People tend to go a bit nuts on vacation.

- Make sure you hunt for the best prices, especially when purchasing big-ticket items. The Internet has made comparison shopping easy, even for things like used cars and appliances. Check out the new auction sites for real bargains on electronics, airline tickets, vacation packages and much more. Don't be afraid to bargain, and ask for a discount when you pay cash. Look for and wait for sales. Don't buy on impulse. A 10-percent-off sale is like earning 14 percent or more on an investment, because you have to pay tax on the investment gain. Pay cash for big-ticket items, even cars. You will buy less that way, and the bills when leasing or paying off a car loan are ultimately much higher.

- Shop around for insurance—life, auto, dental, house, disability. The variance in premiums can be huge. The Internet helps here too. Use term life insurance and save for yourself. Go for ten- to twenty-year level-term policies, and shop around for quotes; there is stiff competition among insurance companies. Make sure you also have disability insurance. For a young person, it is more likely that you will become disabled than that you will die within the next twenty years. Take advantage of any insurance offered by your employer; group rates are usually better than individual. At some point after retirement, you might consider long-term-care insurance to cover an extended stay in a nursing home or custodial care in your home. Be careful, though: these policies are very complicated and often a rip-off, so you will need sound advice from a trusted, qualified professional.

Don't buy junk insurance policies like extended warranties on consumer products, life insurance on children's lives or credit life insurance, which pays off consumer debt if you die. Also look into saving money by boosting the deductibles on your auto and home insurance. You can afford to do that when you save regularly; you won't be wiped out by a leaking roof or car problems.

- Potentially one of the most significant ways of saving is by reorganizing household debt. Pay off high-cost consumer debt as soon as possible. You might consider consolidating credit card balances and auto loans and refinancing them to get a lower monthly rate. If you go through this debt consolidation, don't sign up for more credit cards and spin back into a debt binge. Instead, make a point of socking away the money you were previously paying in interest.

  Refinance your mortgage, where possible, to pay the lowest rates. Remember, you can assume that interest rates will remain low because of continuing low inflation. If anything, interest rates on government bonds could edge down further, to about 4$^1/_2$ percent. Don't change your monthly payments when rates come down; just pay off more of the principal. Amortize your mortgage over the shortest time frame you can; fifteen years is much better than the standard twenty-five. Use all windfalls—tax refunds, unexpected bonuses and gifts—to pay down your debt, beginning with the highest-rate non-deductible loans. In a deflationary world, it does not pay to be in debt, because you are paying it back in appreciating dollars.

- Invest fully in all tax-advantaged retirement savings vehicles, like RRSPs and employer- or union-sponsored registered retirement plans. These allow you to save in pre-tax dollars. This means that for every $1 you fork over, the government is picking up as much as 53 percent of the tab, assuming you are in the highest tax bracket. That frees up money you can then use to pay down your mortgage or other debts.

  Take full advantage of Registered Education Savings Plans (RESPs) to save for your kids' or grandkids' education. You can contribute up to $4,000 per child per year into a RESP and the government will add an additional 20 percent, up to a maximum of $400 per year if the child is under the age of eighteen. The contributions you make to the RESP are not tax-deductible, but the funds in the RESP—including those contributed by the government—earn tax-free income while they remain in the plan. When your child withdraws the funds to pay education expenses—which include not only tuition fees but also books, lab fees, equipment, accommodation and transportation—the income earned in the plan and the amount of the government contribution will be taxed as regular income at your son or daughter's tax rate. The idea is that they will be in such a low tax bracket that, even though the income becomes taxable, the tax bill will be minimal.

There is a maximum lifetime contribution per beneficiary of $42,000. However, if your child does not choose to go on to post-secondary education, then the RESP must be terminated no later than the end of the year in which the plan has its twenty-fifth anniversary. You can even transfer it into your RRSP if you have the contribution room and certain conditions are met. This makes the RESP far more attractive; it used to be that you forfeited the earned income if it was not used by the beneficiary for education. You can also withdraw contributions from your RESP without tax consequences. There are some issues regarding the type of RESP you set up—pooled plans versus self-directed plans offered by financial institutions. Talk to your financial adviser about the details of each and which would be best for you.

- When approaching retirement, many people think about moving to a place where the cost of living is cheaper. This is at least a consideration. Moving can also cut your tax bill. Some move from high-tax to low-tax provinces.

It's Never Too Young to Start Saving

The sooner you begin to save, the better and the easier it is. Do you know that if you save $50 a month in a tax-free account like an RRSP beginning at age twenty-five, by the time you are sixty-five you will have $175,000? I have assumed an 8 percent annual return, which is conservatively consistent with long-term stock market performance. If you save $100 a month over the same period, you will have $350,000 at sixty-five, and if you save $284 a month you will be a millionaire from this source alone. If the money you save is for an RRSP, you will have a tax savings of between 30 percent and 53 percent each year, depending on your tax bracket and the province you live in.

If you do the same thing at age forty-five—save $50 a month—your nest egg at retirement will be only $29,500; $100 a month will give you $59,000. It would take a whopping $1,686 a month, or just over $20,200 a year, beginning at age forty-five to accumulate a million dollars in twenty years at an annual rate of 8 percent (see figure 15.1). The maximum annual RRSP contribution today is only $13,500, or $1,125 per month, which would be worth $670,000 in twenty years. To make up the additional $330,000 to accumulate a cool million dollars, you would have to save the remaining funds outside of the RRSP, with no income tax deduction on this amount. Any interest or dividends earned on this money would also be taxable.

These examples demonstrate the power of compound interest, particularly tax-free compound interest. The bottom line: it takes at least $1,686 in monthly saving to accumulate a million dollars by age sixty-five if you begin at forty-five and only $284 monthly if you start at twenty-five. Quite a head start.

FIGURE 15.1

How Much Do I Need to Save Each Month to Reach $1 Million when I Hit Age 65?

Assuming 8% Rate of Return

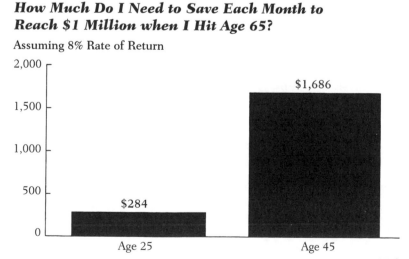

SCA©

Teach Kids to Save

A fellow from Shawnee, Kansas, wrote to the *Wall Street Journal* personal finance column recently to say that in 1967, while on vacation from college, he spent the summer loading boxcars and was paid $1,600. Following his father's advice, he bought thirty-seven shares of AT&T. In early 1999, after the breakup of AT&T and various spinoffs and the reinvestment of dividends, the portfolio was worth in excess of $142,000. His dad gave him good advice.

Ever since my son, Stefan, was born, I have tucked away all those little gifts of money he has received from his grandparents and others. Five dollars here, twenty dollars there. When the government used to send me those baby bonus cheques (family allowance payments) years ago, I deposited those in his account too. Over the years the money has added up. Initially, when interest rates were very high, I put it in a high-yield GIC. As rates came down, I started buying small quantities of stock.

At age thirteen, for his bar mitzvah, he received cheques amounting to about $2,000. In late 1995, I took the cash and some of his savings and bought Stefan one hundred shares of Bristol Myers, the U.S. pharmaceuticals company. It cost $3,120 Canadian. In early 1999, just over three years later, that investment was worth nearly $38,000—a gain of close to $35,000. My cousin Mike, an investment adviser in Springfield, Massachusetts, gave Stefan twenty-five shares of Genrad, a U.S. automotive parts company, in 1994. At the time it was trading at about US$3.25. When we sold the stock in early 1999, it traded at nearly US$20. All of our investments haven't been profitable, but the blockbusters like these have more than made up for the others.

Watching this happen, I have now started to give kids stock for birthdays, Christmas, baby gifts. Even one share of Disney or BCE or Microsoft could get the ball rolling. Some take a real interest, but even if they don't, their parents appreciate it.

Last summer, Stefan had his first real job; he was a counsellor at an overnight summer camp. He earned $620. He suggested we invest the money—honestly, it was his idea. He put it in a global science and technology mutual fund in September 1998. As of May 1999—seven months later—it was worth $780 on paper. He knows he has taken a big risk, investing it in a very aggressive mutual fund. It has already seen a 30 percent correction. He knows its value can fall, maybe even plunge. But he is investing for the long run. The top holdings of the fund are Microsoft, IBM, Merck, Cisco and Pfizer; he says he's not worried.

Saving for Financial Security and Freedom

All of us wonder how much we need to save. How much is enough to be secure, to have some of the things we want, to retire in comfort? This is not an easy question to answer. Some aspire to be wealthy, others want a sufficient nest egg to cover those rainy days. Some people just don't worry about it, assuming things will take care of themselves. We all fall somewhere along this spectrum.

In Part I, we saw that Thomas Stanley and William Danko, the authors of *The Millionaire Next Door*, have studied the affluent in the United States and have developed a rule of thumb to determine who is wealthy. They define wealthy people as those who have "net worth (assets minus liabilities) excluding inherited wealth equal to their age times their pre-tax annual household income from all sources except inheritances divided by ten." So, if your gross family income is $100,000 at age sixty-five, Stanley and Danko would consider you wealthy if your net worth were at least $650,000. If your income were $200,000 at the same age, you would not be wealthy with a net worth of $650,000. Wealth is relative to your age and income. In the case of the $200,000 income, you would not be considered by the authors to be wealthy unless your family net worth was $1.3 million. What you need to save and accumulate depends on the lifestyle you are accustomed to.

The authors suggest that if you are not yet wealthy but want to be someday, you must live frugally. You must live below your means. They recommend you never purchase a home requiring a mortgage that is more than twice your family's total gross annual income. And remember, mortgage interest is tax-deductible in the U.S. For cities like Toronto and Vancouver, with very expensive housing, following that rule could be quite difficult, particularly early in your career. You could, however, start small with a condo and then work your way up; or you could postpone your purchase until you have saved for a substantial down payment and your family income has increased; or you could move to a distant suburb where house prices are more reasonable. Many young families do all of these things to reduce the mortgage burden; the ones who don't may never get out from under the debt. A good overview of the issues involved in home ownership may be found in the book by Margaret Kerr and JoAnn Kurtz, *The Complete Guide to Buying, Owning and Selling a Home in Canada.*

Of course, there are many families that have no aspirations to be wealthy. Even so, having a savings cushion will make life a lot more pleasant. That way, losing your job, facing an unexpected home maintenance predicament or experiencing serious car problems won't become the disasters they would otherwise be. And who knows if you will work long enough for one employer to collect a pension generous enough to support your lifestyle? Who knows what government pension support will be available many years from now?

The Baker Family Isn't Leaving It to Chance

Bill, aged thirty-two, and Angela, aged twenty-eight, have been married for five years and have an eighteen-month-old baby boy. Bill is a research analyst with a bright career ahead and Angela works part-time. Their gross family income from all sources is $100,000, well above average, and they have significant upside potential. They want to buy a house as soon as they can, and then they would like to have a second child.

They currently live in a rented condo in downtown Toronto and pay $1,500 a month in rent. Their net worth is an impressive $125,000 in the form of a late-model car, RRSPs and other investments. They can withdraw up to $20,000 per RRSP tax-free to purchase their first home if they pay it back in equal annual instalments over a fifteen-year period.

Bill has accumulated this net worth by saving as a student from summer jobs, maximizing his RRSP contributions and investing aggressively, mainly in U.S. stocks. For example, Bill bought technology stocks like Sun Microsystems in 1995 and has also invested in U.S. strip bonds, which have appreciated with the fall in interest rates and the rise in the U.S.–Canadian dollar exchange rate.

Bill and Angela are shopping for a house. They know that the monthly carrying costs of a mortgage, property taxes and other house-related expenses will be greater than today's $1,500 monthly rent payment unless they move to a distant suburb. Difficult as this may be, given Bill's seven a.m. job start each day, they feel it is worth the sacrifice. They also expect child care costs to rise with another baby.

According to their calculations, their monthly all-in house costs would be affordable with a mortgage of no more than $250,000. Their dilemma is to determine what kind of house they can afford. They must decide how much of their savings they are willing to liquidate to buy a house within a manageable distance from work. The farther away they move, the cheaper the house, but the more likely it is they will need a second car—another expense. Bill and Angela have decided to look for a house that costs roughly $325,000, is located less than twenty kilometres from work and is near a subway line.

They plan to postpone purchases of furniture and other house-related durable goods so that they can continue to contribute the maximum allowable to their RRSPs. They plan to use the tax refund and any earnings growth to replenish their RRSPs and to gradually pay down their mortgage. They are well on their way to long-term financial security. Over the next five years they will have little discretionary income, but with great career prospects and smart investments, they will continue to build their net worth.

A Single Gen Xer With a Plan

Todd Kerr, aged twenty-eight, grew up in Delhi, Ontario, a small rural town one and a half hours southwest of Toronto by car. The region, which has long depended on tobacco farming, has been in decline for a decade. Once catering to rich tobacco farmers, Delhi was a bustling place. Todd's grandparents owned a bakeshop and made a very nice living. His parents were both high-school teachers and retired comfortably on their pensions and other savings. As the demand for tobacco waned, however, the region's wealth diminished and the young people started moving away. The farmers have shifted increasingly to ginseng and vegetables, but nothing could fully replace the big cash crop, tobacco.

Growing up, Todd watched these developments and realized his future would not be in Delhi. He wanted a career with income potential and the likelihood of job growth. Todd entered the computer science program at the University of Waterloo, a world-class program in this field. He received bachelor's and master's degrees in computer programming and then set off for the big city, Toronto. He has been there for three years.

His first job was at one of the chartered banks, with a starting salary of $37,000. It was a good job but somewhat dull, and it didn't engage Todd's entrepreneurial spirit. When a small investment firm offered him a job on a high-tech money management team, he jumped at it. Today, Todd earns $63,000 a year—$50,000 in salary and the rest in a discretionary bonus based on the firm's performance and on his. Todd loves his job and the people he works with and, best of all, he knows he has meaningful upside potential.

He rents a small apartment in downtown Toronto for $1,000 a month and still lives with his grad-school furniture. Indeed, he says he continues to live and eat like a student. His only splurge has been the purchase of a one-year-old Acura Integra. He bought the car nine months ago when he traded in his 1991 Honda Accord. He has a $15,000 car loan at the prime rate of interest, now 6 1/4 percent.

Todd is a saver. He has maxed out his RRSP contribution for his three years of employment by making a lump-sum contribution at the beginning of each year and investing the money in equal monthly amounts to dollar-cost average. Too many people wait until the very last minute, two months after the end of the RRSP year—March 1, 2000, for the RRSP year 1999. This reduces their accumulated wealth in retirement and doesn't allow them to dollar-cost average. They are making an investment of up to 18 percent of their income at one moment in time—maybe the wrong time for the particular investment that is right for them over the long run. Coming up with the lump sum may be very difficult, and it is certainly more difficult than saving a set amount each month. Many are forced to borrow the money for the RRSP contribution and then are tempted to spend the tax refund rather than pay down the debt. Furthermore, the refund only covers half of the loan at most. Clearly, it is better to pay yourself first from each paycheque.

Todd invests in equity mutual funds and maximizes his foreign content at 20 percent in both U.S. and international equity funds. Todd puts enough of his RRSP contribution into his company RRSP to get the full corporate matching. The firm contributes a maximum of 3 percent of his income as long as he matches that amount. The rest he puts into a self-directed RRSP because he likes the wider array of investment vehicles from which he can choose. Todd now has nearly $25,000 in his RRSP. If he never saves another nickel (which he will), that money will be worth almost $450,000 when he turns sixty-five, assuming an 8 percent average annual rate of return—another example of the power of tax-free compounding.

In addition to his RRSP saving, Todd has recently enrolled in a share purchase plan of BCE stock administered by the company. He sends $200 a month in post-dated cheques to the company's transfer agent which are used to buy BCE shares with no commission, and the dividends are automatically reinvested. Dividend reinvestment plans are an easy and cost-effective way to amass a stock holding over time. Todd will have to pay the tax on the dividends each year, but he is willing to do that out of current income. Todd says he chose BCE because of its long-term growth potential; he sees it as a high-tech company with tolerable volatility.

Todd inherited stock from his grandparents five years ago, valued then at $75,000. Recognizing the expertise required to manage this amount of money and feeding a personal interest, he enrolled in a financial planning course offered through home study and has become a Certified Financial Planner. His inheritance is now worth $120,000 and is currently invested in Newbridge, QLT, Linamar (an auto parts manufacturer), CIBC, Bombardier and BCE. He reinvests all of the dividends. At an average 4 percent after-tax total return, this money will be worth close to $500,000 when Todd turns sixty-five.

Todd is a terrific example of an Xer with a firm financial plan. He could be living at a far more extravagant level, but instead he chooses to sock his money away for the future. Don't get me wrong: he likes to have fun and is very pleased that he bought his slick car, but he enjoys the investment process and really does his homework. In time, Todd says, he will buy a house and start a family, but he doesn't seem to be in a hurry.

These Xers show that starting early is a huge advantage, but with declining income growth and rising tax burdens, the process can be difficult. Many believe that things will take care of themselves—"eventually, I will save." Many put off saving until the kids are gone. Wait until your fifties and you could be sorry, particularly if you do not have a company pension. Relying on Canada Pension and Old Age Assistance could be dicey. Most of the Xers I talk to don't trust that today's level of government pension money will be there for them. Wait too long and you could find yourself out of a job in your peak earning years, or needing to amass larger sums than you expected to achieve financial security. The next chapter looks at how much you might need. As you will see, this may be more than you think.

How Much Do I Need to Retire and How Do I Get There?

Obviously, not everyone is as well organized financially as Bill and Angela Baker or Todd Kerr. Most Canadians underestimate what they will need for retirement. A survey conducted by Toronto-based Marketing Solutions in November 1996 and reported in the *Financial Post Guide to Investing and Personal Finance*—a very good basic primer on financial planning—found that 60 percent of Canadians have never tried to estimate how much they will need in retirement. Most "grossly overestimate how early they can retire." The younger the person surveyed, the earlier they expected to stop working.

I remember working with an institutional equity salesman in the early 1980s who was twenty-nine and said he wanted to retire at forty. He talked about it all the time. I wondered if he hated his job. He is forty-four now and never mentions it.

How much you need to save for retirement depends on a number of uncertain factors. How much will you spend each year in retirement? How long will you live? What will the rate of inflation be over the period? What will the rate of return be on your investments? How much money will you earn from other sources—from a company- or union-sponsored pension plan and from government retirement benefits? Are you willing to die broke, eating into all of your initial capital, or are you intent on leaving an estate to your heirs?

We cannot know the answers to most of these questions for sure, so my strategy is to err on the conservative side. I'd much rather have saved too much than too little. I could always go on a whirlwind tour around the world, finance my grandchildren's education and create a charitable foundation if I have too much money, but heaven help me if I have too little. Poverty in old age is a horrifying prospect, and too many old people, if not poor, are insecure about their finances. Some suggest that government benefits of about $28,000 annually before tax are enough for most couples. I don't think so, at least not in expensive cities like Toronto, Vancouver and maybe even Calgary; and not if your pre-retirement family income was above $60,000 a year. Many people feel that depending on children for old age care is undesirable. Preventing that eventuality—the loss of independence and the burden on your family—is worth the sacrifices today.

How Much Income Do You Need in Retirement?

Estimate how much income you will need before tax in retirement. Experts say that for most families it is between 40 percent and 70 percent of their pre-retirement family income; that is a wide range. The higher your pre-retirement income, the lower the percentage needed after retirement because so much is taken by taxes, work-related expenses and savings. Remember, in retirement your kids are gone, your house is likely paid for—you may even downsize or move to a cheaper locale—and work-related expenses are gone, as are payroll taxes like Employment Insurance and Canada Pension Plan premiums. Your income taxes may be lower and you do not have to save for retirement. You might, however, take up some expensive hobbies and travel a bit more, so keep that in mind.

According to actuary Malcolm Hamilton, a principal with William M. Mercer, Ltd., people won't notice much of a change in lifestyle in retirement if they can replace roughly 50 percent of their gross working income. I think it depends greatly on your retirement plans and your individual family circumstances. At 70 percent of income, the retired couple will have some extra money to put away in case of emergencies or to splurge a bit. For those of you who want to travel or spend part of the year in the U.S. or elsewhere outside the country, the risk of further Canadian dollar erosion is notable. Planning on closer to 70 percent of pre-retirement income rather than 40 percent might make sense. Clearly, each family's situation is unique, so the advice of a qualified financial planner is very useful.

For younger families, estimating retirement income needs requires some guesswork. You haven't yet hit your peak earning years and you don't know your ultimate living expenses. The good news is, the earlier you start to save, the more you accumulate, providing a cushion for early miscalculations. The Boomers by now have a pretty good idea of their household expenses and can make better estimates of their post-retirement pre-tax income requirements. Calculate that figure, keeping in mind that you still have to pay taxes in retirement. What pre-tax income do you need in retirement to pay for your desired lifestyle?

Income from Pensions and Government Benefits

Now determine how much retirement income you will have from a company- or union-sponsored defined-benefit pension plan, that is, the kind that pays you a guaranteed percentage of your top annual salary for every year of service. As of 1996, about 37 percent of working Canadians were covered by these pension plans, but that ratio is falling. Just under half of those covered work for the public sector and have a retirement benefit equal to 2 percent of earnings for each year of service. This is considered to be quite generous, and most private sector plan members have lower benefits. Fewer and fewer people stay with one employer for twenty-five or thirty years—long enough to receive the maximum retirement payout. Most people early in their careers should not assume they can rely fully on this source of retirement income.

Next, make an assumption about your government retirement benefits. In 1999, the maximum annual CPP benefit at age sixty-five was $9,020 per person. You can take the benefit beginning as early as age sixty, but you get less annually over the course of your retirement. The maximum Old Age Security (OAS) benefit was $4,929. These benefits go up each year by the rate of inflation, and both are considered taxable income. The most a couple could receive annually from the government in 1999 was $27,898. So, if your pre-retirement family income is below the average family income level of about $60,000, this might be enough to maintain your lifestyle in retirement. Keep in mind two things, however: if one of you dies, your benefits might decline by more than your living expenses; and if you are just beginning your career today, you might be wise to assume that this much money (in inflation-adjusted terms) won't necessarily be there for you when you retire. There are no guarantees that government retirement benefits won't be significantly altered when the bulk of the Boomers retire in twenty to twenty-five years.

Betty and Joe's Story

Betty Bloomfield and her husband, Joe Sterling, live in Edmonton. They are both in their late thirties and are perplexed about their financial future. Betty is a hairdresser making about $25,000 a year (in a good year) and Joe is a waiter earning about $22,000 annually. Because both rely so heavily on tips, their income is uncertain. Nevertheless, they have been able to save roughly $20,000 over the years in their RRSPs and in a bank savings account. They rent a small apartment and have no children, but they would love to buy a home. With government-assisted mortgages they could make the down payment, but it would wipe out their savings. What should they do?

The home ownership decision is always about lifestyle rather than investment. Since they want a home, it is reasonable for Joe and Betty to buy one, keeping in mind a long-term goal of paying down the mortgage by the time they retire. This might mean that virtually all of their savings goes towards mortgage repayments rather than an RRSP; but, given their pre-retirement income of under $50,000 a year, they would experience little change in lifestyle if they lived on the $28,000 annual CPP and OAS payments from the government. This is particularly so if their house is paid for. The equity in the home gives them a safety cushion as well, allowing them to consider a reverse mortgage if necessary in the future (more about that below).

Two-Pension Families

If you are a two-pension-plan family, you might be in great shape without much additional savings. This is especially true if your debts are paid off, you don't plan on living outside Canada or travelling extensively and you never need either nursing-home care or auxiliary in-home care for an extended period of time. Remember, however, that OAS benefits are clawed back at a rate of 15 percent on income greater than $53,215. Therefore, a person making more than about $85,000 annually will not receive any OAS benefits.

Keeping all of this in mind, you can estimate your income shortfall in retirement. For example, assume your family income today is $120,000 and you decide you want to plan for 60 percent of that in retirement, or $72,000. You have no defined-benefit pension plan, but you will get CPP and OAS of an estimated $28,000. The shortfall for you is $44,000 a year. How much money do you need to have saved the day you stop working to generate that much income in retirement?

How Much is Enough?
Your Retirement Nest Egg

I have calculated some rough rules of thumb to answer this question. If you make the following assumptions:

- you retire at age sixty-five and live to age ninety—twenty-five years of retirement;
- your average annual rate of return on your investment portfolio is 8 percent before inflation; and
- inflation is 3 percent annually over the course of your retirement,

then *you will need savings equal to fifteen times your required annual pre-tax retirement income if you are willing to die broke* (*excluding the value of your house*). Under this scenario, you must be willing to dip into your capital over the years, spending your last cent in your ninetieth year. With the above example of a $44,000 income shortfall, you would need savings of $660,000 on your last day of work.

If dying broke bothers you and you are reticent to dig into your capital at all, then the rule of thumb becomes: *You will need savings equal to 22 times your annual pre-tax income requirement if you want to die rich.* In the above example, that would be $968,000 in savings. In both cases—dying broke or dying rich—we are assuming you remain at least partially invested in stocks; otherwise, an 8 percent nominal return is unlikely. The lower the return, the higher the savings multiple. It is safe to assume that higher inflation would mean higher nominal interest rates, so errors on that score are less troublesome.

To provide another example, if you desire $100,000 in post-retirement income from your investment portfolio, you will need a retirement nest egg of $1.5 million if you are willing to use up all your capital by age ninety, or $2.2 million if you don't want to touch your capital. Most people will choose something in between. These calculations can be adjusted for different retirement ages and different rate-of-return assumptions. See my Web site (**www.sherrycooper.com**) for spreadsheets that allow you to make these calculations, and see a financial planner for a detailed analysis.

The bottom line here is that some families might not need to accumulate huge sums of wealth to retire comfortably, but many do. Fortunately, the power of compound returns helps a lot, especially the tax-free compounding available in an RRSP. The sooner you start saving, the easier it is. Once you have determined how much you need to accumulate by the time you retire, you can work backwards to see what that means in terms of monthly contributions to an RRSP and an investment account. My Web site shows you how.

Annuities

There are other options like annuities and reverse mortgages, both of which have their pluses and minuses. An annuity is longevity insurance.

Generally, it is a contract guaranteeing lifetime income—fixed or variable, depending on the terms. An annuity can be bought with a single lump-sum premium or with periodic payments over a pre-specified period. Annuities have three advantages: they provide lifetime income; fixed annuities guarantee a set amount of income; and the income is partly tax-free because it is seen as a repayment of capital if the annuity is purchased with funds that originated outside of an RRSP (otherwise the full amount is taxable).

Like everything else, however, you pay for the security of a defined income. Guarantees cost money, often more than they are truly worth in hindsight. That's what the insurance company actuaries determine. They are betting on actuarial probabilities about your life expectancy and rates of return on investments. The insurers certainly build into the premiums a margin of safety for themselves. The main drawback is that you could die soon after buying an annuity, not collect much income and have the bulk of the money end up with your insurance company rather than your heirs. Other disadvantages of annuities are that they are usually irrevocable; the income, though guaranteed, might not keep up with inflation; and the income is only as good as the solvency of the insurer. Despite these disadvantages, annuities might make sense for some. They should be considered carefully with the help of an independent professional adviser.

Reverse Mortgages

Reverse mortgages offer an income-generating option for people over the age of sixty-two with substantial equity in their house and little other investment money. They are currently available only in Ontario, British Columbia and Alberta, but that may be changing. You can borrow 10 percent to 45 percent of the appraised value of your house. The younger you are (over the age of sixty-two), the lower the proportion of equity you can borrow; this is to help ensure that the value of the mortgage never exceeds the future value of your home. You can receive the money as a lump sum or as a regular stream of income (or some combination of the two). The income derives from a life income annuity and is, therefore, tax-sheltered; it continues as long as you or your spouse live in the house. The loan is paid back at death or when you choose to sell.

The fees and costs of these loans are higher than for regular mortgages. Generally, the cost is four percentage points over the current Treasury bill rate, adjusted annually. Today that would be 8½ percent, well above the traditional mortgage rate. The people who benefit the most from reverse mortgages are those who are house rich but cash poor. They are not for people who intend to move soon or who want to leave the full value of their home to their heirs. It is probably advisable to wait as long as you can before getting a reverse mortgage, to maximize the value of your potential income and estate. Once again, consult a qualified professional before taking action.

While reverse mortgages provide an income-enhancing option for those who have saved little, they are not a desired prescription. It is clear that saving 15 percent of gross income over the course of a thirty-year career makes a lot more sense. It is never too late to start, however, and most people's ability to save increases with age, particularly as incomes peak and family expenses wane. Most people will save the bulk of their retirement nest egg in their fifties. The trick is to get as much of a head start as possible and to work as long as you can. Retirement in your fifties is a pipe dream unless you have been working for one employer for thirty years and have a generous defined-benefit pension plan. That was the case for the Millisons.

John and Amy Millison—Semi-Retired on a Government Pension

John, aged fifty-nine and his wife, Amy, aged fifty-seven, say they feel comfortable and secure about the future. Their real beef is that the better they have looked after themselves, the more the government has clawed back benefits John says he paid into for a lifetime. "Besides RRSPs," John says, "the only tax shelter the government hasn't taken away is a home-based business."

John is a retired major in the Canadian Armed Forces living in

Winnipeg. He retired four years ago at the compulsory retirement age of fifty-five. He has a bachelor of science degree in electrical engineering and a master's in aeronautical engineering. Upon retiring from the military, John set up a mechanical repair business at home. His daughter Jean, aged twenty-six, says he works harder today than he did before retirement, but he sure does love it.

Amy is a registered nurse and has worked part-time for the past seven years. She earns just under $30,000 a year and still contributes to an RRSP. John earns $45,000 annually from his military pension, and his new business brought in another $18,000 last year after expenses. He too contributes to an RRSP.

Their joint family income is augmented by $7,500 in rental income, bringing the total in 1998 to $100,500. Over the years they have invested in rental properties in Winnipeg, Arizona, Toronto and Florida. These are worth about $360,000 after the mortgages. Including their RRSP investments of $165,000, their mortgage-free home valued at $300,000 and cars worth about $20,000, the Millison family's net worth is $845,000. They are a high-net-worth family according to the Stanley–Danko criteria of age times income divided by ten.

They are travelling, trying out new hobbies and generally enjoying life. Most of their RRSP investments are in equity mutual funds, but they intend to shift more of this money to fixed income investments over the next ten years.

Boomers Have to Save

Many Boomers have it a lot tougher than their parents in saving for retirement. Take Doug Rizika, a thirty-eight-year-old chartered accountant, and his wife, Robin Dalio, aged thirty-three. They bought their first house in 1991 for $240,000. Doug worked at the time for one of the chartered banks, which does offer a defined-benefit pension plan, but he left to join a small accounting firm seven years later. Over the past three years his income, which is bonus-based, has risen substantially, but now he is on his own in terms of RRSP saving. As well, his income is highly variable, rising in good years and falling in bad ones.

Robin quit her social-work job in 1994 when their first child was born. Their second child came along in 1996. With the two boys, their 1,500-square-foot house was feeling pretty cramped. In 1998, they bit the bullet and sold it for $215,000, taking a $25,000 loss. This was a far cry from Doug's parents' house-investment experience. His dad was a civil engineer with Environment Canada in Ottawa and his mom was a part-time kindergarten teacher. They bought a house in Ottawa for $15,000 in 1950 with a 3 percent National Housing Authority mortgage and sold it thirty-five years later for $200,000. This, along with his government pension and lifelong savings, allowed his dad to leave his government job in comfort at fifty-five. Doug is going to have to work a lot longer than that.

He and Robin are careful with their money, and Doug's future is bright. Their new house cost $385,000 in a suburb of Toronto. Doug's commute is an hour by GO train, but they love the house. Their original mortgage on the new house was $240,000, but they are paying it down at a pace of $38,000 a year. In addition, they are putting the maximum $13,500 a year into an RRSP. Today, they have about $150,000 in RRSP savings and $75,000 in other investments. Assuming an 8 percent rate of return, that $225,000 will be worth $1.8 million when Doug turns sixty-five. If he maxes out his RRSP contributions between now and then, he will have another $1.2 million, or a cool $3 million in total. They are doing just fine.

The Wealthy Boomers

So are Paul Grogan, aged thirty-seven, and his wife, Donna Joseph, aged thirty-five. When they were married in 1991, someone gave them David Chilton's book *The Wealthy Barber*, which recommended that they save 10 percent of their income, paying themselves first. They took this advice to heart. Donna's brother is an investment adviser with a mutual fund company. He helped them set up a portfolio of mutual funds that met their investment goals and risk profile. They hold mostly equity funds, both Canadian and international.

Paul is a computer graphics designer for a small company and

Donna works part-time from home as a technical writer and management consultant. They have two children, ages four and seven. Before the kids were born, Donna worked for a large management consulting firm in Toronto, but now she is on her own. She is working only thirty hours per week now, with Paul's mom and dad helping with baby-sitting, but she hopes to step that up when both kids are in school full-time. They own a home in Whitby, Ontario, an hour's commute for Paul to Toronto. The house cost them $171,000 in 1991. Today, their mortgage is $117,000. They are looking for a larger home now because Donna could use a separate office. They are willing to spend up to $230,000. They figure they will sell their place for about what they paid for it in 1991—no windfall there.

Their combined annual income is currently about $100,000. They have approximately $100,000 in their RRSPS and $15,000 in a savings account. They invest $600 a month in their RRSPs and pay down their mortgage by $8,000 a year. Their goal is to have $1 million by age fifty-five. At the rate they are saving today, they will fall short by about $250,000, but if Donna starts working full-time when the kids are older and they sock away more money, their goal is within reach.

Timing the Market

The real moral to these stories is to have a plan, start young and save. Save every month, year in and year out, and invest in a diversified portfolio of high-quality investments. It does not make sense to try to time the markets, actively reallocating your funds between stocks, bonds and cash as your forecast of future returns changes. This is a controversial subject. Some, like James O'Shaughnessy in his book *How to Retire Rich*, suggest that you should rebalance your portfolio annually to take advantage of sectors that have fallen significantly in value but are showing some early signs of potential outperformance. Others, like U.S. stock market gurus Ned Davis and Marty Zweig, have built huge money management and research businesses dedicated to developing market timing strategies and stock selection techniques. However, few succeed in timing the markets successfully over a long period of time.

Evidence of this is seen in the better long-term performance of strategic balanced mutual funds—those that invest in a set proportion of stocks, bonds and cash—over tactical balanced funds, which actively shift asset allocation based on management expertise. Over the fifteen years ending in 1998, according to the analysis by Portfolio Analytics Ltd., Canadian strategic balanced funds posted a compound annual return of 9.1 percent, compared with 8.5 percent for the market timers in the tactical balanced funds (see table 16.1).

TABLE 16.1

**Mutual Funds Fifteen-Year Top Performers
(1983–98)**

Fund	Compound Annual Return (%)	15-Year Standard Deviation
Fund Categories		
U.S. Large Cap	13.9	15.8
U.S. Equity	13.7	15.9
U.S. Mid-Cap Equity	13.3	16.1
International Equity	11.5	14.2
Americas Equity	10.7	16.4
Canadian Bond	10.5	6.2
Global Equity	10.4	15.6
North American Equity	10.3	14.4
Fixed Income	10.0	5.2
Canadian Dividend	10.0	9.7
Canadian Diversified—Growth	9.9	16.0
Bond & Mortgage	9.8	4.7
Canadian Diversified—Value	9.6	13.9
Regional Equity	9.4	16.0
Canadian Small-Cap—Growth	9.4	15.2
Canadian Large-Cap	9.2	13.8
Canadian Large-Cap—Neutral	9.2	13.8
All Funds	9.1	11.2

Fund	Compound Annual Return (%)	15-Year Standard Deviation
Mortgage	9.1	3.3
Canadian Balanced (Strategic)	9.1	9.1
Balanced	9.0	9.7
Canadian Diversified Equity	8.8	14.1
Canadian Large-Cap—Value	8.7	13.2
Canadian Large-Cap—Growth	8.7	14.2
Canadian Diversified—Neutral	8.6	14.0
Canadian Balanced (Tactical)	8.5	11.6
Canadian Short-Term Bond	8.4	3.7
Other Country Equity	7.6	21.2
Japanese Equity	7.6	21.2
Canadian Money Market	7.2	1.1
Money Market Overall	7.2	1.1
Canadian Small-Cap	6.8	14.7
Canadian Small-Cap—Neutral	6.4	15.5
Canadian Small-Cap—Value	6.2	13.3
Canadian Real Estate	4.5	3.0
Specialty	3.6	8.2
Canadian Gold/Precious Metals	1.5	21.2
Canadian Resource Sector	1.4	22.4
Canadian Sector Funds	1.4	22.2
Asia–Pacific Rim Equity	1.0	22.6
Global Precious Metals	1.0	23.8
Market Benchmarks		
S&P 500	18.2	13.3
Scotia Capital Long Bond	14.1	9.2
Scotia Capital Mid Bond	12.0	6.9
Scotia Capital Universe Bond	11.9	6.5
Scotia Capital Government Bond	11.9	6.5
PAL Balanced IV	11.4	8.5
TSE 100	11.2	12.7
PAL Balanced I	11.1	8.9
TSE 300	11.0	13.1
TSE 200	10.2	17.6
Nesbitt Burns Small Cap	8.7	16.1
Average 5-Year GIC	8.4	0.6
Canada Savings Bond	7.0	0.7
CPI	3.0	1.1

Sources: **Pal Trak; Nesbitt Burns**

John Bogle, chairman of the Vanguard Group of Investment Companies, has said in reference to market timing that, "In thirty years in the [money-management] business, I do not know anybody who has done it successfully and consistently, nor anybody who knows anybody who has done it successfully and consistently. Indeed, my impression is that trying to time the market is likely not only not to add value to your investment program, but to be counterproductive."

An analysis by Burton Malkiel, author of the classic book *A Random Walk Down Wall Street*, shows that from 1970 to 1994, mutual fund managers—professionals in the business—were essentially incorrect in their allocation of assets into cash in every market cycle. In other words, they became more cautious, shifting more money into cash, at troughs in the stock market. Conversely, they almost invariably became less cautious, reducing cash allocations, at market peaks. If they can't do it, you have to ask yourself, how can you?

Obviously, being out of the market when it crashes, like in October 1987, is a good thing, but the stock market doesn't issue invitations when the time is right to reinvest. Unless you know just when to get back in, analysis shows that you will do no better than those who follow a "buy and hold" strategy. Transactions costs (commission fees) and capital gains taxes can quickly offset the potential gains. Reinvesting dividends when the markets go down can help to offset the negative effect of temporary sell-offs. This is particularly the case for those holding a diversified portfolio of stocks, especially in the U.S. Why do I say especially in the U.S.?

Relative Financial Market Performance— Canada vs. the U.S.

The Canadian economy was once among the strongest in the world, and this was reflected in our stock market. From the end of World War II until the late 1970s, the Canadian economy grew at a pace above that in the United States, as we have discussed. The resource sector was strong and that, along with the manufacturing sector boosted by the 1965 Auto Pact, led to sizable gains in the economy and the stock market. From 1956 until 1981, compound annual returns in Canadian stocks as measured by the

Toronto Stock Exchange (TSE) 300 were 9.2 percent. This compared with 8.0 percent for the U.S. S&P 500. Resource stocks did well back then, with compound annual returns over the period of 9 percent, well above the returns of 6 percent on Treasury bills. I make that comparison because since 1982 you would have been better off in cash (Treasury bills) than in resource stocks, and without taking on the added risk.

FIGURE 16.1

TSE Underperforms S&P since 1980

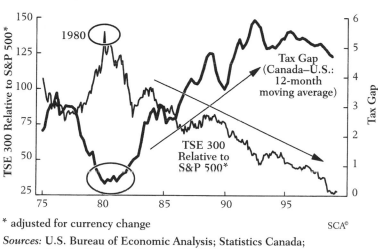

* adjusted for currency change   SCA©

Sources: U.S. Bureau of Economic Analysis; Statistics Canada;
Standard & Poors; Toronto Stock Exchange

The world changed, however, as we showed in earlier chapters. Canada is now the fallen global growth leader, and that has been reflected in our relative stock market performance. Our fall has been even more dramatic when we adjust for the decline in the Canadian dollar. The Canadian stock market has underperformed the U.S. markedly since 1980 (figure 16.1). Over that period, Canada made a number of governmental policy moves that have spelled our ultimate financial decline. We have talked about these. Canada's generous social welfare system introduced in the 1960s, while the pride of Canadians, proved to be more than we could afford. It led to the spectacular increase in budget deficits in the seventies and eighties, which in turn promulgated the upward movement in tax rates. While Thatcher was cutting taxes in Britain and Reagan was doing the same in the U.S., Trudeau and later Mulroney and Chrétien were raising them in

Canada. The tax gap between Canada and the U.S. is at historically high levels.

Canadian personal income tax rates are still below those in France or Sweden, but the U.S. is our number one trading partner and the primary lure for our skilled workers and growth businesses. The U.S. is also attracting our investment capital, with Canadians sending record volumes of funds to the U.S. stock market, even with the foreign content restrictions on RRSPs and the sub-70-cent Canadian dollar. For households, for businesses and for capital gains, the tax gap with the U.S. have rarely been wider, and it is destroying us. Our corporate tax rates are actually higher on average than virtually everywhere else in the industrialized world. This is killing our living standards, it is killing our competitive position and it is killing our entrepreneurial spirit. Our tax rates discourage foreign investment and make it difficult to entice much-needed talent north of the border.

The relative dearth of foreign investment in Canada has been a big negative. The discouragement of foreign direct investment, beginning with the Foreign Investment Review Agency (FIRA) in 1973 and the National Energy Program in 1980, has had a lingering legacy. The situation has deteriorated in the nineties, reducing egregiously our share of the growing volume of foreign business investment worldwide. We have fallen sharply behind our NAFTA partners in this regard. The government's own research shows that business investment by foreigners, even takeover activity, boosts jobs, global reach and economic activity. It also imports new technology and innovation.

Canada has substantially underperformed the other major industrialized countries of the OECD in manufacturing and total productivity gains largely because we have not shifted sufficiently to a knowledge-based economy. We are not as productive and we are not as competitive. We are behind in the innovation race, and this too is reflected in our stock market. We are still too dependent on low-value-added, low-tech manufacturing and traditional resource businesses. The resource sector represents 20 percent of the TSE, down from 31 percent five years ago, but this reduced presence is only because of the relative decline in resource stock prices, not because of a fundamental shift in our economy to growth industries. Government subsidies to declining sectors do not reduce the jobless rate. Instead, they slow the pace of progress, slow the shift to growth sectors. While nearly 32 percent of the U.S. stock market is in the fast-growing science and technology sectors, those sectors represent only 14 percent of the TSE (figure 16.2).

FIGURE 16.2

TSE Resource-Heavy, Tech-Light
Equity Market Weightings, March 1999

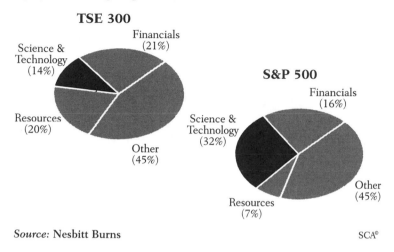

TSE 300
Financials (21%)
Science & Technology (14%)
Resources (20%)
Other (45%)

S&P 500
Financials (16%)
Science & Technology (32%)
Resources (7%)
Other (45%)

Source: Nesbitt Burns   SCA©

For investors saving for retirement, the underperformance of the Canadian stock market is a big problem—a very big problem—because we are forced by government regulation to keep 80 percent of our retirement savings in Canada. This RRSP imprisonment is costing us big time, but innovative new investment vehicles are now available to allow you to legally exceed the foreign content limits. We will discuss these below.

Relative Performance—The Facts

Those who watch American news programs, CNN or CNBC, or who read the American press, know the euphoria associated with U.S. stock market performance over the past fifteen years. Household net worth in the U.S. has risen more than 50 percent since the end of 1992, thanks to the stock market. As of the end of 1998, the S&P 500 had posted total returns in excess of 20 percent annually for an unprecedented four consecutive years. Performance continued strong in the first quarter of 1999. The S&P has had only one losing year in the past seventeen, while the TSE 300 has had five over the same period. The top ten stocks in the S&P 500 as of mid-1999 were Microsoft, General Electric, IBM, Exxon, Wal-Mart, Intel, Cisco, MCI Worldcom Inc., AT&T and Merck—all world leaders in their industries.

The tech-heavy Nasdaq composite index—containing more than five thousand stocks—has boomed as well, up 40 percent in 1998, posting four consecutive years of massive gains and continuing its uptrend well into 1999 despite repeated substantial, even unnerving, corrections. There have been huge excesses in the U.S. stock market, particularly in the technology stocks, and nowhere has the mania been more evident than in Internet stocks. Unprecedented valuations for companies that have little or no earnings are obviously unsustainable; these stocks will continue to be subject to appreciable correction, maybe even a crash, but a correction is healthy. In every past upwave in the long cycle, the stocks of the breakthrough technology of the day surged, then corrected—even crashed—only to resume a more sustainable pace of growth. This was evident with the canals, the railways, the automobile, electricity, radio, airlines, television, biotech and now Internet stocks. As we have said many times, expect volatility. Not all Internet companies will survive, but the fundamental underpinning for the Internet is real.

American financial advisers can say without equivocation that stocks outperform bonds and cash over long periods of time. All U.S. financial planners tell their clients that if they are under fifty, they should invest most of their money in a diversified portfolio of stocks. A very conservative (maybe even too conservative) rule of thumb is to hold a proportion roughly equivalent to your age in bonds and the rest in stocks depending on your risk tolerance, liquidity needs, etc.; so if you are thirty years old, hold 30 percent in bonds, and if you are fifty, hold 50 percent in bonds. They generally recommend a core holding of a broad-based index of stocks, the performance of which could be enhanced by investments in specialized stock funds or individual stocks—but the core holding is key.

On a total return basis, the S&P 500 has not posted two consecutive losing quarters in fifteen years—wow! In Canada, we saw multiple quarters of negative returns in 1984, 1990 and as recently as 1998. The 1998 decline attracted many Canadians, in the 1999 RRSP season, to the guaranteed-initial-investment promises of segregated funds. Within less than two years of the 1987 stock market crash, the U.S. market was back to a new high; it took the TSE six years to recoup the 1987 losses.

Table 16.2 shows that the S&P 500 has enjoyed a compound annual return in Canadian dollar terms of 18.3 percent since the end of the recession in 1982, the beginning of this bull market. The TSE, in contrast, has gained only 10.8 percent annually, underperforming long-term bonds—those with maturities of ten years or more—which have posted compound annual total returns of 14.9 percent over the period. The compound annual return on the universe of bonds over the same period was 12.8 percent. Taking on the greater risk of stocks in prefer-ence to bonds has not paid off in Canada.

TABLE 16.2

Sectors of Canadian Stock Market and Other Securities

Compound Annual Total Return, 1982–May 1999

(C$ terms except where noted)

Sector	Total Return (%)	Sector	Total Return (%)
S&P 500 (U.S.$ terms)	**18.3**	**TSE 300 Index**	**10.8**
Utilities	16.9	Industrial Products	10.7
Banks	16.7	Merchandise	10.3
Financials	16.0	**T-Bills**	**8.3**
Communications & Media	15.7	Paper & Forest Products	7.8
Long Bonds	14.9	Metals & Minerals	6.3
Consumer Products	14.8	Transportation & Environment	6.2
Managed Futures	14.0	**Resources**	**5.1**
Pipelines	13.0	Gold & Silver	4.1
Bond Universe	12.8	**Oil & Gas**	**4.1**
Conglomerates	12.7	Inflation	3.4
Ex. Resources	12.5	Real Estate	−4.5

SCA©

Looking at returns year by year, the TSE outperformed the S&P in only four out of the past sixteen years, twice—1987 and 1993—because of a surge in gold stocks, and twice—1983 and 1996—because of a run-up in other sectors. It might happen again in 1999 as oil and gas stocks, base metals and forest products surge from depressed levels. In 1983 the conglomerates like Brascan and Power Corporation, along with the newspaper stocks and Canadian Pacific, had stellar performances. In 1996, top performers included the utilities like BCE, led by gains in Northern Telecom, the bank stocks, real estate, and once again conglomerates like Power Corporation and Canadian Pacific. The real estate sector was the worst performer over the period, despite the good performance in 1996, posting a compound annual return of –4.5 percent.

Resource Stocks—High Risk, Low Average Returns

Excluding the resource stocks from the TSE improves our overall stock market performance. The TSE ex-resources posted compound annual returns of 12.5 percent, still paling in comparison with bonds. Only the utilities stocks at 16.9 percent, the bank stocks at 16.7 percent and the financials (which include bank stocks) at 16.0 percent have outperformed long bonds in Canada, coming closer to the stellar stock market returns in the United States.

Resource stocks showed compound annual returns of only 5.1 percent. This means that since 1982, you would have been better off taking no risk in cash-like Treasury bills that earned 8.3 percent than taking a huge risk in resource stocks. The low average returns, however, mask huge volatility. In some years resource stocks were up dramatically, and in other years the losses were just as dramatic (figure 16.3). This is important for the economy, and confirms what we have already asserted in earlier chapters: too much of our economy remains devoted to high-risk, low-return resource industries. The resource sector was a safer bet in the twenty years before 1982, when the global economy was racked by ever-rising inflation. Since 1982, inflation has been on a long-term downtrend and the resource sector has underperformed on average over the period.

FIGURE 16.3

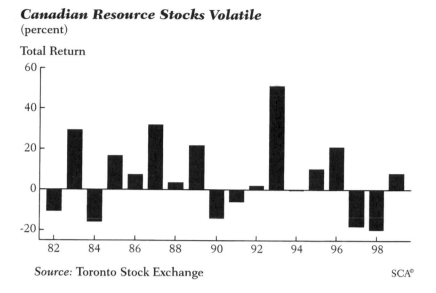

Canadian Resource Stocks Volatile
(percent)

Total Return

Source: Toronto Stock Exchange   SCA©

The weakest resource returns were in oil and gas, at 4.1 percent. However, this again masks enormous volatility. The energy sector did very well in 1989, 1992, 1993 and 1996. It has also moved up considerably in the first half of 1999 as oil prices rose, owing to OPEC supply cuts and a rebound in economic activity in Asia. The precious metals stocks, primarily gold stocks, also underperformed over the period, with compound annual returns of only 4.1 percent. The golds are highly volatile, posting huge gains in 1985 (50.4 percent), 1986 (23.0 percent), 1987 (42.8 percent), 1989 (34.7 percent) and 1993 (105.4 percent), and huge losses in most of the other years.

Resource stocks overall follow that same pattern, driven by the golds and the energy stocks. Big up-years are followed by big down-years—with gains over the period since 1982 rather disappointing overall. They are obviously not for the faint of heart. They can augment returns in good years, but they kill returns in bad ones. Knowing which will be which is the trick, and it isn't easy. Betting too long on the resource sector can be devastating to your performance.

Just for interest, I ran the same table going back as far as the data will allow, which is 1934. With almost sixty-five years of data, the picture was only slightly better for the Canadian stock market. We still underperformed U.S. stocks in Canadian dollar terms—13 percent compound annual returns for the S&P 500 versus 10.6 percent for the TSE 300. Over this extended period, Canadian long bonds continued to beat stocks; bonds posted an 11.2 percent compound annual return.

As you see in figure 16.4, all of the world's commodity-producing countries posted sub-par stock market performance over the past ten years, a period of falling inflation. While commodity prices will likely continue to rise as the economies of Asia, especially Japan, rebound, I believe this will be a relatively short-lived phenomenon. Global technological innovation points to a continued secular rise in the supply of commodities and commodity substitutes, lower costs of production and lower prices.

In 1998 alone, the total return on the TSE was a meagre -1.6 percent, compared with 38.2 percent on the S&P 500 in Canadian dollar terms. Even excluding the resource sector, the TSE was up only 2.9 percent, still underperforming bonds at 9.6 percent, while the S&P ex-resources surged 35.8 percent. This tells you why you must maximize the foreign content in your RRSPs; why you must invest in U.S. and foreign stocks or mutual funds outside of your RRSP; and why even young people can't necessarily look to the TSE 300 stock index as the only component of a core portfolio.

FIGURE 16.4

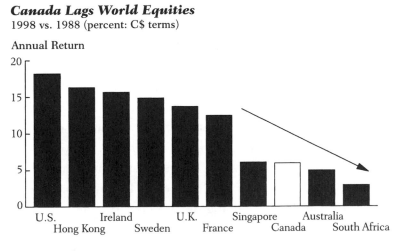

Canada Lags World Equities
1998 vs. 1988 (percent: C$ terms)

Source: Bloomberg   SCA©

Bond Market Returns

Long-term Government of Canada bond yields today are almost 5³/₄ percent. If my analysis about the technology revolution and continued low inflation is correct, they are headed for 4¹/₂ percent over the next few years, maybe even a bit lower and even sooner. If it were to happen all in one year, which is unlikely, the total returns on bonds would be over 20 percent that year. The decline in interest rates is likely to be more gradual, and there will be considerable volatility; rates may even rise sharply for intermittent periods. I believe that yields will remain low for many years to come, and the capital gains on bonds and bond funds will diminish. So, over the next fifteen years, Canadian stocks are likely to outperform bonds.

Bond investments carry risks beyond just the market risk of a general rise in interest rates. Even when overall interest rates trend downward, there are *credit risks* and *reinvestment risks*. Interest rates will fall to the 4¹/₂ percent range for the highest-quality triple-A government credits, but there could be intermittent risk in lesser-quality sectors. We saw in August 1998, when Russia defaulted on its debt, that interest rates on lesser-quality credits—all issuers other than the federal government—spiked, creating capital losses in lower-grade bonds. Most fixed-income mutual funds include lesser-quality credits to boost the income from the fund. That means you are taking more risk. These credit risks can even affect government bond yields when the world shifts to U.S. Treasuries in a flight to quality, as it did in 1998.

The reinvestment risk arises because as interest rates fall, the coupon payments and maturing bonds are reinvested at lower and lower interest rates. You can't maintain the same returns. Strip bonds—zero-coupon bonds—alleviate this problem. There are no coupon payments; you buy the bond at a discount to the ultimate face value, implying a certain constant rate of return. The value of the bond in the marketplace fluctuates with movements in interest rates. These bonds are particularly sensitive to interest rate movements, but if you intend to hold them to maturity to guarantee a rate of return over a long period of time, then you are unconcerned about the market risk.

Strip bonds should be considered only in tax-free accounts like

RRSPs, however. In taxable accounts, you would owe tax on the implicit interest income you receive annually, even though you don't actually get the money until you sell the bond or until it matures. Many people use strip bonds to guarantee a certain sum of money at a pre-specified time in the future. You can "ladder" strip bond investments—staggering the maturity dates—to give you a set income stream in retirement. You normally wouldn't do this, however, until you have amassed a substantial sum in your RRSP.

These are very complicated issues. Clearly, for Canadians, there is a place in most portfolios for fixed-income investments. You should discuss this and other portfolio investment issues with a trained professional.

A Word about Mutual Funds

Mutual funds are a good vehicle for regular periodic investment, because they give you diversification and convenience that would otherwise be difficult to obtain with relatively small monthly investments. This process allows you to dollar-cost average—invest a fixed amount at regular intervals and smooth the cost of the shares that you buy over time. You are buying when prices are high *and* when prices are low. You are not trying to time the market.

You can choose from a wide array of funds, according to your goals, life circumstances and risk profile: stock, bond, money market, balanced (including both stocks and bonds), real estate and mortgage funds. There are funds that are actively managed and others that replicate an index of stocks or bonds. Most of these fund categories are available for Canada only, for the U.S. or for other countries and regions. For example, you can buy a Canadian equity fund, a U.S. equity fund or a Pacific Rim equity fund. Table 16.1 shows you the fifteen-year compound annual returns in each mutual fund category in Canada.

Actively managed equity funds come in different flavours:
- *Growth funds* seek long-term capital appreciation, with dividend income more or less incidental. They look for companies with rapidly expanding sales or profits.

- *Value funds* seek a combination of growth and income, often focusing on stocks with above-average dividends and below-average price-earnings ratios. They favour stocks that are cheap compared with their assets or earnings.
- *Equity income or dividend funds* seek to provide a major portion of total return through income, investing in stocks with dividends that are generally well above average. In Canada, this would emphasize the preferred shares, which act more like bonds than stocks, or common stocks of banks, utilities and pipelines, which are interest-sensitive and pay dividends. The tax treatment of dividends is more favourable than of interest income, which is treated as ordinary income.
- *Broad-based specialty funds* focus on the major sub-sectors of stock markets, such as small-company stocks, aggressive growth stocks, global stocks or U.S. stocks.
- *Concentrated specialty funds* invest in the stocks of a single industry, such as financial services, oil and gas or resources.

Over the past five years, growth funds have outperformed value funds. Large-capitalization stocks, the stocks of the largest companies, have outperformed small-cap stocks, the stocks of the smaller companies, which are generally less liquid. This may be because of the growing popularity of mutual funds, which, as they get larger, can only invest in the stocks of companies that can trade easily in huge lots. During the ten-year period ending in 1984, however, small-cap stocks outperformed.

You should pay attention to the portfolio characteristics of your mutual fund: the top ten stock holdings and the turnover. The higher the turnover—the purchase and sale of securities in the fund's portfolio— the higher the transactions costs and the greater the likelihood of taxable capital gains. This is important if you are investing outside an RRSP.

Keep an eye on the performance of your mutual fund(s) relative to comparable funds and relative to the matching overall market index. Make sure to compare like against like—compare a fund with others in its peer group. If your fund *consistently* underperforms others in its class, switch funds. Look at the fund's track record in absolute and relative terms. Most investment dealers provide research on mutual funds. Discuss the best one for you with your investment adviser. Remember, however, that the hottest sectors last year are often the underperformers this year. Hot funds never fail to cool off. And don't believe in the fund managers who are lionized by the press; they too rise and then fall, that is, regress to the mean.

What you want to do is pick the best performers within the particular mutual fund category that suits your goals, time horizon and risk profile. Look at ten-year performance records or, for newer funds, the performance over the life of the fund. Invest principally in broadly based mainstream funds where you can get substantial diversification. If income is a consideration, look at dividend funds. Hold roughly your age in bond funds depending on your risk tolerance and liquidity needs. Limit narrowly based equity funds like small-cap, Asian, emerging market or resource funds to no more than 20 percent of your overall equity holdings; they are quite volatile and it is very difficult to beat the market by trading sector or specialty funds short-term. Finally, maximize the foreign content in your RRSP. We have seen how much better U.S. markets have performed. You want to have the full foreign content limit of 20 percent of your RRSP in foreign stocks, primarily U.S. When that limit is increased, increase your foreign exposure, if for no other reason than diversification; remember, Canada represents only 2 to 3 percent of global financial markets. There are now ways to legally exceed the limits, as I will show you below.

Equity Index Funds

You might consider an *index fund*, one that tracks the overall stock market—the Toronto Stock Exchange or the Standard and Poors 500 or even the broader U.S. stock market index, the Wilshire 5000. Over the past five years, the index funds have outperformed the universe of actively managed equity mutual funds in both Canada and the U.S. This has in part been reflective of the outperformance of large-cap stocks, which dominate the indexes more than the typical stock fund. Furthermore, the management fees are much lower on index funds. That doesn't, however, mean that all actively managed mutual funds underperform; it means you must do your homework or get advice from a trusted professional.

Do not actively trade your funds. You are investing retirement money for the long term. Do not fixate on the weekly, monthly and quarterly performance numbers—it will drive you crazy and needlessly churn your account. Instead, look at the three- and five-year performance data and the relative long-term ranking of your fund—first through fourth quartile. This information is published in the business section of the newspapers at the end of each quarter, or your investment adviser can provide all the info you need. In addition, it is available on the Internet at sites linked to my own, along with a whole host of other important information: the size and age of the fund, the experience and longevity of the fund manager.

Pay attention to the cost of owning the fund, including front-end sales charges (front-end loads), redemption charges (back-end loads) and expense ratios (the management expense ratio—MER). These costs are often overlooked and they can be substantial, meaningfully reducing your long-run rate of return. It is estimated that for the typical Canadian investor, each percentage point skimmed off your return in annual management expenses reduces your nest egg by 20 percent over the long run. See my Web site (**www.sherrycooper.com**) to calculate the effect of management fees on long-run total returns. The typical MER on index funds is now 1.0 percent, but some are as low as 0.5 percent, compared with over 2.3 percent on actively managed Canadian stock funds. Make sure that the extra fees are worth it. You can test their value in a down market: when the stock market declines, you are paying the manager to protect your investment. Check the performance of your fund in 1998. If the fund didn't outperform the TSE, which was down 1.6 percent, you might reconsider. Actively managed funds have more trouble beating the index when stocks are rising.

Segregated Funds

Expense ratios and sales charges are also important considerations in choosing today's popular *segregated accounts*. Seg funds, also known as guaranteed or protected mutual funds, guarantee at least 70 percent of your principal investment over a pre-specified period—usually five or ten years—while offering some upside potential tied to the stock market. These often carry large fees—in essence, the premium for the insurance. Guarantees cost money. Insurance companies, banks and mutual fund companies sell these funds. There is a widespread misconception that you can withdraw your money from a seg fund at any time and be guaranteed the value of the initial investment; this is not true. Read the fine print, because the guarantee often applies only after a minimum holding period of five years.

Insurance company actuaries have calculated that there is less than a 5 percent chance they would have to pay out on a ten-year guarantee of initial capital investment. The stock market doesn't usually decline over ten-year stretches, not even the Canadian stock market. Over a five-year term it is possible—it happened in the five-year period beginning in 1973—but it is still uncommon.

Fixed Income Funds

These funds invest primarily in interest-earning securities like bonds—federal government, provincial and corporate. They may also invest in mortgages or occasionally in preferred shares providing high dividend yields. The volatility of fixed income funds tends to be lower than for dividend funds and much lower than for equity funds. As we have seen, Canadian long bond funds—those investing in Canadian securities with maturities of ten years or more—have outperformed the TSE 300 over the period since 1982. This is not likely to continue in the future, as bond yields have already fallen to low levels and the downside in interest rates from here is limited. Historically, however, Canadians have not been paid for taking on the increased risk of stocks over bonds. This is not true in the U.S., where the S&P 500 has, as we have seen, substantially outperformed bonds over long periods of time.

Bond funds can be differentiated by the maturity of the underlying securities: *long/mid-term bond funds* invest in bonds with maturities of five years or more, while *short-term bond funds* invest in fixed-income securities with maturities of less than five years. Short-term bond funds tend to be slightly less volatile than longer-term funds. There are also *mortgage funds*, which invest in residential and commercial mortgages; volatility is about on par with short-term bond funds. International fixed income funds are also available.

Money Market Funds

These funds invest only in short-term (maturities of one year or less) money market instruments like Treasury bills, commercial paper, certificates of deposit and short-term government bonds. These funds have very low volatility. They earn rates of return close to money market rates, which today are roughly 4$^{1}/_{2}$ percent. They may be seen as cash equivalents and sometimes offer limited cheque-writing capability.

Balanced Funds

These invest in a combination of stocks, bonds and cash. They are generally less volatile than stock funds because of the stabilizing effect of the income from the bond portfolio, but they are more volatile than bond-only funds. *Strategic balanced funds* keep their asset weightings relatively stable and generally maintain a minimum proportion in each asset class. *Tactical balanced funds* alter the proportions of the fund invested in stocks, bonds and cash based on the manager's view of the markets. These are the market-timing funds discussed earlier; they have generally underperformed the strategic funds over the past fifteen years, confirming our assertion that it is very difficult to time the markets.

Real Estate Funds

These invest in commercial and industrial real estate or real estate securities, such as Real Estate Investment Trusts (REITs).

Managed Futures Funds

These funds invest in futures contracts on commodities and financial securities including stocks, bonds and currencies. The managers can be short or long the underlying futures, meaning they can be betting prices will fall or rise. The volatility here is relatively high, but the returns are not highly correlated to stock market or bond market returns. This means that managed futures act independently of other asset classes, so they offer diversification in a balanced stock and bond portfolio. In that way, they can reduce overall portfolio volatility and enhance portfolio returns historically. They also give you exposure to global markets but are considered Canadian content in RRSPs. They should, however, represent no more than 10 percent of your portfolio; are generally of interest only to those with sizable investment portfolios; and should be held for the long run because of their volatility.

Individuals can buy managed futures certificates of deposit that have principal protection for a minimum investment of $2,000. The terms are usually around six years and at maturity you are guaranteed to receive no less than your original investment. After the first year, investors can usually redeem semi-annually at the price reflecting the performance of the program since issuance, but in the first two years there are redemption penalties. Historically, the returns on managed futures have been somewhat higher than for stocks and bonds; compound annual returns were about 14 percent from 1980 through 1998, so it may be warranted to take on the enhanced risk for greater return in a small portion of your portfolio.

Mutual funds and other investment vehicles are the sole subject of many books, some of which I have listed in the bibliography. The issues can get complex and require analysis. Even if you have the time and the inclination, it is still wise to consult a financial professional for advice.

Maximizing the Foreign Content in Your RRSP

We have seen the importance of maximizing your exposure to foreign, and particularly U.S., equity investments in your RRSP. The real need is to get exposure to foreign equities. I wouldn't recommend using your foreign content to buy exposure to foreign bonds. They help to limit your Canadian dollar risk, but Canadian bonds, as we have seen, have performed very well. Looking ahead, our budget surpluses and debt repayment help ensure that our performance in the bond world will likely be at least as good as elsewhere. In fact, outside of the U.S., the credit risk in bonds could be substantial. So, optimize your U.S. and foreign equity exposure.

Innovation in the investment industry has helped to make the 20 percent rule less binding. Here are a number of ways to increase your foreign content:

- Invest in Canadian equity mutual funds that hold 20 percent of their investments in foreign stocks. These still count fully as Canadian content but would increase your foreign exposure to a maximum of 36 percent.
- Invest in Canadian securities whose return is linked to a foreign equity investment. Many financial institutions and investment dealers offer these products—notes linked to the U.S., European or global stock markets. Just beware of fees.
- There are derivatives products that count as Canadian but track foreign stock markets through the use of futures contracts on those markets. Typically, the managers of such funds put 80 percent of their portfolios into federal or provincial Treasury bills. The rest of the money is invested in futures or options contracts tied to the performance of international securities or various market indexes. For example, a number of fund companies and banks offer mutual funds tied to the S&P 500 through futures on the S&P index. A few segregated funds track foreign stock markets, including the U.S. Nasdaq index. More of these types of investments are being offered all the time, and they are becoming quite popular.

- Investing in labour-sponsored funds increases your allowable foreign content. However, these are investments in start-up companies and, to date, their performance hasn't been great. These venture capital funds offer investors federal, and in some cases matching provincial, tax credits. They count as small-business property in an RRSP, so you can boost your foreign content by three times the amount you invest up to a maximum of 40 percent. For example, if you are an Ontario resident and you invest $5,000 in a venture capital fund, the tax credits amount to as much as $4,015 if you are in the top tax bracket and you can have extra foreign investments of $15,000, as long as you don't exceed the 40 percent limit. These should be seen as long-term investments, however, because start-ups are risky and often take a long time to pay off. They should represent only a very small portion of your portfolio.
- Invest in a fund that holds bonds issued by the World Bank. These bonds can protect you from a decline in the Canadian dollar because they are denominated in a wide variety of major foreign currencies. Revenue Canada regards these bonds as domestic content because Canada is a member of the World Bank. Keep in mind, however, that the Canadian bond market has actually performed quite well, notwithstanding the long-term fall in the loonie; it is our stock market that has historically underperformed most of the rest of the world.
- Invest in managed futures funds for up to 10 percent of your portfolio. These give you exposure to global markets but are considered Canadian content. Remember, though, that these funds are volatile and should only be considered by long-term investors.

These investments, like all others, should be seen in the context of your overall financial strategy. This should, of course, be individually determined based on your unique goals, time horizon and risk profile.

Investment Strategy

Investing can be very emotional. That is why I believe that ongoing investment of 15 percent of your gross income is the best way. Once you have amassed a sizable nest egg, you can assess the value of professional management available to high-net-worth investors. The fees might be more cost-effective and the portfolio strategy can be customized to your needs over time. Until then and even beyond, the trick is to accumulate.

We often do not have enough self-discipline to control our spending and saving. At the same time, we are far too confident in our ability to pick winning stocks and forecast markets. We fret too much about short-term performance, even though we are supposedly investing for the next twenty or thirty years.

Successful investment is not about finding some magical investment strategy. I am convinced there isn't one. Instead, investing is about devising a plan that allows you to meet your long-term financial goals without panicking during periods of market turbulence. And there will be many of those periods in the years to come.

There are no magicians. With every year that passes, we see more star fund managers who burn out, no-lose propositions that fizzle, market gurus who fall into disrepute. Settle on a mix of stocks and conservative investments like bonds, invest your money monthly or with each paycheque, and then forget about it. Most investors don't do this. For many it is more about entertainment than making money.

Active trading strategies rarely work. Unless you are a professional money manager, don't do it except in a small trading account that you earmark for entertainment purposes. Don't do it in your core holdings; the costs in terms of commissions and mutual fund expenses are huge. It is almost impossible in a taxable account to use an active trading strategy to outperform an index fund over long periods of time. You might get better pre-tax results, but once you figure out the capital gains taxes of up to nearly 40 percent generated by frequent trading, you will likely find you would have done better if you had parked your money in an index fund.

Invest in Yourself

The basic message is to put your investment strategy on long-term automatic pilot and spend your time investing in yourself. As I have said repeatedly throughout this book, we are living in a time of rapid change, spectacular innovation and tremendous potential prosperity. As Canadians, we have not enjoyed the fruits of the boom to the same degree as our neighbours to the south, but better times are coming.

I believe that we will do the right things. We will cut taxes, we will encourage innovation and growth, we will let the dying industries die so that others will pop up in their place. We will redeploy our financial and human capital to the growth areas of the future. We want a better outlook for our children, for ourselves. We are an exceptionally resourceful, productive and adaptable people. Our relative economic performance has dipped, and this has taken its toll, but we will respond and adjust. That does not mean we will abandon our social welfare programs or reject our notions of equity and fairness. We will always help those who cannot help themselves. It does mean we will create an environment of growth and prosperity. We will provide the framework—the educational and training opportunities—for all to prosper. This and this alone will drive the jobless rate down and ensure economic and financial prosperity.

Each able-bodied person among us must take care of himself or herself. Invest in yourself. Lifelong education is key. Commitment to quality is key. The belief that we each run our own personal services company in a rapidly changing, competitive world instills the right sense of purpose. The risks are there, but the opportunities are huge. We live in exciting times. We will prosper and grow rich as a country and as individuals.

Selected Bibliography

Demographics

Adams, Michael
   Sex in the Snow: Canadian Social Values at the End of the Millennium (1997)
Anderson, Clifford
   The Stages of Life (1995)
Barnard, Robert, Dave Cosgrave and Jennifer Welsh
   Chips and Pop: Decoding the Nexus Generation (1998)
Cheung, Edward
   Baby Boomers, Generation X and Social Cycles (1995)
Chevreau, Jonathan
   The Wealthy Boomer (1998)
Cork, David, with Susan Lightstone
   The Pig and the Python: How to Prosper from the Aging Baby Boom (1996)
Dychtwald, Ken, and Joe Flower
   Age Wave: How the Most Important Trend of our Time Will Change Your Future (1990)
Foot, David K., with Daniel Stoffman
   Boom, Bust & Echo: How to Profit from the Coming Demographic Shift (1996)
Mitchell, Susan
   American Generations: Who They Are. How They Live, What They Think (1998)

Russell, Cheryl
  The Master Trend: How the Baby Boom Generation is Remaking America (1993)
Smith, Walker, and Ann Clurman
  Rocking the Ages (1997)
Sterling, William, and Steven Waite
  Boomernomics: The Future of Your Money in the Upcoming Generational Warfare (1998)
Strauss, William, and Neil Howe
  Generations: The History of America's Future 1584 to 2069 (1991)
Strauss, William, and Neil Howe
  The Fourth Turning: What the Cycles of History Tell Us about America's Next Rendezvous with Destiny (1997)

Long Wave

Beckmann, M., and W. Krelle
  Lecture Notes in Economics and Mathematical Systems: Technological and Social Factors in Long Term Fluctuations (1989)
Beckmann, M., and W. Krelle
  Lecture Notes in Economics and Mathematical Systems: Life Cycles and Long Waves (1989)
Berry, Brian
  Long-Wave Rhythms in Economic Development and Political Behavior (1991)
Metcalfe, Stanley J.
  Evolutionary Economics and Creative Destruction (1998)
Schumpeter, Joseph A.
  The Theory of Economic Development (1997)
Schwartz, Peter
  The Art of the Long View: Planning for the Future in an Uncertain World (1991)
Shilling, A. Gary
  Deflation (1998)
Shuman, James, and David Rosenau
  The Kondratieff Wave (1972)

Future Trends

Beck, Nuala
Excelerate: Growing in the New Economy (1995)

Beck, Nuala
Shifting Gears: Thriving in the New Economy (1998)

Beck, Nuala
The Next Century: Why Canada Wins (1998)

Burstein, Daniel, and David Kline
Road Warriors: Dreams and Nightmares along the Information Highway (1996)

Celente, Gerald
Trends 2000: How to Prepare and Profit from the Changes of the 21st Century (1998)

Crane, David
The Next Canadian Century: Building a Competitive Economy (1992)

Davidson, James Dale, and Lord William Rees-Mogg
The Great Reckoning: How the World Will Change in the Depression of the 1990's (1991)

Dyson, Freeman
The Sun, the Genome and the Internet (1999)

Gates, Bill
The Road Ahead (1996)

Henderson, Hael
Building a Win-Win World: Life beyond Global Economic Warfare (1996)

Kelly, Kevin
New Rules for the New Economy (1998)

Madrick, Jeffrey
The End of Affluence: The Causes and Consequences of America's Economic Dilemma (1995)

Naisbitt, John, and Patricia Aburdine
Megatrends 2000: Ten New Directions for the 1990's (1990)

Pfeiffer, William J.
Roadkill on the Information Highway: The Future of Work in Canada (1998)

Popcorn, Faith
   *The Popcorn Report: Faith Popcorn on the Future of Your Company,
   Your World, Your Life* (1991)
Popcorn, Faith, and Lys Marigold
   Clicking: 17 Trends That Drive Your Business and Your Life (1997)
Richard, Judy
   Workforce 2020: Work and Workers in the 21st Century (1997)
Rifkin, Jeremy
   The Biotech Century (1998)
Shapiro, Carl, and Hal Varian
   Information Rules: A Strategic Guide to the Network Economy
   (1998)
Simon, Julian L.
   The Ultimate Resource 2 (1996)
Tapscott, Don
   Growing Up Digital: The Rise of the Net Generation (1997)
Tapscott, Don
   *The Digital Economy: Promise and Peril in the Age of the
   Networked Intelligence* (1997)
Tapscott, Don
   Creating Value in the Network Economy (1999)
Wolman, William, and Anne Colamosca
   *The Judas Economy: The Triumph of Capital and the Betrayal of
   Work* (1997)
Worzel, Richard
   Facing the Future: The Seven Forces Revolutionizing Our Lives
   (1994)

Economic History

Berton, Pierre
   1967: Canada's Turning Point (1997)
Blaug, Mark
   Great Economists before Keynes (1986)

Buchholz, Todd G.
  New Ideas from Dead Economists: An Introduction to Modern Economic Thought (1989)
Colombo, John Robert
  1999: The Canadian Global Almanac (1998)
Evans, Harold
  The American Century (1998)
Fischer, David Huckett
  The Great Wave: Price Revolutions and the Rhythm of History (1996)
Gould, Stephan J.
  Full House: The Spread of Excellence from Plato to Darwin (1996)
Lipset, Seymour Martin
  Continental Divide: The Values and Institutions of the United States and Canada (1983)
Morton, Desmond
  A Short History of Canada (1983)
Perry, Harvey
  A Fiscal History of Canada: The Postwar Years (1989)
Rothbard, Murray N.
  Classical Economics: An Austrian Perspective on the History of Economic Thought, Vol. II (1995)
Wilber, Ken
  Sex, Ecology, Spirituality: The Spirit of Evolution (1995)
Wilber, Ken
  A Brief History of Everything (1996)

Stock Market Booms

Davis, Bob, and David Wessel
  Prosperity: The Coming 20 Year Boom and What It Means to You (1998)
Dent, Harry S., Jr.
  The Great Boom Ahead: Your Comprehensive Guide to Personal and Business Profit in the New Era of Prosperity (1993)

Dent, Harry S., Jr.
  The Roaring 2000's: Building the Wealth and Lifestyle You Deserve in the Greatest Boom in History (1998)
Yamada, Louise
  Market Magic: Riding the Greatest Bull Market of the Century (1998)

Global Economic Comparisons

Drucker, Peter
  Post-Capitalist Society (1993)
Institute for Management Development International
  The World Competitiveness Yearbook (1998)
Johnson, Chalmers
  MITI and the Japanese Miracle (1982)
Krugman, Paul
  Pop Internationalism (1998)
Krugman, Paul
  The Accidental Theorist (1998)
Organization for Economic Co-operation and Development
  OECD Economic Outlook (1998)
Prestowitz, Clyde
  Trading Places: How We Are Giving Our Future to Japan and How to Reclaim It (1993)
Thurow, Lester
  Head to Head: The Coming Economic Battle among Japan, Europe and America (1992)
Van Wolferens, Karel
  The Enigma of Japanese Power (1990)
World Economic Forum
  The Global Competitiveness Report (1998)

How to Manage Money

Blix, Jacqueline, and David Heitmiller
   Getting a Life: Real Lives Transformed by Your Money or Your Life
   (1997)
Bogle, John C.
   *Bogle on Mutual Funds: New Perspectives for the Intelligent
   Investor* (1994)
Burton, Makliel
   A Random Walk Down Wall Street (1996)
Chilton, David
   *Wealthy Barber: The Common Sense Guide to Successful Financial
   Planning* (1989)
Down, John, and Jordon Goodman
   Barron's Dictionary of Finance and Investment (1995)
Eisenson, Marc, et al.
   Invest in Yourself: Six Secrets to a Rich Life (1998)
Financial Post
   Guide to Investing and Personal Finance (1998)
Heinzl, Mark
   Stop Buying Mutual Funds (1998)
Kerr, Margaret, and JoAnn Kurtz
   *The Complete Guide to Buying, Owning and Selling a Home in
   Canada* (1997)
Lee, Dwight R., and Richard McKenzie
   *Getting Rich in America: 8 Simple Rules for Building a Fortune
   and a Satisfying Life* (1999)
Lynch, Peter, and John Rothchild
   *Learn to Earn: A Beginners Guide to the Basics of Investing and
   Business* (1995)
Morris, Kenneth, and Alan Siegel
   *The Wall Street Journal Guide to Understanding Money and
   Investing* (1994)
Orman, Suze, and Linda Mead
   You've Earned It, Don't Lose It (1994)

Orman, Suze
   The Nine Steps to Financial Freedom (1997)
O'Shaughnessy, Jim
   How to Retire Rich (1998)
Pape, Gordon
   Retiring Wealthy: How to Beat the Coming Retirement Crisis
   (1999)
Pollan, Stephen M., and Mark Levine
   Die Broke (1997)
Pollan, Stephen M., and Mark Levine
   Live Rich (1998)
Powers, Richard
   Gain (1998)
Sarlos, Andrew, and Patricia Best
   Fear, Greed and the End of the Rainbow (1998)
Seigel, Jeremy
   Stocks for the Long Run: The Definitive Guide to Financial Market
   Returns and Long-Term Investment Strategies (1998)
Stanley, Thomas J., and William D. Danko
   The Millionaire Next Door: The Surprising Secrets of America's
   Wealthy (1996)
Tobias, Andrew
   The Only Investment Guide You'll Ever Need (1998)
Turner, Garth
   2015 after the Boom: How to Prosper through the Coming
   Retirement Crisis (1996)
Turner, Garth
   The Strategy (1997)
Turner, Garth
   Garth Turner's 1999 RRSP Guide (1998)
Turner, Garth
   The Defence (1998)
The Wall Street Journal
   Guide to Understanding Money and Investing (1998)

Mutual Funds

Chand, Ranga
  Chand's World of Mutual Funds: Your Guide Through the Maze of Mutual Funds (1998)
Chevreau, Jonathan, and Stephen Kangas with Susan Heinrich
  Smart Funds 1999: A Family Approach to Mutual Funds (1998)
Farrell, Paul B.
  Mutual Funds on the Net: Making Money Online (1997)
Kelman, Steven
  Understanding Mutual Funds: Your No Nonsense Everyday Guide (1998)
Newsome, Mark
  The Canadian Mutual Fund Bible: A Complete Guide (1997)
Stenner, Gordon, and Adam Annett
  Stenner on Mutual Funds: The Complete and Authoritative Guide to Mutual Fund Investing in Canada (1999)

Miscellaneous

Barlow, Maude
  The Fight of My Life: Confessions of an Unrepentant Canadian (1998)
Goleman, Daniel
  Working with Emotional Intelligence (1998)
Gray, Kenneth, and Edwin Herr
  Other Ways to Win: Creating Alternatives for High School Graduates (1998)
Lipsey, Richard, et al.
  Economics, Ninth Canadian Edition (1997)
McQuaig, Linda
  The Cult of Impotence (1998)
Nader, Ralph
  Canada Firsts (1992)

Sowell, Thomas
    The Economics and Politics of Race (1983)
Sowell, Thomas
    Knowledge and Decisions (1980)
Updike, John
    Rabbit Is Rich (1981)

Index